TIGER
TIGER!
TIGER!

The Lindt Café Siege

The incredible inside story of the two days

that traumatised a nation

and one man's journey of resilience and hope

By 'Officer A'

The book they wanted to ban

.theend

Copyright notice

Tiger! Tiger! Tiger! © 2022

ISBN 978-0-473-65599-0

https://www.tigertigertiger.book.com

Cover design Ignacio Querejeta

The End Authority Limited

Trading as The End Publishing Ltd

68 New North Road, Eden Terrace, Auckland 1021

Aotearoa New Zealand

Email publishing@theend.co.nz

Web www.theend.pub

All rights reserved. No part of this publication may be reproduced, copied, or stored in a retrieval system, or transmitted, in any form or by any means, electronic, mechanical, by photocopying, or recording or otherwise, without the prior written permission of the copyright owner.

For my three beautiful daughters

Dear David,

Enjoy!

signature Ben ..... Officer 'A'

24/12/22.

The suppression of
Tiger! Tiger! Tiger!

Readers will notice that some details in this book have been deliberately blanked out. These 'banned' words, phrases, and minor descriptions are currently the subject of legal suppression. Over the course of the coronial inquest into the Lindt Café siege, the New South Wales (NSW) State Coroner made a substantial number of non-publication orders. Many were related to the Tactical Operations Unit (TOU) and granted at the request of the NSW Police Force through public interest immunity. Orders relevant to *Tiger! Tiger! Tiger!* cover police methodology and the deployment of specialised equipment, as well as the suppression of an operator's full name and identity. (With their approval, my TOU mates have only been identified by an alias.)

One such order, still in force, is specific to the non-publication of my identity. (This includes photographs and drawings.) (For the purpose of the inquest I was simply referred to as 'Officer A.') Right now, if I were to publish my full name, I would be in breach of this order. However, despite numerous well-intentioned requests to both the coroner and the police hierarchy, I was not provided with relevant requirements but rather referred to an extensive list of limited-detail, public-domain non-publication orders. Importantly, these orders only relate to the Lindt Café siege and subsequent enquiry.

Unlike the restrictions placed on me by the NSW Coroner, I have been informed that *Police Regulation 2015* specifically bans me from disclosing privileged information that derives from my capacity as a member of the NSW Police Force (despite no longer serving). For these reasons, from the beginning, I have been very careful in how I wrote about certain details, especially those that could potentially compromise an officer's safety or operational effectiveness. Many of my best mates still serve in the TOU. I would never increase the risk to them or any other serving police officer. I believed that I had successfully achieved this. My good intentions were clearly shown by my briefing of all parties prior to publication. Surprisingly and disappointingly, I was met with official silence, stonewalling, and then with what could be interpreted as veiled threats of imprisonment and crippling fines if I were to publish my book in an unredacted form.

The truth is, there is nothing in *Tiger! Tiger! Tiger!* that a Google search and countless YouTube clips wouldn't reveal within minutes. These open-access sources yield far more detail than anything I have written. Even movies or popular television shows about Special Weapons And Tactics (SWAT) or special forces expose detailed methodology and the use of specialised equipment. And then there are countless online computer games such as *Call of Duty* that rely on the input of ex-special forces soldiers to create authenticity and realism. I put this argument to the decision makers. They refused to acknowledge common sense.

And so, in this first edition, I have temporarily masked some details and pushed forward with publication. Importantly, there are pending applications to remove both current restrictions and general suppression. Notwithstanding, I've chosen to leave my story intact. This is because included in the suppression list are details that have been widely broadcast on Channel 9 *A Current Affair*, ABC (the national broadcaster) *4 Corners*, and even an episode of the Seven Network's *The Force* together with countless other news stories and press articles. Significantly, several books, written by ex-NSW police officers, including one by a former TOU operator, were not opposed, according to my understanding. Were these programs broadcast and books published with the knowledge of the police hierarchy? Because, at the very least, they set a precedent for the free publication of my story in its entirety. An example is the demand to remove 'all references to methods of entry into strongholds'. This was despite the police hierarchy inviting *A Current Affair* to film and report on a comprehensive TOU capability display that included every one of the tactical methods of entry written about in this book.

Rest assured, however, that despite a concerted effort to suppress *Tiger! Tiger! Tiger!*—especially a firsthand account of the bravery of my TOU mates—this story will be told.

ACKNOWLEDGEMENTS

To my publisher, Terrease McComb of The End Publishing Limited I say thank you for recognising the importance of my story. Special recognition is also extended to my editors Dr Rob Goodfellow and Mr Peter O'Neill OAM of Cultural Consulting, to my family and friends, as well as my good mates and colleagues, without whose unfailing encouragement and support this book would not have been possible.

Finally, I'd like to acknowledge the following people for their timely endorsements—Tony Abbott AC, Prime Minister of Australia (2013 to 2015), Mike Baird AO, Premier of NSW (2014 to 2017), Ray Hadley OAM, Nine Radio broadcaster, Louisa Hope, Lindt Café siege hostage survivor and Dawn O'Neil AM, former CEO of Lifeline and Beyond Blue.

This is a remarkable book that I couldn't put down and finished reading through a haze of tears. If you want to know about life as a cop—from general duties to tactical operations—you must read it. It's all there: the adrenalin, the exhilaration, the terror, the mateship, as well as boredom and the frustration with bureaucracy, judiciary and the 'higher ups'. Finally, there's coming to terms with Post-Traumatic Stress Disorder (PTSD) and never again being able to do what was loved and lived for. Ben ▮▮▮ has done much, suffered much, and overcome much. Reading *Tiger! Tiger! Tiger!* is like listening to a mate by your side taking you through the things most of us wonder about but never experience. May others be inspired to take on life in the same way.

Tony Abbott AC, Prime Minister of Australia (2013 to 2015).

Against what standard does one judge a man demanded to stare down death to save strangers. Who will dare say that they could have done better.

New South Wales State Coroner Michael Barnes, Coronial Inquest Findings.

FOREWORD

Do you remember what you were doing the day of the Lindt Café terrorist attack? For those of us held captive and those poised to rescue us, there remains a shared bond, a moment in time, a common grief, and a unique terror. For this reason, the New South Wales Police Tactical Operations Unit (the TOU) will always hold a special place in my heart.

After the siege I spent three months in hospital and many more in rehabilitation. My mother, Robin, who was also wounded, spent the years until her passing in 2018 trying to get over what happened to her. Some wounds are not visible. Trauma can take its own sweet time before it grabs your heart and shakes your innards out. And there you are, imagining that for all you've experienced, and all you've seen, and all the hits you've taken, somehow, you're special enough to get away with it. Ben ███'s story explains that no matter how tough, trained, skilled or brilliant you might be, Post-Traumatic Stress Disorder (PTSD) can still get you in the end.

I'm so grateful for this honest account of what happened to Ben and his TOU mates. Even after all these years, I find many questions remain unanswered. This extraordinary book has helped fill those gaps, and in doing so it has brought me great comfort.

Louisa Hope

October 2022

PREFACE

I first got the idea for *Tiger! Tiger! Tiger!* after my psychologist encouraged me to record past traumas as part of Post-Traumatic Stress Disorder (PTSD) therapy. However, my motive for writing this book is that a front-line, unfiltered account of the courageous actions of the Tactical Operations Unit (TOU) in response to the Lindt Café terrorist attack needs to be told and, in doing so, my hope is that it might also provide closure for everyone involved.

Tiger! Tiger! Tiger! is my all-in story about an Aussie SWAT cop and his mates (the 'boys in black') who risked everything to save the Lindt Café hostages. It will challenge what you thought you knew about the siege but, more than that, it shares the significant moments in my life and policing career that led to Lindt: the reality of everyday policing, our selection and training, my role as a TOU operator and sniper, as well as the TOU's involvement in countless high-risk and life-threatening operations—protecting the community and arresting the worst in society, always faced as a team of professionals with loyalty and mateship.

Writing *Tiger! Tiger! Tiger!* has been personally confronting. I'm not the sort of person who is normally comfortable with talking about how I feel. But as I began to recall operational details about the Lindt Café siege, and write them down, I surprised myself at how emotionally honest my descriptions were. In doing this, I've revealed far more than I ever imagined or intended. This is because I have another story to tell. Like other emergency service officers, I've paid a high price for my service. I know first-hand the heartache and hurt this can cause and the terrible toll it takes on the lives of our families and loved ones. So my other purpose in telling the story of a front-line TOU officer is to explain my personal resilience. This is because, if I can find a way of living with the psychological damage done to me in the line of duty, then there is another message in this book: one of hope.

'Officer A' (Ben)
October 2022

PROLOGUE

"Alpha team, prepare to initiate the Emergency Action," our sergeant yelled. The lives of the hostages were now in the hands of the Tactical Operations Unit alone. "Ready yourselves boys, we're about to go in." *Boom.* Another shotgun blast went off inside the café.

"What the fuck is happening in there?" I said out loud. "Is he executing hostages?" It took every ounce of my strength and discipline not to break rank and run in. I was like an over-wound watch spring.

"Just give us the order for Christ's sake," one of the younger boys in the stack called out.

"Hold!" our sergeant roared.

Boom. A third shot went off inside the café. I felt the blood pulsing in my ears. Over the sergeant's radio I could hear: "Hostage down, white window two. Repeat, hostage down, white window two." I checked my ▉▉▉▉ laser pointer and light source one final time and, with a single sharp slap of my left palm, I confirmed that the magazine of my M4 was firmly seated. I was completely focused. I slowed my breathing and stared at the café entrance door just waiting for the code word…

Around The Campfire

When I meet someone for the first time and get asked to tell them a bit about myself, I usually say: "I have three daughters and I live in ███████████████" but what they really want to know is: 'What do you do for a job?' So, I usually answer: "Nothing special. What about you?" This is because experience has taught me that some people have preconceived ideas about police officers, and this can make them feel uncomfortable.

I've always been proud of being a cop, but I never offer it up straight away. If I do, it often leads to a list of all-too-familiar questions like "There was this speeding fine I got a few years ago. I think the cop's name was Peter Smith, you *must* know him." I usually just let that one go.

If they press me, I say: "We're actually the third largest police force in the world." I work in the Tactical Operations Unit ... the TOU, not the highway patrol."

"Is the TOU like SWAT?"

"Yeah, pretty similar, ay," I continue.

And then they usually ask: "So, you're in the riot squad then?"

"Nope, definitely not," I add, shaking my head and smiling.

Another question I often get is: "Have you ever shot anyone?"

"Nah," I just don't want to talk about that.

Then the conversation awkwardly moves on to: "So, what sort of jobs do you actually do then?"

And I answer: "Basically, the TOU are NSW Police's response to all high-risk operations, like sieges and hostage situations."

"Armed robberies?"

"Yeh, that too. Basically, any job where someone has a weapon and is willing to use it on the cops." Then you see them thinking—because this always provokes a reaction.

"Terrorism incidents? Are you the ones that did the Lindt Café job?" Inevitably, the next question is, "Were you involved?" And then, they offer their opinion on how the operation should have been conducted.

When we're asked to describe ourselves, most people think about what they do for a job—because that's such a big part of who we are, especially for a police officer. (When cops 'clock off' for the day, they still have the same powers and responsibilities to intervene if they witness a crime or a person needs assistance.) But I'm much more than that. Who I am, my story of resilience and how this played out during and after the Lindt Café siege, started long before I became a police officer. And so, to get a true understanding of my journey— an adrenalin-charged career in police tactical operations, constantly exposed to confrontation, violence and death—I want to take a few pages to describe where it is that I'm coming from.

*****

I was a happy kid living in a world of my own imagination. I built miniature motocross tracks in the sandpit and made the noises of a two-stroke motorbike at full throttle while I won the fantasy AMA 250cc supercross championship—overtaking the great Jeremy McGrath on the final berm to cross the finishing line unopposed. But there was no podium celebration in my imaginary world, no lifting of the trophy above my head to the roar and approval of the crowd because, even at that age, it was never about recognition. When I did occasionally snap out of my pretend world, it was to watch *Bush Tucker Man* on ABC television—because Major Leslie James Hiddins was my hero. (We were rural, and the antenna would only pick up the

ABC, so that was that.)

I grew up on five acres n the Hawkesbury, one and a half hours north-west of Sydney, and was free to have all sorts of adventures with my younger brother Luke and baby sister Leah. I was surrounded by animals: chickens, cows, dogs, ducks, goats, guinea pigs, horses, and rabbits. I'd often capture lizards and mice in the grain shed and keep them safe as pets until my mother convinced me to release them.

My mum was always caring for injured wildlife. One day I walked into her ensuite bathroom and found a flying fox hanging from the shower head. He looked at me and squawked. I looked at him and shrieked. We cared for 'Batty the fruit bat' until he regained his strength and released him back to his mates. (He returned every night to eat nectarines in the tree outside my bedroom window.)

My father was a country boy who grew up on a 3,000-acre sheep farm. He believed in hard work and the outback, so much of my childhood was spent in the bush. My mother was from the North Shore of Sydney, so she was a city girl. She introduced me to culture and people through art galleries, museums, and trips to the 'big smoke', but her true passion was nature conservation and the work of Sir David Attenborough. Soon enough it became my passion too.

I spent a lot of time with my grandfather around an open fire brewing billy tea and baking damper—smothered with 'Cocky's Joy' (Golden Syrup—which has always been popular on outback stations) and listening to bushranger stories. My grandfather was a great source of family history (and just about everything else for that matter). I learnt from him that my surname ▮▮▮ comes from the Middle English ▮▮▮— an occupational name for someone who traded in gold coins. He also told me that I was related to the universal human rights advocate and writer Annie Besant, and to the prolific 19th century novelist and historian Sir Walter Besant, his brother William Henry Besant (an accomplished mathematician) and Cecil Rhodes, the founding prime minister of what was once called the Cape Colony. I was also a descendant of English free settlers and Irish convicts—together with Aboriginal and Afro-Caribbean ancestors from the very first years of the Botany Bay Colony, New South Wales.

"Was Ned Kelly a hero?" I asked my grandpa one night as the two of us quietly sat around a campfire.

"Well Benny boy, you have both English and Irish ancestors—and others besides. The English and the Irish have very different versions of the Ned Kelly legend. The Irish see it as the story of someone who fought against English mistreatment of Irish settlers. To them Ned was a hero. Your English ancestors have always sided with the police who say he was a criminal. Let me tell you the story from both sides and you can decide for yourself." From that moment, I admired people who could present a balanced argument and then leave it up to you to judge the evidence for yourself; and I mistrusted those who clearly had their own agendas.

There were many campfire stories about my family. My great-grandfather had been a soldier in the famed 4th Australian Light Horse Regiment during the First World War and was in the Battle of Beersheba—one of the last massed cavalry charges in history. (Actually, the Light Horse were mounted infantry.) He also served as a radio operator in the battles of Megiddo and Gaza in what was then the Ottoman Empire and later British Palestine. Like many of my fellow Generation Xers, I was raised on the ANZAC traditions of loyalty, mateship, sacrifice and service, which made my generation self-sufficient, resourceful and individualistic.

My grandfather had been a flight engineer in the Royal Australian Air Force (RAAF) during the Second World

War. Sometimes, if I pestered him, he would tell me a story. "Grandpa, please tell me about the bombers?" I'd ask.

"Well Benny boy, a lot of our fellas didn't make it back you know."

"What do you mean Grandpa? Killed?"

"Our chances of surviving over Germany were very low," he replied, looking past me to somewhere long ago and far away. "Incredibly low." Apparently, his best mate had flown so many missions that, according to Bomber Command, he was supposed to have died two-and-a-half times over. My Grandpa told me about one bombing mission that his friend was on where a German fighter shot their plane up badly. One engine was knocked out. There was smoke trailing from another, and the pilot was hit by shrapnel in the leg. "My friend was next to him in the cabin. He forced his thumb into the jagged wound to stop the blood flow from an artery." I grimaced. It might seem like too much detail for a kid but now my grandfather was on autopilot—not telling me a story anymore but talking out loud to himself.

"Imagine just a few years older than you Benny, fighting the freezing cold, cramping for hours, saturated in blood."

"Did they make it Grandpa?" I whispered, hoping against hope for a happy ending.

"Yes, my boy, they did. The pilot flew the bomber back to safety in England and they all survived."

My grandfather's war stories had a lasting impact on me. Every time these men strapped on a flying suit, they did so in the knowledge that their chances of survival were poor and that eventually most of them would pay for their service with their lives. And yet, they turned up for duty day after day—year after year.

My grandparents were a big part of my childhood and my grandfather's stories were the raw stuff of my imagination.

They lived on our property in a caravan while they were building a house. The daily routine for my younger brother and sister and I was to wake up early and run over in our slippers and dressing gowns. (My parents assured me that they weren't *Star Wars* fans and that it was a pure coincidence that I was named Ben, aka Ben Kenobi, that my brother was called Luke and that my sister's name was Leah.)

My grandmother would make us Weet-Bix with hot milk and honey for breakfast while my grandfather told us stories about the American Wild West. He never seemed to tell the same tale twice. Then hour upon hour I acted out my own Western movie adventures with home-made stagecoaches fashioned from bedsheets and cardboard boxes—always ending in a big O.K. Corral-like gunfight.

My grandmother, bless her, made me a cowboy outfit with a little leather waistcoat, embroidered chaps and a gun-belt bandolier complete with a hip holster that held my trusty cap gun at the ready—and to top it off I sported a well-worn, Aussie-made, Akubra hat. My liberal-minded mother tried to take my toy guns away but when she found me with sticks shaped like rifles, playing the same games, she realised that there probably wasn't any point.

My mum had a great love of horse riding. She had a Quarter Horse of her own named Jollian. We three kids had a pony that we all shared. His name was Tarago. One of my favourite movies was the Australian classic, *The Man from Snowy River*, based on Banjo Paterson's famous poem of the same name. The climax to the film was when the rugged mountain man chased a mob of wild brumbies (wild horses) off a steep mountain ridge that no other rider would dare to take on. I re-enacted the scene over and over dressed in full Western attire. I rode our eager pony down the bank of our dam, leaning right back in the saddle, cracking my home-made stock whip above my head. But all creatures have their limits. One day, I was chasing imaginary outlaws on horseback, as you do, and I drew my cap gun to fire and discovered that Tarago had his limits too. He was a sturdy animal with a good temperament but the sudden and unexpected shocks—*Bang. Bang. Bang*—were more than he was bred to bear.

From an early age, it was clear that I had a fascination with guns—pretend ones of course—especially my cap gun, but also spud guns, water pistols and a John Wayne-inspired lever-action toy Winchester rifle. The barrel and working parts were made from hard grey plastic simulating the steel components with a faux woodgrain plastic stock. (When I was a kid, toys were still made in Australia.)

I was born to be competitive—from soccer (both indoor and outdoor), to racing skiffs at the Royal Sydney Yacht Squadron, to schoolboy rugby league and rugby union, to swimming and baseball. But my real passion was motocross—dirt-bike racing. My mother preferred us to ride horses. The compromise was that my brother and I rode our pushbikes around a little figure-of-eight track making motorbike noises, before, one day, she couldn't say 'no' any longer. My father bought my brother and me a Kawasaki KX60. I loved it. The problem was my brother did too. Dad eventually bought me another bike, a Suzuki RM80, and so began my motocross journey.

We quickly got bored of riding around the paddocks; we needed jumps—so we made our own. Dad worked in excavation and occasionally he'd drop off a load of soil. It was like all our Christmases had come at once. My jump-building obsession involved a sunrise to sunset commitment—every chance I got. Often my mother had to come out in the dark and drag me home for dinner. My determination far outweighed almost every other consideration—including food. The exception was, as the eldest child, I was always looking out for my younger siblings. A concern for the vulnerable and later a protective attitude towards my colleagues, including being elected TOU Police Association Branch Chairman, was a trait I carried with me into my policing career and into the firefight at the Lindt Café.

There was no greater adrenalin rush than motocross—lined up with 30 other bikes, revving to the max, completely focused on the starting gate, just waiting for it to drop. Then *Boom*, the roar of bikes as I accelerated to get the holeshot. Thirty finely tuned machines racing flat chat into the small first corner rarely allowed everyone to make it around. There were often crashes with me being involved in my fair share.

The rest of the race was pushing to pass your opponents, riding as hard as both your bike and your body would allow: focus, attack position, airtime, brake slide. Motocross was loud and raw with every possible sequence and combination of decision-making under pressure. I learnt that mistakes have consequences. This focused my mind. I thrived.

Motocross was a family affair and most Sundays saw us driving all over the State to compete. The only break my poor family seemed to get was when I was physically injured—in hospital or recovering at home: concussions, fractured limbs, and torn ligaments—but I always got better.

General Duties

Serving as a general duties (GDs) police officer exposed me to the worst of society and, sometimes, the very best. This made me both a cynic and an optimist at the same time. It showed me the distance between my natural optimism and the reality of having to deal with so many damaged people. I was disappointed by those who looked for excuses to hurt themselves and others but, on the other hand, I was impressed by individuals who overcame adversity. Six years as a 'street cop' confirmed my darkest beliefs about human nature but also challenged my many stereotypes. These experiences were like steps on a journey to those fateful few seconds between life and death in Martin Place, Sydney, 12 years later.

The graduation ceremony was held at the Police Academy in Goulburn—one of three classes to finish in 2002. My family were there to celebrate the occasion. I stood on the parade ground in full dress uniform, lined up with all the other new recruits. The NSW Premier, Bob Carr, and the NSW Police Commissioner, Ken Moroney, both gave inspirational speeches and the crowd applauded. We all removed our hats and threw them into the air with a loud cheer. We were now sworn NSW Police Officers.

My first appointment was Bankstown Local Area Command (LAC). At the time, the area was known for its gang violence, especially drive-by shootings. One of my lecturers at the academy, who had once been stationed there, described the LAC as "a confronting place to work, with the highest level of crime in the State." I put down Bankstown as my number-one choice and, of course, I got it. I was 21 years old.

I walked into the police station in uniform, full of pride and still on a high from the graduation ceremony earlier that day. The waiting room was crowded. At the front counter was an overworked female constable. She glanced up from calming an angry, red-headed man who was telling her how disgusted he was with the police. He was swearing in her face, but she didn't seem troubled in the slightest. "You one of the new blokes?" she questioned me without looking up again.

I smiled and replied, "Yes, hello, my name is Ben. Ben ███."

She turned her head slightly and yelled, "Sarge!"

I heard a male voice call back, "Yeah?"

"Another new bloke."

A big man appeared from a side entrance next to the counter. He must have been seven feet tall because he had to duck to get through the doorway. He looked me up and down and motioned to follow him down a corridor before he turned into an office and sat down. The sergeant then pulled out a set of keys and a padlock which he slid across the desk. "The gun safe is over there and this is the key for your brief drawer. You'll find out more on Monday. Be here at 7.00 a.m.," he said.

I paused before simply replying, "Yes sergeant," but really thinking, 'Is that it?'

"Good," he replied. His expression said it all, 'That's it, you can bugger off now'.

On Monday morning, I joined a group of young men and women from very diverse backgrounds. It was an election year and the government had upped the intake of recruits. We were summoned to a briefing room where we waited for further instructions. Fortunately, there was at least one familiar face. 'Apps' and I shared a rental in Goulburn during our training and we'd become good friends. He was born in the Philippines, migrated to Australia as a teenager, and grew up in Cabramatta. He was short and stocky, with a shaved head and tattoos. There always seemed to be a cigarette resting in the corner of his mouth. He called me 'brother' and his large extended family embraced me like a son.

When I first met Apps, I was living in a motel. To pay for it, on weekends, I'd drive home and work in my mate 'Big Nick's' tree-lopping business. It was hard work, and on Monday mornings I kept falling asleep in lectures. Apps came to my rescue and offered me a room in his unit. He couldn't cook to save himself but his mother sure could. Her signature dish was *Adobo*, one of the most popular dishes in the Philippines. (No more peanut butter sandwiches and two-minute noodles for me.)

In Bankstown, our group was soon greeted by two female education duty officers. They formally introduced us to the station superintendent, detectives, highway patrol officers, and members of the plain-clothes proactive team who specialised in drug- and gang-related crime. We were also introduced to our field training officers who'd show us the ropes. I was assigned to Constable 'Hardy'. She was of average build and wore reading glasses. Her dark hair was pulled up in a high ponytail and tied off with a rubber band. I had expected a big man like the sergeant.

With the oversight of Charles Sturt University, the academy had redesigned the policing curriculum to be more academic and less 'hands-on'. However, after the station briefing, I was quickly told by Hardy, "Whatever you think you've learnt at the academy, a lot of it's bullshit." She must have noticed the shocked look on my face. "Well, some of it is anyway," she continued. "What I mean is that your real training to be a cop starts … now."

Within minutes of the induction ending, I was on the road with Hardy patrolling the streets of Bankstown. I was assigned observer status. The other officer in the car was a fellow probationer who had already been in the job for six months. His name was 'Gus'. He was just under six feet tall and about my age with Ken Doll meets Astro Boy gelled dark hair and a Zoolander perpetual five o'clock shadow. He always seemed to be lost in his own mind as if he didn't have a care in the world, but he had a sense of humour and a good nature. I liked him immediately and so did everyone else; but more than that—I trusted him.

Bankstown LAC is culturally diverse. It is so large that it includes 23 suburbs and 12 postcodes, an airport, and the Villawood Immigration Detention Centre. There's a sizeable Vietnamese and Pacific Islander community (as well as an older Anglo population); however, it is now predominantly the home of migrants from the Middle East, especially Lebanon. The first time I overheard two men speaking in Arabic, I was convinced that they were about to punch on. Hardy assured me that they were 'just having a chat'. I was also lucky to work with an Australian-born Lebanese cop. He educated me about how brutal life had been in Lebanon during the civil war and how complex the Bankstown migrant community was. He also introduced me to Middle Eastern food, especially my favourites: kibbeh, kousa and kafta and the shisha water pipe.

After my initial six-week probation, I was trusted to patrol 'two-up' in the police vehicle. I enjoyed working with my mentor and hearing her street cop 'war stories'. My attitude towards women in policing had already changed from expecting to work only with men, to thinking that working in teams with women was a good thing, to not thinking about it anymore.

The two of us were patrolling the streets of Greenacre—a neighbouring suburb of Bankstown. The area was known for the horrendous, systematic gang rapes coordinated by the Skaf brothers—scumbags Bilal and Mohammed. When investigating crime in one housing commission block on Greenacre Road, we were expected always to call for backup. Police cars had been targeted with bricks and rocks and officers surrounded and attacked by large groups of locals with baseball bats, iron bars and even fireworks. I caught a glimpse of a young man, about my age, riding a high-performance road bike. It was a new black Yamaha R1. "Bloody hell he's only in his undies and no helmet," Hardy said in disbelief. The man stopped and stared in our direction. He then aggressively revved the accelerator, clearly considering his options.

Hardy pulled our car up just short of him, blocking a potential exit. Suddenly, he dropped the bike, smashing it onto the concrete before running down the road towards the housing complex. I gave chase. "Ben, wait!" Hardy yelled out, but—too late. I was young and full of adrenalin and completely focused on chasing this guy down. He had a head start on me, but I was determined. I sprinted after him with public housing apartment blocks to my left and right. It was then I noticed the rows of scowling unfriendly faces watching me from the windows and balconies. Groups of angry people started to gather at the front of their units—just like in the 2001 movie *Training Day*. The POI ('Person of Interest' in police jargon) ran into a cul-de-sac before he veered into an open garage and disappeared through an internal door. He momentarily glanced back at me before slamming it shut.

I kicked the door as hard as I could. It burst open. Inside, an old Lebanese man with a walking stick wearing a brown fedora took one look at me, held his right hand to his heart, and collapsed onto a couch. I looked down, trying to take it all in. I saw the POI at the far end of the unit. He ran through another door slamming it shut as well. A woman then appeared in a burqa. She started screaming something in Arabic before she too held her chest and collapsed onto the floor. 'What the hell's going on here?' I thought, looking past her. The door was locked.

I took a step back, kicked it open as well, and was immediately confronted by the man who was now facing me with nowhere left to run. We stared at each other before he lifted his hands in a fighting stance. I struck first, taking him by surprise, with a tackle my junior rugby league coach would've been proud of. Then he hit me with an elbow to the side of my face. I wrestled his arms around behind his back and handcuffed him. My heart was racing. It took a few moments to compose myself. I could hear sirens in the distance. As my breathing slowed, I waited for a break in the voices on the police radio before managing to get on. "Bankstown 15, urgent, I require backup, POI in custody."

"Bankstown 15, what's your location?" responded the operator. I immediately thought, 'How can I explain where I was?' I'd been warned that the location was dangerous, and that backup was always required. The operator again called over the air, "Bankstown 15, repeat, what's your location?" I paused, trying to figure out a way to describe exactly where I was and then answer the more difficult question of why I was on my own. The guy then tried to head butt me while screaming for help from his mates. If I couldn't get assistance and quickly, I was in real danger. I positioned myself, facing the bedroom door. If anyone answered the man's call to attack me, I'd now see them coming. He continued to struggle violently.

"Radio, I'm in the rear bedroom of ... ." At that exact moment Hardy burst in, like the cavalry of my Wild West boyhood adventures.

"You owe me," she said, out of breath, pointing her finger in my direction and smiling before transmitting our location. "We'll need to have a chat about this later," she added in a more serious tone. That was the first of many times Hardy saved me from a dangerous situation—and from myself.

More police arrived. As I walked the offender out of the

room, I noticed our backup talking to the elderly man in the fedora and the woman in the burqa. Both had made a complete recovery (they'd been 'playing dead'). It was my first big arrest. One of the other cops patted me on the shoulder as much to say, 'good work'. I was reflecting on this when a large group of agitated, angry, and very annoyed men began surrounding us, yelling, and screaming in Arabic. Hardy added, "You know the bike was stolen?"

"I presumed it was," I replied.

"And this lot aren't very happy with you, are they?" she continued with an approving look that said, 'Today we won'. A fellow officer was speaking with the crowd in Arabic attempting to calm them down. It wasn't working.

The sergeant cautioned us, "We'd better clear out before the locals go 'berko' and we have to lock up half the neighbourhood."

"Ben. Let's go!" Hardy added with a sense of urgency. "You don't want to get a reputation as a shit magnet." But I didn't see it like that. For me, the job had everything: new challenges every day, camaraderie, teamwork, service and, on this day, running down a crim and making an arrest—securing the crook in the back of the paddy wagon, slamming the door, and locking it shut.

We arrived at the van dock at Bankstown police station. The custody sergeant was sitting behind his desk hunched over a keyboard like a question mark. I gave him a brief rundown of events. I was so happy with myself. He took one look at me and, without showing an ounce of interest said, "Here's the form, fill it out."

"Are you sure you want to do this charge. It's a lot of work for someone so inexperienced," Hardy said.

"Of course, I do, if that's ... okay?" I replied, in what must have been an annoyingly enthusiastic voice.

"Come on then or we'll be here forever," she continued, resigned to her fate.

The rest of our shift was taken up with searching the POI, completing the charge on the police computer system, taking offender photographs from the front and side, and then fingerprinting, before having everything verified by the custody sergeant. My lack of experience made it an even longer ordeal. Hardy was extremely patient. The inspector less so—police budgets are always tight in relation to overtime.

But this was just the beginning of the paperwork tsunami—that inescapable process of preparing a brief of evidence for court: my statement, the victims' record of events, witness subpoenas, producing interview transcripts, collating other police documentation, forensic testing and organising court dates. The theft of a motorcycle wasn't a hard brief to compile but, as a probationary officer, what it showed me was how much paperwork was involved in modern policing. It wasn't what I expected.

The sheer volume of administration in such a busy command means that you must complete it all at work and usually in your own time. Meanwhile there's an expectation that you engage in proactive policing, including knife and drug searches, licensed premises inspections, patrols of public places and schools and the surveillance of critical infrastructure that could be a possible terrorism target. I struggled with time management. The paperwork threatened to overwhelm me. Hardy again came to my rescue—and, in her own unpaid hours, got me up to speed.

There are many times in a GDs police officer's career where you feel more like a record keeper than a trained law enforcement officer and that 'real policing' is almost an afterthought. Then, on top of this, there's the stress of constant scrutiny, especially monitoring and oversight. Minor complaints—most of which are retaliatory or vindictive, are dealt with internally by an inspector or above. For more serious complaints, there's the professional standards command (Internal Affairs) and the police integrity commission (PIC), with the ombudsman overseeing everything. (The PIC was disbanded and reinvented as The NSW Law Enforcement Conduct Commission (LECC). This means that NSW Police Officers are the most paperwork-burdened, oversighted, regulated and complained-about profession in the State—but, despite all that, I loved—*almost*—every minute of my four years in GDs and two years in the plain clothes unit.

*****

My first 'deceased job' in Bankstown was a suicide on the train tracks. The man's dismembered body was spread over at least 100 metres. After removing shocked commuters from the scene and once the forensic investigators had finished, our work began. I was directed to assist another probationary officer—my now good mate Gus—to gather up the body parts and place them into plastic evidence bags. It was gruesome beyond words. We were especially careful to follow blood exposure protocols. "Watch out mate, pull your gloves up, he might have AIDS or something," Gus said placing a severed hand into a bag.

"Hey, Ben, have a look at this," Gus continued excitedly, picking up a leg, "The impact has stripped his shoes and socks off."

"Yeah, awesome," I replied, fighting back waves of nausea.

Another job involved managing the body of an intravenous drug user who had overdosed on a couch in her unit in the full sun. It was summer and the curtains were wide open. She'd been there for days before neighbours noticed the smell.

My partner and I rolled her over at the request of the crime scene investigators. The young woman was lime green on the exposed side and completely black on the underside. The stench was almost unbearable. I'd known the smell of decomposing animals when I was a kid—a dead kangaroo or a wombat on my pop's farm but this was different. It is something that you can never get used to—or forget. It's a smell so penetrating that your uniform must be bagged, binned, and replaced. A senior officer saw me wincing. "Here, try some of this," he said, handing me an almost empty jar of Vicks VapoRub. "Put a smear on your top lip, just below your nostrils." It was only *slightly* better than nothing.

Then, just to complete the trifecta, my partner and I were called to remove someone who had died in the bathtub. This time the body had been undisturbed for weeks rather than days. The person's human form had turned into a sort of thick soup. We needed a bucket to scoop the remains out. My partner muttered what must have been the understatement of the century, "This is so gross."

I replied, "I don't think I'll ever be able to unsee this." But that was just one of many confronting GDs experiences that could never be unseen.

"What's for dinner?" my offsider teased me, attempting to lighten the mood.

"Mum's making a salad," I replied.

"Thank God for that!"

I quickly discovered that police and paramedics work closely together. A close bond exists, based on trust and a mutual respect of each other's skill sets and the awareness of how testing and gruesome each other's job can be. From horrific car accidents to drug overdoses, to preventing the mentally ill from hurting themselves or others, to having to deal with deceased persons, we attend jobs together. Paramedics have assisted me countless times over the years. In turn, if an ambo ever requested backup, I'd make it my priority.

I had one such job where a heroin user had overdosed, and the ambos requested assistance before giving intravenous Narcan. (Narcan is administered to reverse the life-threatening effects of a narcotic overdose—heroin and morphine but, increasingly, street fentanyl and OxyContin.) When I arrived on the scene, one paramedic was giving first aid to a 30-something man on the ground and her offsider was trying to calm down his irate friend. "This one's going to go off when we *Narc* him. Last time he went apeshit," the young paramedic in her late 20s said.

"Let's get it done then," I reassured her.

"Thanks for coming so quickly," she continued with an appreciative smile.

"Too easy," I continued.

The Narcan was administered and the man immediately lived up to his reputation. His eyes opened wide, like a switch had been turned on, springing to his feet in one motion like an overstretched rubber band. With pure rage in his eyes his attention quickly turned to the female paramedic who was holding the now empty Narcan Min-I-Jet syringe.

"You wasted me fuck'en hit yer fuck'en bitch!" he squealed as he threw a punch straight towards her face. I grabbed hold of his arm, midair, just before impact and pushed him to the ground. He fell hard but immediately jumped back up again, this time growling and snarling like a wild animal. I was now clearly the focus of his rage. He then drew his head back, sucked air violently through both nostrils and spat right at my face through his methadone-ravaged blackened dolphin teeth. I ducked to the side—just in time but not before a gooey blob of blood-streaked loogie hit me just above my shirt pocket. Now I was the one who wasn't happy. I grabbed hold of his hoodie and again threw him to the ground—before handcuffing him. Later, in the back of the paddy wagon, he tried to engage me. "Sorry chief, didn't mean it. I just can't help me self. I get fuck'en agro when I waste a hit." ('Chief' is a common term used to address an authority figure by people who have spent time in gaol.)

There's a friendly rivalry between each emergency service. Cops and paramedics always enjoy stirring up Fire and Rescue. "Sorry we had to wake you guys from your beauty sleep, but we just couldn't put this stolen car doused with petrol out with our little fire extinguisher," I said with a smile as the crew were still rubbing their eyes and not looking happy about the late-night call-out. But, when faced with a life-threatening situation involving fire, you wanted them around. (Although not generally superstitious, emergency service officers all know not to ever say the unspeakable 'Q' word (for 'quiet'). If someone did carelessly say it, it always seemed to result in an immediate surge in the number of jobs.

Then there are emergency department (ED) nurses and doctors. They always seem to be overworked with full waiting rooms and ambulance stretchers lined up the corridor, into the parking bay and down the road. Every time I had to attend the ED at either Bankstown or Liverpool hospitals, there'd be at least one mentally ill patient going ballistic, while another family were yelling and crying demanding attention. Or else, there was someone acting out and collapsing onto the ground in a well-practised fit, attempting to jump the queue.

For some reason, there was often a patient running around completely naked. There was one time where a middle-aged woman was scraping lumps of faeces from her bare

Tiger! Tiger! Tiger!

backside and then throwing the larger chunks at the horrified clerical staff. Her distraught but well-presented daughter was trying to calm her down. But it was the admission clerks who were the most disturbed by it all. They had the unmistakable look on their faces of, 'I didn't sign up for this ... shit'. To the untrained eye, it was chaos but, as my experience grew, I realised that it was, in fact, organised chaos.

Later, I was involved in a foot pursuit where I was directly exposed to contaminated blood. The police radio operator's description was: "Bankstown 17 POI Caucasian, heavy build, approximately 190 centimetres, wearing a black hoodie, dark long pants and bum bag, white runners." The man had just committed a home invasion and assaulted the occupants with a baseball bat before running off with cash. I spotted him jogging along the side of the railway tracks. I pulled myself over a high cyclone fence, cutting my hand on some wire in the process. I sprinted, somehow keeping my footing on the loose blue metal ballast and ironbark sleepers. As I cornered the offender in a backyard, I recognised his face. "Billy, I know it's you. You've got nowhere to go," I said struggling to catch my breath.

Billy was a local drug dealer, standover man and all-round ratbag. It ended in a violent exchange of blows. He struck first, splitting my lip. My boxing coach would've yelled at me, "████████, never forget to block the first punch." I got Billy's blood all over me, including in the open wound on my hand. He was both HIV and hepatitis C positive, which meant I had to endure six months of testing, not knowing if I'd contracted anything before I was cleared (My good friend sustained a needle stick injury from an intentionally placed syringe in the boot handle of the police vehicle.)

However, the everyday work of a GDs police officer isn't always so dramatic. Rather, it is ordinary human tragedy that tends to define the job. This is often emotionally traumatic but, at the same time, it can be surprisingly life-affirming. The baby was a six-month-old boy. His parents were a hard-working Western Sydney blue-collar 'Aussie battler' couple—a factory worker and a cleaner. I had to explain that an autopsy was required for a suspected cot death. The little boy was dressed in a pale blue onesie with his blonde hair perfectly combed to the side. His face was as pale as a sheet. The sergeant had chosen my female partner and me because, at the time, neither of us had children. We watched as an older ED nurse adjusted the baby's bedding to ensure that he was 'comfortable', which is something I've noticed nurses do with deceased adults as well. The nurse's hands were trembling, and her eyes were swollen with tears. She came back several times to do this and we had to ask her to stop. Her emotional cup was clearly overflowing. The parents pulled a small blanket up to their son's chin and then sat quietly next to the cot holding hands and looking down, as we waited for the doctor to complete the paperwork. I often thought about the couple and their little boy, especially years later after I met my wife, and we had children.

The constant exposure to physical danger is one thing, but it is other people's trauma that seems to take the greater toll on a police officer's mental health, and all front-line responders for that matter. This is especially true of murders, suicides, serious road accidents, sexual abuse cases, gunshot wounds and knife attacks. Young children, women and the vulnerable elderly were always the hardest for me to cope with.

It was a Wednesday around midnight. There had been a lull in the number of jobs, which in Bankstown was rare. My junior partner 'Tommy' and I had taken the opportunity to catch up on a mountain of outstanding paperwork. "Isn't it time for our break?" Tommy said, looking up at the clock from behind the ancient computer monitor. "I could really do with a proper coffee," he added, yawning. "Ben, what do you say we head over to Krispy Kreme and get a latte?"

"I might top-deck my doughnut with a scoop of mango ice cream," I replied enthusiastically.

"Now you're talking, man," Tommy said, obviously starting to feel more awake.

"I thought you were on a diet?" I added with a cheeky grin.

"I'm starting as soon as these night shifts are over."

While we bantered, I was typing away and listening to the police radio at the same time. This is a skill that police officers develop. I heard a priority job come over the station intercom: two high pitched beeps. In cop speak, it was a 'double beeper'. An emergency triple 0 call had come in from a lady reporting that she'd been stabbed and that the man was still in her house. I looked at Tommy, we nodded to each other, and I said, "Let's go!" The address was only a couple of streets away. I drove with lights and sirens deliberately off and pulled up out front as quietly as I could. We ran to the front door that was slightly ajar. I drew my firearm and Tommy passed me a torch. (GDs Glock handguns don't have a light source.) I held it with my left hand positioning it under my right, which was holding my weapon and activated the torch. My heart was pounding. There was no backup. I took a deep breath. We nodded to each other and stepped inside.

The house was in darkness. I shone my torch down the hallway with my finger on the receiver of my pistol. Using hand signals, we went from room to room clearing the ground level. I pointed to the stairs and we moved quickly and quietly towards them. I signalled to Tommy with my index finger pressed to my lips in the universal sign to 'hush'. He went left and I went right. I cleared an upstairs bathroom before noticing the last door on the left, at the end of the hallway, was open. I could see a faint light coming from inside.

I gently pushed the door open, revealing the entirety of the dimly lit room and a scene of horror. A woman in a night dress was lying on her side, curled up in the foetal position on a double bed, facing away from me. I eased my way in before standing at the base of the mattress. She was saturated in blood with a large red circle surrounding her, soaked into the white linen. I glanced up at the walls and ceiling that were splattered in blood. I paused momentarily in a state of near shock, trying to take it all in, grappling with the realisation that I'd been too late to save her.

Suddenly and unexpectedly, the woman rolled her head slightly, moaned and looked straight at me. She was still alive and holding a cordless telephone to her ear against a mess of blood-soaked hair. Tommy came in beside me. "We need paramedics here. Now!" I stood by the woman's bedside, looking into her eyes which were filled with raw terror. "The ambulance is coming. You're safe now," I said in a strained but reassuring voice. I held her trembling hand as she attempted a pain-wracked smile. I made a gesture that I wanted to assess her wounds, but she just tightened her grip on my fingers. The terror now left her eyes, and I knew I was at least comforting her. But I needed help to save her life and I needed it now.

The ambos arrived quickly and worked methodically. She still wouldn't release her grip, so I stood by her, doing my best to keep out of the way. They checked her vital signs, before removing her night dress. It was then that I could see the full extent of her injuries. There were too many deep puncture wounds to count. The woman was placed on a stretcher with two intravenous drips running into her arm and rushed to hospital. I took a deep breath and sat on the bed with my head in my hands trying to process it all when Tommy burst back into the room. "You okay man?" I immediately replied, "Yeah, let's go."

The backup crew had located a shirtless man in a nearby park with a bloody knife in his hand. He matched the description the woman had given: 'Caucasian, heavy-set with scruffy brown hair'. The detectives told me that the suspect had an extensive history of mental illness and was well known to them for randomly stabbing a teenage girl in the face in the street some years earlier. He told detectives that the reason he attacked the elderly woman was because "She'd pruned some shrubs on her property without asking him." It was so disordered (and he wasn't even a neighbour). He'd waited until dark, climbed up the guttering of the two-storey house and onto an upstairs balcony, entering through an unlocked window before casually walking into the woman's bedroom. She was reading by the light of a bedside lamp at the time and didn't notice him until it was too late.

The widow, who was aged in her late 60s, lived alone. She had a close and caring extended family—Lebanese Maronite Catholics who, later in Liverpool Hospital, told me about her life in war-torn suburban Beirut before she fled to Australia as a refugee. In one word, they described her as 'tough'. Later, the lady told me that the only way she could get the man to stop stabbing her was to 'play dead'. When her attacker finally left, she mustered all her strength and rang emergency triple 0. I was impressed by her courage. Even as he was killing her, she had the inner strength to do what needed to be done. After an extensive stay in hospital and then rehabilitation, which included retraining for brain damage sustained through a stab wound to her skull, in a show of character, she refused her family's pleas to move in with them. But the truth was, she was never the same again, always obsessively checking that her doors and windows were locked, forever battling the effects of her emotional and physical trauma.

The lady's daughter was very sweet. She said, "You cops see the worse in society, don't you?"

I replied, "But we also get to meet good people too, like you and your mum."

The case affected me. I had nightmares about it for weeks but, like a lot of terrible experiences in GDs, I just locked it away. Most cops do. Tommy experienced other ordeals besides, especially working in the NSW Child Sex Crimes Unit. Years later, when I was working in the TOU, Tommy was one of two undercover cops involved in a 'buy-bust' operation of drugs and firearms. We made the arrest at night in a public swimming pool car park in Sydney's west. One of the offenders had a semi-automatic pistol down the front of his pants. As he fumbled for the weapon, I deployed my Taser. The probes flew right past Tommy's head, striking the offender in the chest, instantly incapacitating him. We arrested everyone just to make sure Tommy's cover wasn't blown. (He was wrestled to the ground and handcuffed as well.) I was worried I might've been too rough with him. "Sorry about that mate. You all good?" I said, back at the station.

"No problems," he replied, shaking my hand. "Just another day at the office," he added with a forgiving smile.

*****

It was a routine 'break and enter' investigation. I knocked on the door and heard a female voice say, "Just hold on," and then, "Please come in officer." The woman unlocked the security screen while adjusting her colourful hijab. Her home was very tidy with large white polished floor tiles and Persian carpets, enormous silver picture-framed scenes from Mecca and the Haj and clean marble benchtops. The woman called to someone in another room. A man entered.

"Sorry, Constable ▇▇▇, is it?" She asked, looking up at my name badge. "This is my husband, Mohammad."

The man warmly cupped my hand and said, "Please, *habibi*, take a seat. I insist," gesturing with a welcoming sweep of his arm. *Habibi* is an Arabic expression meaning 'my friend', 'my brother', or 'my love'. I often heard it said in people's homes. Mohammad sat on a white leather couch facing me across a glass-topped stainless-steel-framed coffee table. He was dressed in smart, dark charcoal grey trousers, and a black long-sleeve Mandalay-collar style cotton shirt. His perfectly polished black slip-on leather shoes were left at the door. He had a kind face, a close-cropped haircut, and a large, full black beard. He called out something in Arabic and three children appeared. The two boys politely shook my hand. The little girl just stared at me from behind her mother.

"Hello there. What's your name?" I asked.
"My name is Fatima."
"Are you a little shy?"
"Yes. Are you a policeman?"
"I am a policeman and I'm here to help your daddy. Have you started school yet?"
"No, next year," the little girl smiled, clearly now more relaxed with me.
I replied, "That's exciting, Fatima."
"Your children are very polite," I commented to her father.
"Yes, yes, thank you. I teach them to respect the police."
"Good man."

Mohammad showed me a smashed side window and we went through a list of what was stolen. I walked back into the lounge room where a plate of homemade baklava, a small blue porcelain cup of strong Turkish-style coffee and a glass of cold water were waiting for me. That was one of the good experiences I had in Bankstown, but then there were others.

We pulled up to the front of a run-down fibro public housing residence with no garden or trees. It might've been the home of any petty thug—anywhere—but it was in Bankstown. There were two cars parked on the overgrown front lawn. One was a brand-new Subaru WRX with extensive illegal modifications, complete with a Lebanese flag displayed in the back window and a small gold *Quran* pendant hanging from the rear-view mirror. The other was a black Range Rover with dark window tints and a personalised licence plate that started with the letters 'LEBO'. There was also an expensive fishing boat resting on a trailer parked on the median strip and a jet ski in an open carport. I knocked on the door. A dog barked and snarled. From inside I heard someone say, "Wait bro, till I lock me pitty away ha." The man then yelled, "Shut da fuck up," and I heard a dull thud. The dog yelped and whined, and the barking stopped. "Come in chief," he continued, looking me up and down.

"You know pit bulls are illegal don't you?" I said, checking to see that the dog was okay.

"Nah bro, he's an American staffy."

The air was stale with cooking oil and tobacco smoke. There were McDonald's hamburger packaging, doner kebab wrappers and empty takeaway Coke cups with lids and straws strewn across on the floor amongst dirty clothes and an overflowing bowl of cigarette butts. The sink was full of unwashed dishes and a saucepan of what looked like last night's leftovers. There was a woman in a black hijab sitting on the tiles with a group of children watching an Arabic-language movie on a massive flat-screen television. She didn't look up or acknowledge me.

The man was stocky, even muscular, with a long beard and a freshly shaven moustache. He was wearing an ill-fitting baseball cap with oversized sunglasses and dressed in white Everlast pants and a blue Canterbury Bulldogs singlet that revealed his sleeve-tattooed arm. He was draped in jewellery: a thick chunky silver necklace, an enormous silver wristwatch and silver diamond-studded earrings. Strung across his neck was what looked like a Louis Vuitton manbag.

"So, bro, liss'enn. Some dog tried steal'en me boat last night. Lucky me pitty chased them fuck'en junkies off ha." (It sounded like he wasn't up on the politically correct terminology like 'substance dependent person', 'habitual user' or 'addiction sufferer'.)

"Did you say pitty?" I continued.

"Nah bro, Staffy."

"Did you get a look at them?" I asked, note pad and pen in hand.

"Nah bro, that's your job ha."

"So how do you know someone was trying to steal it?" I continued patiently.

"Look bro, I'm not fuck'en stupid ha. Seriously, youse say'en I'm a fuck'en idiot? Them pricks were suss-en out me boat ha."

"All right, did you get a licence plate number?"

"Nah bro, liss'enn, seriously," he continued, before pausing with a pained look on his face like he was trying to explain something to a two-year-old. "It was a ute ha. I seen'em fuck'en dogs look'in at me boat. Yer got it bro?" His intention, however, was to have the boat 'disappear' for insurance purposes. I had seen it in GDs many times, especially with motor vehicles. The reported attempted theft was almost certainly a ruse to support his false claim.

In one operation, off the Rabaul Road boat ramp on the Georges River, together with police divers and a large crane, Gus and I were part of a task force that pulled 27 cars out of the water in one day. Most of them reported stolen and the subject of insurance claims—and there were plenty more where they came from, we just ran out of places to park them all. To add to this, criminals driving tow trucks were picking up cars right off the street—to order—by phone—and then scrapping them the same night to destroy the evidence.

I went through the motions. "Okay, so let's start with your name."

"What da fuck has that got to do with it bro? Seriously. Liss'enn. Youse coppers just gotta find them deadshits ha?" Gus started to say something but then stopped himself.

"If you'd like me to make a police report, I'll need your full name," I continued.

"Me name is Abdul ▮▮▮▮. That's all youse gett'en. Swear to God bro. Now youse find them pricks before I call me cousins and it gets full hectic." I didn't appear to be getting anywhere and I hadn't been offered any real information. A young boy got up from watching television. He would only have been five years old. He had a rough-cut mullet-style haircut with a long-braided rat-tail running down the middle of his bare back. He walked right up to me and, before I could say 'hello' he spat out the words, "Fuck'en pig!"

Gus just rolled his eyes and said, "Bloody hell. Let's get out of here man."

And that was Bankstown. As my Australian-Lebanese mate said, "The community is complex."

'Who Would Be A Cop?'

After four years in GDs, I was ready for something different. I completed the riot squad course allowing me to work part-time shifts. The full-time unit didn't interest me. I'd rotated through the highway patrol and the detectives, but they weren't for me either. I also did the mountain bike course which I loved—and who wouldn't. It was the best way to get around the CBD and surprise drug dealers. My partner and I even had competitions to see who'd ride down the steepest stairs onto railway station concourses.

Once, I got into a bicycle pursuit with a well-known local shitbag. I activated the ridiculous sounding siren on the bike as I chased him through a scrum of startled pedestrians in Bankstown's Chinatown, before knocking him off his bike. Not long after that, I was accepted into the proactive team, mostly working undercover, specialising in drug and gang-related crime. (The best part was that I was no longer a slave to the endless jobs broadcast over police radio.) It was a small, close-knit group of both men and women and, to top it off, Gus had been selected too.

Gus and I became inseparable. We had very different upbringings, but we effortlessly bounced off each other. He was the loveable larrikin, a man who people just wanted to be around. I can't recall him ever offending anyone although he constantly 'took the piss' out of everyone, especially through the most random and peculiar nicknames. But, if he finished off with his trademark cheeky grin, then all was forgiven. (Gus always took the time to have a chat, even if he didn't particularly like a person. This isn't something I'm particularly good at.)

"You do love the shit chat, don't you?" I said.

"Look, isn't it just easier to be nice to everyone?" he

replied.

"Yeah, true but to be honest, I don't need to. I'm nice to everyone vicariously through you man," I said with a smile.

*****

One mid-afternoon, we were patrolling an outdoor pedestrian mall searching for a local gang. Two of their known members had outstanding arrest warrants. I stopped and turned to look at Gus. "Bloody hell, you do realise the reason we wear plain clothes is to be undercover, don't you? You stick out like dogs' balls. You're not heading out to Northies at Cronulla," I said shaking my head.

He laughed. "Come on man, seriously, I wouldn't be seen dead wearing black Everlast gear and a white hat with a manbag, would I? And Jade would never speak to me again. Besides, you've got the homeless man look down pat," he continued with his usual cheeky grin.

"Says Antonio Banderas over here," I shot back.

"Look, I told you, I'm half Welsh and half Scottish. I've got the Celtic dark hair, like Colin Farrell." You can say it all you want but I'm not Mexican and I'm not Spanish either."

"So, what's it going to be for lunch then *amigo*? Burritos or paella?"

Gus's wife shared his love for fashionable clothes. She was a 'Shire girl' from Sutherland, south of Sydney. Their personalities were the male and female equivalent of each other—two sides of the same coin. She had styled light-brown hair with porcelain-doll skin and a perfect smile. Her claim to fame was she'd once been a Qantas poster girl. One word defined her: bubbly. The two of them—Gus and Jade—were in love, to the point of being nauseating.

"Dear God, Jade. You're obviously not looking at the same bloke I am? You can't keep your hands off him." I said with a look on my face like I had a piece of lemon in my mouth.

"Benny, he's a gorgeous specimen, isn't he? Just ask him. He'll tell you," she smiled.

Gus was laid-back about everything but when 'shit got real' he switched on. He was the man I wanted next to me in an operation. On one job, a woman high on drugs was involved in a long police pursuit from a neighbouring command before eventually crashing her car. What made the job different was that we found the woman's partner, dead, underneath her, on the driver's seat. He'd earlier overdosed and died. She then climbed on top of his dead body and continued to drive around like that for hours.

"I'd like to think that Jadey would at least pull me out of the seat before she kept my car," Gus said with a smile.

"I'd help her out with that one, hombre. For sure, don't you worry about that," I replied in our usual harmless bantering way.

I drove our unmarked Holden Commodore at Mach 1 under lights and sirens before screeching to a halt outside a local pub known for regular weekend brawls. A fight between two groups of men had spilled out onto the street. A scrum of Pacific Islanders was punching on with a larger pack of Middle Eastern wannabe gangsters. Although outnumbered and wearing plain clothes, Gus and I glanced at each other, nodded, and ran in.

As back-up police arrived, the Lebanese men made a quick exit. The huge Islander guys were fired up on the drink and now turned their attention to us. After more than a few haymaker punches were thrown, with the two of us ducking and weaving, I pulled my OC (pepper) spray and emptied the contents, concentrating on the two biggest and most aggressive of the group. Both men hollered in what sounded like a war cry as they rubbed their faces. But, instead of slowing them down, it just seemed to make them wilder, throwing more mad punches, now into the abyss. Gus and I picked our timing and crash-tackled both to the ground as we fought through the secondary contamination of pepper spray. We soon led the two away in handcuffs. I looked down at my hand. It was covered in blood. Someone from the Lebanese gang had stabbed one of the Islanders in the back during the brawl. The big man hadn't even noticed.

"Tough bloody fella," I said shaking my head in disbelief as I watched the ambos do their work.

"Yeah, that guy's head's even bigger than yours," Gus said as he rubbed the pepper spray out of his eyes.

"Yeah, right-o dickhead," I replied with a smile. "Tougher than those so-called gangsters stabbing the Islander in the back," I continued shaking my head.

*****

Most people join the police force with good intentions. Part of my motivation was to help people. Early in my GDs career, I went out of my way to help intravenous drug users. Their stories were so tragic, but they always seemed to let me down. Later, during my time in the plain-clothes proactive unit, one of our targets was the most active youth gang in Bankstown. It was made up of Middle Eastern men, mostly aged between 16 and 22, who were robbing commuters as they got on and off the trains, sometimes at knifepoint. Operational intelligence was that they were also dealing in drugs and stealing cars. Our methods were to observe and arrest key individuals but also to interrupt and interfere with general gang activities. They always treated us with contempt and hostility. One of them was a 16-year-old Syrian refugee.

The boy was short and weedy compared to the others and easily recognisable, even from a distance, by his longer than usual modified-mullet hair style—cut straight across at the front, shaved at the sides above the ears, and very long at the back. (It's called a 'skullett'.) I managed to separate him from the others early on. When I did, he didn't carry on with the same mouthy bravado. We had many chats and developed a rapport. He had a sad story. His father and most of his extended family had been killed in the Syrian Civil War. He escaped with his mother and two younger sisters.

"I just got in with the wrong crowd bro. I'm gonna sort my shit out. Seriously. Swear to God bro," he said using exaggerated hand gestures to convince me.

"Good," I replied.

"I'll show youse ha," he added.

I made it my mission to get him away from the gang and support whatever good decisions he promised to make. One night, weeks later, a priority job came over the police radio. There was a brawl at Bankstown railway station. Gus activated the sirens and I put the blue flashing light on the roof of our unmarked car—a silver Ford Falcon. As we pulled up, a crowd of young men scattered in different directions. I noticed a familiar face. It was the Syrian boy. I yelled out, "Hey bro, get over here." He had a ripped shirt and was breathing heavily. "So, tell me man, seriously, what happened?" (In the Bankstown LAC, it was often necessary for plain clothes officers to use street language for basic communication—but never while in uniform. The reason was that it lured our targets into a false sense of security, which we then used to our advantage.)

He replied, "Those fuck'en FOBS jumped us bro." ('FOBS' was the street name in the area for Pacific Islanders—who strangely used the same term to describe themselves. (It is slang for 'Fresh Off the Boats'.) There was a long history of violent conflict between the gang and the local Samoan 'bloods'. To complicate things, Samoans hate Tongans and vice versa, and they both hate New Zealand Māoris, and all the Pacific Islander gangs hate the Lebanese.

I took the boy's details and told him that I'd be in touch. No one was saying anything, and the gang dispersed. The area was clear. We headed to the station master's office and viewed the CCTV footage. The camera showed three Pacific Islander teens walking onto the concourse. They were then approached by the gang. There were seven of them. Words were clearly exchanged before a fist fight broke out.

Our team were on a high level of operational readiness due to a recent brawl resulting in a gang member having his skull fractured from being repeatedly struck with a cricket bat. A couple of days later, we were patrolling the outdoor mall when I again recognised the Middle Eastern gang. A loud-mouthed all-round grub named Ahmed stepped forward. "Why youse dogs always hassling us bro?"

I said, "You know why."

He sneered, "Nuffin fuck'en else better to do ya fuck'en dog!"

I calmly replied, "You're always up to something and, if you swear at me again, I'll write you a ticket." Ahmed spat on the ground and muttered something under his breath. We searched the three of them for knives and drugs; all had previous weapons charges.

"See Offf-iss-sa, nuffin, ha," he said in a snarly,

mocking tone. I managed to get the Syrian boy away from the group.

I said to him, "You been avoiding me bro?"

"Nah bro, I've been around just chill'en."

"The CCTV footage from the other night showed a very different story to what you told me man."

"Nah bro, those FOBs were trying to staunch us ha," he insisted.

"That's not true man. You guys started it by gettin' in their face first."

He said, "Nah, bro, seriously, those fuck'en FOBs are try'in to move in ha."

"Look man, I've been reasonable with you, haven't I?" He just nodded. I continued, "I'm telling you, you're on a slippery slope. You understand me? Keep hanging out with these gronks and you're going to end up in gaol."

He just grunted and said, "Yeh."

"Where you living?" I continued.

"Me Mum's," he replied, looking down at the ground.

"You sure? I was there the other day and she said you haven't been there in weeks."

"Alright, bro, I'm stay'en at Ahmed's crib."

I shook my head. "Really bro? You don't seem to learn. Look, I can sort you out but you're going to have to listen to me." His face was expressionless. "This won't end well, hundred per cent. Here's my card, ring me. You going to think about it?" He took it, put it into his top pocket, and nodded passively. A week later he was arrested and charged for robbery with a knife. I bumped into him after he got out of the juvenile correction centre. He didn't want to talk. I said, "The offer still stands bro. Look after yourself." He just walked away.

The gang was broken up. Our unit had other targets

and priorities. Some of the members were in gaol and others had moved on to more serious crimes—as they do. My female partner and I were acting on a tip-off that there were two underage girls being prostituted from a garage in one of the local housing commission blocks. They were aged 13 and 15. The girls were initially hostile to us but, after a bit of kindness and a lot of patience, they began to cooperate. They were both heroin-addicted and homeless. Fortunately, my partner was able to find them some crisis accommodation. I pleaded with the girls to provide the names of the two guys who were pimping them in exchange for drugs. My heart sank. One of them was the Syrian boy. The detectives took over the case. I was disappointed, but, worse than that, I felt a sense of utter futility. All I was left with was the harsh life lesson: 'You can't help people who don't want to be helped'.

*****

My partner from the proactive unit and I were at court for a case involving a 17-year-old charged with weapons possession offences. NSW Children's Court dictates that cops must attend in plain clothes as a uniform is considered intimidating to young offenders. Most, however, are far from bothered. We had watched some live CCTV footage of a group of young men in a car park at night. They were moving a baseball bat and what looked like knives from one car boot to another.

    We pulled over a carload of them in our unmarked vehicle. As I approached the gang, I noticed a familiar face. It was the same young guy that we had given evidence against the week before. We searched the car and found the baseball bat but there was also a cricket bat, a one-metre-long sword and scabbard, a butcher's knife, a metal bar, and a sickle—which is a long crescent-shaped metal blade with a wooden handle. One of the young men admitted that the gang were on their way to fight 'the Parramatta boys'. We arrested all four and interviewed them at the station with their respective support persons present. The boys refused to speak to us.

As we sat outside the courtroom, I noticed the young offender jive in with his entourage. His name was Ali. He glanced towards us and with a big idiotic grin said to his mates, "Look at these useless dickheads. Swear to God bro." Then he turned to us and said, "I don't know why youse dogs bovver charging me. Me barrister says I won't get nuffin. Nuffin ha. Why youse even here?"

I replied, "I'm getting paid to be here, that's why."

He then turned his attention to what we were wearing. "Obviously not enough money eh bro? Losers ha, dress'in in those shit clothes. Where'd ya get 'em, fuck'en Kmart? Fuck'en op shop ha?" (He was really enjoying himself. If he'd spoken to me on the street like that, it would've been a different story—and he knew it.)

Then he continued with, "Don't forget, youse dogs work for me ha. I pay yer fuck'en monkey wages bro."

"If you say so," I replied. The truth was that Ali hadn't finished school, never worked a day in his life and so had never paid a cent in tax. Together with his extended family, he lived in subsidised public housing with most of them on long-term sickness benefits. Ali had no prospects in life beyond the immediate flashy rewards of drug dealing and, in his heart, he knew it. He was later convicted of being a key player in a large-scale illicit drug syndicate.

"I wouldn't get out of bed for the pocket change they pay yer bro," he said, forcing out a humourless cackle.

"Of course, you wouldn't," I replied.

Finally, it was my turn to give evidence and I received the usual grilling by his defence solicitor—who repeatedly called me a liar—which is their usual practice. I sat down and watched the rest of the proceedings. I was convinced we would get a conviction. The CCTV footage, the number and type of weapons found in the car and the criminal records of all involved were seemingly indisputable.

Ali went into the witness box for questioning with a cocky look on his face, dressed in a schmick new jacket, which he wore like a suit of armour. He admitted straight up to putting the items in the car. That should have been the end of it. His taxpayer-funded legal aid solicitor then began to question him. First, it was about the baseball and cricket bats. Apparently, the young guy had recently taken up both sports. (He must have forgotten to bring the balls with him.) He then went on to explain that he'd also started mowing lawns, which he said required the use of a wheat-harvesting sickle, not to mention a metal bar and a butcher's knife; God knows what for—the edges? The magistrate seemed genuinely transfixed by his story. The defence lawyer then requested that a video be shown to the court. My offsider whispered to me, "This ought to be good."

The court was then treated to a poorly made home movie of a Shiite religious ceremony. The defence solicitor proceeded to tell the magistrate, with a straight face mind you, that the young person was a devout Shiite Muslim who required a knife and a sword for 'strictly ceremonial purposes'. Now I'd seen it all. The court was adjourned while the magistrate considered the evidence. The police prosecutor came over and had a chat with us. "No one of sound mind could possibly believe that story—could they?" she said. After a brief intermission we returned to court.

"All rise."

We stood and bowed as the magistrate entered the chamber. As she began to read out her findings, I couldn't believe what I was hearing. All charges were dismissed. The police prosecutor didn't look surprised. I don't know why I was. As we were walking out, a car drove by and we were bombarded by the gang's jeers and obscenities, "Fuck'en loser cops," and "Eat shit off-iss-sa ha," all to the previously banned soundtrack of N.W.A's rap, *Fuck tha Police*—a local favourite. (Radio triple j and ABC staff went on strike, playing it continuously for 24 hours to make their point, until it was put back on air.)

Police are the most scrutinised of all professionals. Judges, it seems, may be the least. As young Ali was 'flipping me the bird', and yelling "Fuck you pig," I recalled another case in the same court with a different magistrate. She arrived late carrying a large handbag. Peeping out of the front zipper was the fluffy brown face of her rat-sized pet Pomeranian. I could imagine that the magistrate was an ex-defence solicitor who lived in a leafy, wealthy, harbourside suburb like Double Bay or Potts Point or Vaucluse—a mere 45-minute drive from the crime-ridden alternative universe of Bankstown, Greenacre, and Telopea Street, Punchbowl.

Whilst everyone was standing, the magistrate set the dog down on the courtroom floor. The little mutt was clearly at home. I found it hard to pay attention to the proceedings; the dog was just so distracting. The police prosecutor and the defence solicitor didn't appear fazed in the least. The dog then cocked its hind leg and urinated—twice, and then, as I anticipated, it did a curly little turd in the corner. I sort of expected someone from *Australia's Funniest Home Videos* to leap out with a microphone and tell me that I was being secretly filmed for my reaction. Outside, I asked a court officer about what I'd just witnessed. He said, "Yeah, she's been doing that for ages. Did it do a crap in there?"

I said, "Yeah, and pissed twice."

"Bloody great!" he said in an exasperated tone. "She makes us clean it up too. They're a law unto themselves those magistrates."

"That they are, but what can we do?" I said with a shrug of the shoulders.

In another court, I observed the elderly magistrate shuffle in and sit down. He reminded me of Montgomery Burns from *The Simpsons*. No sooner had the prosecutor begun reading the charges than I saw the magistrate's head nodding forward—and then he fell asleep—at the bench. The prosecutor glanced up, took a deep breath, and continued as if nothing was out of the ordinary. When it came time for me to give evidence, I saw the magistrate momentarily wake, look in my direction, reposition himself in his chair and then nod off again.

I finished answering questions and turned to the magistrate who was still asleep—or dead. It was hard to say. The prosecutor waved me down from the witness box and finished presenting his brief. Then the defence solicitor gave his final submission and looked at the police prosecutor who said, "You may as well just continue." There was silence across the courtroom. Everyone just sat there waiting to see what would happen next. I expected someone to call an ambulance.

After what seemed an eternity, a court officer gave the magistrate a gentle shake, before having a brief chat in his ear. The magistrate made a note, shuffled the papers in front of him and began to read the verdict. "After considering all the evidence here today ... I find the offender ... uhm ... not guilty." I laughed out loud. I just couldn't help myself. It was such a circus. The magistrate gave me a death stare. I'd spent days in the office compiling the brief of evidence and all for nothing. I've observed that the longer a magistrate is on the bench, the less likely it seems that he or she will send someone to prison. Is it the sheer futility of it all? The same faces, the same crimes, the same punishments and then the same revolving door? Cops call it the 'legal system' and not the 'justice system' for a reason.

In GDs, I came across one good magistrate. I still remember his name. His intention was to clean up the area. All the defence solicitors went out of their way to have their cases moved to other courts. When the magistrate did issue what police prosecutors thought were more appropriate sentences, he was complained about until he was removed. "Is it any wonder that cops develop an 'us and them' mentality?" Hardy said on the way back to the station. I just replied, "It doesn't help when they're dishing out harsher fines for speeding than what they'd get if they punched one of us in the face!"

The words of my non-police friends ran through my mind like a mantra: 'Who would be a cop?'

*****

An animal complaint was broadcast over police radio. Two aggressive dogs were on the street chasing people. One was a large white bull mastiff cross pit bull. The other was a brindle Staffordshire bull terrier. They were in a driveway carport next to a run-down fibro house with cast-iron security gratings on all the windows. As my partner and I got out of our police paddy wagon, a middle-aged Vietnamese woman ran over to us shouting in short, panicked, breathless bursts.

"Please try and slow down a little," I said, finding it difficult to understand her.

"Two bi do try bye me. Bi danger!"

"I'll speak to the owner and get them locked away," I reassured her.

"You go, dey ki me."

"I'll come back and see you after we've got the dogs secured. Do you understand?" I added.

"Goo, you do."

The bigger of the two dogs immediately locked his eyes on me and, without so much as a bark, started to run in my direction. My partner was standing to my left. He yelled and swung his baton, but the dog wasn't having any of it. It had its target—me—and nothing was going to stop it. I backed away, but as I did, I felt the heel of my boot on the edge of the concrete kerb and gutter. If the dog hit me now, I'd be knocked backwards onto the road and my throat would be exposed. I reached down, and in one motion, grabbed the handgrip of my Glock, releasing the retaining strap, pulling the weapon upwards out of the holster and pointing it towards the dog which was now only metres from me.

There were mere seconds between drawing my gun and taking aim. In that flash of time, I thought about how much I loved my childhood dogs Banjo, Bess, Ned and Spot. I hoped that the dog charging towards me would change its mind. Then everything slowed down. As the dog began its leap, our eyes met. I wanted one clean shot. I pointed my gun, deliberately angling my aim safely downwards, and then I squeezed the trigger. *Bang.* The animal dropped, motionless, dead on the ground, right at my feet.

The other dog immediately disappeared into the car port. The Vietnamese lady ran off down the street waving her arms in the air, screaming hysterically. My partner walked over to me. "Bloody hell ▨, that was insane."

"Tell me about it man. I've never seen a dog do that before."

"That's a serious killer. It wanted you," my partner continued, shaking his head in disbelief.

"*Was* a serious killer," I replied, correcting him, looking down at the dog's lifeless body, securing my weapon.

"You really are becoming a shit magnet, ▨," he added. Investigations later revealed that the dogs were guarding a drug house.

The sergeant soon arrived and separated us. Protocol requires that, if a police officer discharges his or her firearm on duty, there must be separate interviews. I provided my version as did my partner. "Come on is that *really* how it happened?" the sergeant questioned me with a wry, disbelieving look.

"Yeah sarge, it is, exactly. Why?"

"Have you seen where you shot the dog?" he replied, pointing to an entry wound on the animal's forehead. "You got him right between the eyes."

"To be honest, sarge, it happened so fast."

"You really controlled yourself under pressure. You should seriously consider trying out for the TOU."

Selection

It was a large-scale search warrant operation targeting the homes of outlaw motorcycle gang members. I was involved as a part-time riot squad officer. I looked around as the TOU boys roll up. They were hanging off the sides of their imposing V8 Toyota Land Cruiser, jumping into position even before the vehicle stopped. Dressed in black with M4 assault rifles hanging off their chests they looked tough—the real deal. I decided then and there, that's what I wanted to do. I was fit and strong, or so I thought. I went to the gym and played team sports and of course raced motocross but, from that moment on, I trained even harder with the goal of earning my place in one of the toughest, most highly trained tactical operations units in the world.

There was an information day at the ▮▮▮▮▮▮▮ ▮▮▮▮▮ for an upcoming TOU selection course. A prerequisite was that you had to complete three years of policing. As selection was only held every two years, the auditorium was packed with eager prospects. The program began with an impressive promotional video followed by introductions and a display of weapons—assault rifles, sub-machine guns, shotguns, sniper rifles and grenade launchers. An operator who had recently completed his training outlined how difficult the process was and gave a rundown on what would be required of us physically. He said, "I hope you're not here for the money because you'll be paid fuck all more than a GDs cop and you'll always be on call, day and night, deployed all over the state at a moment's notice and this will be hell on your family life."

The TOU Chief Inspector then walked to the podium. He explained that the psychologically rigorous nature of selection had a clear purpose. "The TOU are looking for someone who will not be rattled or overwhelmed in any situation," he outlined to the spellbound audience. "The TOU wants individuals who will overcome extreme adversity with the highest level of skill and resilience. Selection may be brutal, but I can tell you that it's tame compared to what's expected of a trained operator in the field. Thank you."

A mate of mine from Bankstown was also going for selection. 'Smithy' was a natural athlete who played rugby league at a semi-professional level. He had a cheeky, boyish face—a laid-back surfer sort of guy—tall and tanned, with shaved light brown hair and green eyes. He was one of those blokes you could sit next to for an hour, and he wouldn't say a word. What would've been an uncomfortable silence for most people didn't bother him in the slightest. He loved a punt on the horses. When he ate, his left eye twitched. (He now works with troubled kids as a teachers' aide.) We teamed up and trained together once a week for the next 12 months. My daily routine consisted of running 10 kilometres to the gym, then a workout—normally a bodyweight or strongman circuit—then into the pool for a two-kilometre swim before pack marching 10 kilometres home. I also rode my mountain bike an hour and a half at full tilt to work and then home again at night, all the while hoping not to bump into someone I'd arrested during my shift. I took six weeks annual leave leading up to selection to intensify my regime.

*****

It was a family outing in the city. Everyone was interested to know how my training was going. "We all know you're stubborn enough to get through it, don't we?" my younger sibling, Leah said, with a little-sister smile on her face.

"I'll show you stubborn," I replied. "I reckon I can carry you across the entire Harbour Bridge on my shoulders."

"As if," my 23-year-old sister shot back, clearly issuing a

not-so-veiled challenge.

"Well, come over here then," I said, hoisting her up on my shoulders and charging in the direction of the famous Coathanger's linked flight of stairs.

"Benny, put her down, you'll hurt yourself darling," my mother called after me, obviously concerned. Dad and my brother just shook their heads and smiled at each other.

I made it to the top without a break and pushed on along the pedestrian walkway for the considerable length of the world-famous landmark. It was taxing, no question about that, and my sister wasn't exactly light. My shoulders and legs were hurting but I refused to give up. I was on the home stretch and confident I'd proven her wrong when we were suddenly confronted by a security guard demanding that I put her down.

"Told you so," giggled my sister.

"Not funny. You know I would've finished," I replied.

"Okay, fair enough. You always finish whatever you start."

"Right, the security guy has gone," I said. "Let's get back to it."

"You're a classic," my sister said, laughing out loud.

*****

I completed my TOU selection application that included both a physical and psychological evaluation and I qualified for barrier testing. This involved a range of assessments to determine whether I was physically fit enough to even undertake the selection course. There was a set minimum standard for each mandatory activity. As there were so many prospective recruits, the instructors devised a system of accruing points for repetitions over the minimum required to begin the process of culling.

Tiger! Tiger! Tiger!

After a briefing at TOU headquarters, we jumped on a bus to the naval base at ▓▓▓▓▓▓▓▓▓ to commence our activities. This started with chin-ups (heaves), push-ups (press-ups) and parallel bar dips (an upper-body strength exercise) before we started the sit-up trial. Again, we had to complete a minimum number within 60 seconds. The instructor looked at me and snarled, "Nah, they're dog shit, start again." I knew I was doing them correctly; the instructor was just assessing how I'd respond to authority—and to criticism—and to pressure. The thing that concerned me, however, was that I'd only completed the minimum repetitions and failure at any set task meant the dream was over. I put doubt out of my mind, gathered myself, focused and powered on.

We then had to complete a 'beep test' or shuttle run. I was a good runner, despite my size, and managed to get above the minimum standard required to progress. Smithy and I observed the second group as we regained our breath, checking on our competition.

"That albino fella looks pretty fit hey mate?" I said to Smithy as I wiped the sweat off my brow.

"That's 'Z'. I know him from police footy," Smithy replied.

Z's physical appearance was distinctive: close-cropped electric white hair, piercing Latvian Baltic Sea-blue eyes, with heavily Central Coast surfer tanned skin. He was once a brickie's labourer from up the coast before he joined the cops.

After that, we were taken on an agility run that covered several kilometres, including obstacles and workstations. Our second-last test was to fireman-lift and carry a life-sized dummy up and down a four-storey flight of stairs three times—again within a set period. I realised that I was getting fatigued. All my tests had been run back-to-back. Then I noticed that our group had become smaller. In fact, from 200 who had registered their interest, only 100 attended barrier testing.

The final test was a swimming assessment. We were driven to the NSW Water Police wharf at ▓▓▓▓▓ where we had to jump into bull-shark-infested Sydney Harbour with our police overalls and boots on. Despite being a strong swimmer, I found this taxing. I finished the day and completed everything, hoping to find out if I could at least be allowed to attend the selection course. There wasn't even so much as a 'thanks for coming'. So began the nervous wait.

But, at last, success. I was to report to my alma mater, the Goulburn Police Academy, with selection conducted over seven days—or 'hell week' as it's known in the TOU. The program was based on the Australian Army's elite Special Forces or 'SAS' selection course and designed by an ex-SASR trooper and serving TOU member. More than half of the applicants who competed for barrier testing had been culled. Luckily, Smithy was selected as well. The two of us trained even harder.

Finally, the day came. We all stood to attention on the parade ground in our finest dress uniforms waiting for the head instructor to arrive. There were 44 of us including one loudmouth who'd previously kept telling everyone, "The only way I'm leaving selection is if they carry me out on a stretcher." I offered him a piece of free advice:

"You should be careful what you wish for mate."

I noticed another guy in a worn-out, unkempt uniform and scruffy boots. I thought to myself, 'You're really going to cop it, you poor bastard'. Then, as the team of instructors walked towards us, a white ute pulled up and one final recruit jumped out and jogged towards the formation, casually slinging his backpack over his shoulder. Two instructors nodded and smirked at each other; both recruits were now well and truly on their 'radar of pain'.

I made a point of standing next to the guy with the sloppy uniform, hoping he might deflect some of the attention.

I wasn't disappointed. The drill sergeant was ex-army. His uniform was pressed to perfection and the shine from his polished black boots and silver buttons was blinding. He was a tall man of average muscular-sinewy build, with a tanned hard face, deep frown lines and piercing green-blue eyes, nesting like sparrow's eggs in their respective crows'-feet wrinkles. He worked his way methodically down the line before clasping his gaze on the poorly presented recruit. "What the flying fuck do you call this?"

"Sorry staff?'

"Sorry, sorry, sorry. You should be fucking sorry. I'm down here, away from my family on this bullshit course on the off chance we might select a couple of you low-life maggots and you turn up looking like this. Good God almighty! I'm not here to fuck spiders."

"Sorry staff."

"You're not sorry, otherwise you wouldn't be here." Then he paused, looked him up and down, and said, "Your shirt looks like a billy goat pissed on it." (When our uniforms get old, the blue starts to yellow.) The unfortunate recruit must have reacted because the instructor stopped, turned abruptly, and snarled, "What in fuck's name was that? Did you just eyeball me recruit?"

"No staff."

"What the hell does that mean—you piss-soaked farm reject? Are you calling me a liar?"

"No staff."

"So, which one is it? Are you listening to me? Are your ears painted on?" the instructor continued relentlessly, with one rapid-fire insult after another. The recruit paused, and then wisely settled on the path of least resistance.

"Sorry staff?"

"No bullshit! I'm the one who's sorry, bloody sorry I'm

burning my precious time with a flange of useless, no hoper, fucking sub-normal baboons." It was like the famous drill sergeant scenes from the movies *Full Metal Jacket* and *Forrest Gump*. It didn't matter how well prepared you were, you were yelled at. Physical appearance was especially a target. I was 'Shrek' until one of the instructors thought he saw a fleeting resemblance to a Hollywood actor (known for his 'distinctive' appearance).

One of the recruits was a redhead—which is a social burden at the best of times. The guy seemed to constantly grimace against clenched teeth in a sort of tortured smirk. I kept thinking, 'Man, don't do that' but, too late.

"You'd have to be one of the ugliest fucking flame-headed, blue-arsed rangas I've ever seen in my life," the instructor bellowed.

"Yes staff."

"Are you smiling, ginger nuts?"

"Sorry staff."

"I'm sorry too. Deeply sincerely sorry that you were born you knuckle-dragging half-witted orangutan. I'm going to need my sunglasses just to look at you."

"Sorry staff."

"Do you know what I really want recruit?"

"No staff."

"I want you to keep your mouth shut when you talk to me."

Each recruit was allocated a number and expected always to have it displayed. Removing it and handing it back to an instructor was the symbolic way recruits admitted defeat. (US Navy Seals must ring a bell.) We all piled onto a bus and were driven into the bush. This was the calm before the storm. I sat next to Smithy and, for the first time, it wasn't awkward that he didn't say a thing. Then, from the moment we pulled up, it was on—I was screamed at, screeched at and shouted at from every angle, sometimes by all the instructors at the same time.

Our group lined up for equipment: a bullet-resistant vest, a black ballistic helmet, combat webbing containing two water bottles, a replica M4 assault rifle, a respirator (gas mask) in its pouch and belt, and an army camouflage backpack with a 20-kilogram sandbag in it. Each of us was expected to carry everything at once, which was intentionally impossible. Fumbling, falling, and failing were just opportunities to be belittled, demeaned, and berated. "Are you the most uncoordinated sub-human, chimp-faced, missing link to walk the face of God's green earth?" an instructor screamed into my face showering me with a spray of spittle.

"No ... staff," I answered cautiously, trying not to show a negative expression while blinking from the effects of the human sprinkler.

"How about I be the judge of that? What's your name recruit?"

"███ staff."

"What sort of fucked-up Neanderthal name is that? You're ... ," he paused, deep in thought, before looking to another instructor for guidance. "What's that fucker's name sarge, you know ... the actor?"

"John C. Reilly," he advised with some authority.

"That's it! You're the poor fucker's retarded twin brother."

"Yes staff."

"No," he said, correcting himself. "That's still a grievous insult to my wife's favourite actor. You're a paid up, certified, entry level mongoloid."

"Yes staff."

"Now get out of my face."

Our first activity was a timed 10-kilometre pack march.

Failure meant being sent home immediately. Smithy and I had trained for this. We stuck together. It was hard going but we all wanted to make a good impression. Being the first day, it was sensible not to push myself too hard. But I wouldn't slow down. Smithy and I crossed the finish line together in the lead followed by a colleague of mine from my days in the Australian Army Reserve. (Many years later he was my sergeant at Lindt, 'Officer B'.) Four recruits didn't make the time and were sent packing. One was the guy with the unkempt uniform.

There was no time to reflect, and we weren't going to hear anything encouraging from the selection staff. Our group were taken to a field where we had to endure a horrendous strong man circuit including tractor tyre flips, log hauls and heavy rope lifts above our heads conducted in teams, followed by long sprints and extreme bar and weight work. We continued like this well into the night. I was already exhausted, and this was just day one, but the instructors kept pushing to see who would crack first. When most of the group began to collapse, they threw us on the bus, and we headed back out into the bush.

Individually, each of us had to demonstrate our ability to perform regardless of extreme adversity or fatigue. It was dark and freezing cold. It was Goulburn, and it was winter. I could barely see a thing. Regardless, we were expected to erect an enormous white, rectangular, military-hospital-style tent. It took all night. Each recruit was allocated a camp stretcher—a simple aluminium frame stretched with khaki canvas, with each placed in a designated tent space that ran along both sides in two neat rows. I'd just laid down when an instructor stormed in. "What are you lazy, useless, no-hoper pussies doing laying around. It's a lovely morning, rise and shine. Outside with your helmets, vests, and rifles. Get your sorry arses out of here. Thirty seconds."

It was another unrealistic time frame. A couple of rows

of camp beds down I noticed someone was still in their sleeping bag. It was the guy who kept saying, 'The only way they'd get me to leave is on a stretcher'. I watched as another recruit tried to get him up. "Come on mate, we're all hurting, just stand up and I'll help you get your stuff sorted." He just turned over and pulled his sleeping bag over his head and that was the end of him.

The rest of us ran from the tent and lined up for inspection. The instructor screamed until he was red in the face. "Simple instructions, for simple fucking halfwits. What did I tell you to bring out?"

A recruit in front of me stammered nervously, "Ou … ou … our helmets … ou … ou … our vests and ou … ou … our guns … oh shit!"

"Oh shit is right, you dumb arse. Well, are you going to ge … ge … get it then?" the instructor replied mocking the man's speech impediment. The stammering recruit ran back into the tent and re-emerged with his replica M4. We were then directed into the push-up position and made to continue repetitions past the point of exhaustion. One by one, everyone collapsed. The instructor then individually assessed us for our reaction to failure but also how we regathered and powered on.

"You wannabes actually think you can be in the TOU? You can't even do push-ups!" the instructor bellowed, standing over us. Then, as ordered, we did burpees and squats, just to mix it up, until our entire bodies shook. The sergeant turned up and everyone stood to attention.

"You guys look like a bag of wet shit! Did any of you have a shave this morning?" There was silence. "Well?"

"No staff," replied a couple of low voices.

"Do you expect me to work with anyone who looks like a warb?"

"No staff."

Our group were forced back into the push-up position as, one by one, we peeled away to rapid shave with only half a cup of cold water. Meanwhile, our colleagues kept doing push-ups. We then ran to another station where a breakfast of basic army-style hotboxes was provided.

No one said a thing. I glanced around the group, who now looked a far cry from the confident, well-dressed, and determined recruits that first gathered on the parade ground just a day earlier. Each face told a different exhausted story. Some were desperately gathering themselves for the next wave of torture. Others just wanted it to be over; some were at their end.

Next, our group were confronted with a steel double-axle box trailer full of tractor tyres with huge ropes hanging off the front. "Righto dead shits, drag *this* trailer up *that* mountain," the instructor grinned sadistically, pointing towards where he wanted us to go.

"YES STAFF," everyone replied with forced enthusiasm positioning ourselves on one of the ropes. I glanced up at the mountain. It was steep with large sharp-edged grey rocks everywhere and clumps of snow gums and taller, tortured ironbarks. As we took up the tension, the trailer began to move—slightly.

"No, not that way, you bunch of retarded piss ants. Drag it up on your guts. What if someone was firing on you? Maybe I should give you some help?" he added in a condescending tone. We all laid on our stomachs in the commando crawl position trying to work out a way to do it. I pulled with everything I had. The trailer still didn't move.

"Should I just send you girl guides back to your mummies? What's this bullshit?" the instructor taunted. I pulled harder. A couple of guys turned onto their backs and tried it that way. The wheels on the trailer creaked and it began to move. The next three hours were spent like that, all the while being yelled at—just to increase the stress level. My elbows and knees were already bleeding. My bullet-resistant vest and helmet, although heavy, thankfully protected my chest and head.

We then came to a fence. None of us knew what to do. The instructor stood quietly and watched us. "Do you *really* think we've finished for the day?" he taunted us.

"No staff."

"That's good to hear because I've got a news flash for you limp-wristed maggots. Get it over the fucking fence. Now!"

This was one of many tests where the instructor assessed how we worked as a group, especially who the natural leaders and problem solvers were. A couple of guys offered suggestions. I also chipped in. With a group effort, we managed to raise the trailer, but we just couldn't lift it quite high enough. When one of the guys cut himself on barbed wire, our group were forced to put it back down. "If you useless fucktards don't get *this* trailer over *that* fence then you can all bloody well go home."

"Can we take the tyres out of the trailer first staff?" came a reluctant question from an anonymous recruit.

"Halle—fucken—lujah!" exclaimed the instructor. "You're not all as thick as you look." We completed the task—barely.

"Righto, that was fun, wasn't it? Now get that trailer back over here and drag it down the hill," he continued.

Finally at the bottom, my fellow recruits looked the way I felt.

"Did we enjoy that?" he continued.

There was a near-unanimous "No staff," except for one recruit.

"Yes staff."

"Sorry?" the instructor replied. "What was that? Did one of you say, '*yes staff*?'"

He stepped forward, "Yes staff, I did." It was the bloke who turned up late to the parade on the first day. In his mind, I suppose this was a way of currying some favour—but we just thought he was a bit simple.

"So, you enjoyed it did you shit for brains?"

"Yes staff."

"Righto guys, because our little mountain goat here *luvved* it so much, let's leopard crawl back to the top of the mountain again." Together we made our way on grazed elbows and knees over rocks all the way to the summit and then back again.

"So, did you enjoy it this time too recruits?"

"NO STAFF!" came the unanimous shouting reply.

After an allocated five minutes to shovel food into our mouths, we commenced our next activity—the 'Jerrycan run'. "Righto, you bunch of gronks, grab yourselves some cans. I've already filled them with water for you. Good bloke ay? Follow me," yelled one of the instructors before jogging off down a bush track. I took hold of two as I shot Smithy a sideways glance, unable to stop myself after that last comment. I followed with the rest of the group. It didn't take long before the instructor was out of sight. I power walked as best I could. My forearms felt like they were going to explode. I withdrew into myself and kept pushing on. Eventually, I wasn't given the choice and my muscles let go. I was devastated. Then I looked around and noticed that everyone else was in the same predicament. Years of motocross had gifted me forearm endurance and strength. I put my jerrycans down and walked back to help one of the others. This was immediately noticed by two of the instructional staff. They descended on me like hungry vultures. "Are you finding this too easy ▇▇▇?"

"Definitely not staff."

"Then what the hell do you think you're doing? Are you

chromosome-deficient?"

"No staff. I'm helping one of my mates."

"Aren't you aware that you're competing against everyone else here?"

"Yes staff."

"So, you're a simpleton then?"

"No staff."

"I'll give you a tip ███, it doesn't matter if you finish, you won't be selected. I don't like you. None of us do."

"Yes staff," I replied continuing to help my colleague. I was then abused for the entire exercise, but I also noticed the instructors talking privately and taking notes. I was starting to understand that selection went against everything I'd experienced in life. It didn't matter what you did, how hard you tried or what you accomplished or achieved, nothing was ever good enough. It was an alternative universe of humiliation and physical pain with only two possible outcomes: endure or withdraw.

Night fell and the cold set in. My overalls were stained with mud and saturated with sweat. "You guys look like the swamp people," yelled one of the instructors. "Shower time," he announced laughing. He then brought out two buckets of water with small holes drilled in the bottom. We stood in our underpants shaking with hypothermia as the freezing cold water trickled over us in turn. "I want you back here dressed in some sort of presentable condition in two minutes. Got it? Go!"

We were then told to conduct pickets (or guard duty) on a rotating roster throughout the night and count two barrels of spent bullet cartridges by morning. They also provided an old car disc brake and a blunt hacksaw blade. "You're got to completely saw through this steel disc by the end of the week … or no one passes selection. Understood?"

"Yes staff."

After dinner, we were exposed to seemingly endless burpees, push-ups, and squats to the point where I was sure I was going to throw up the little almost inedible food I'd smashed down. All while we were bombarded with unanswerable questions. This was designed around the idea of 'try-fail-never-give-up'. Finally, well into the night, and totally fatigued, the group were directed to bed. I was first picket. "There's no way we can get through this bloody thing in a week," my fellow picket said, sawing ineffectively at the hardened steel with the spent hacksaw blade.

"All we can do is our best," I replied as cheerfully as I could.

"Yeah, you're right, but seriously, no one is going to pass," he replied.

"Just keep trying man. Here, I'll have a g-g-g-go, you count the b-b-b-bullets. I'm at 1293," I said, my bottom jaw chattering uncontrollably with the bitter cold.

The two of us were relieved. I hobbled back to my stretcher, crawled into my sleeping bag, shut my eyes, and fell asleep— instantly. Then, *Bang*. I jumped up in shock. The dark shape of an instructor appeared at the entrance of the tent with a shotgun, smoke still wafting from the barrel. "Righto dipshits, our mates are under attack. You have two minutes to march your sorry arses out of here."

I fumbled to get my full kit on and ran out of the tent and was then marched deep into the bush in the dead of night. Everyone was ordered to take up covering positions where we remained for the next couple of hours. It must have been well below zero degrees centigrade. As we returned, I saw the first light in the sky an hour before sunrise.

Looking down the tent line I noticed how many empty stretchers there were, vacated by guys who had pulled the pin or withdrawn injured. There was a special casualty access team of paramedics (or SCAT) available to monitor our condition and provide first aid. (Everyone was paranoid of being honest with them as they'd likely recommend that we be removed from the course.) One guy had massive bleeding blisters between his legs. He secretly put strapping tape directly on his wounds and refused to give up. (After selection, he had to have multiple skin grafts.) Another suffered heat stroke and spent three days in hospital on an intravenous drip. We also had a shrink lurking around to psychologically assess our reactions.

Any pre-existing injuries were exposed. The TOU obviously didn't want to waste their time selecting someone who was going to break physically later on. I had both feet strapped and wore two pairs of socks to avoid blisters. (My time in the Australian Army Reserve had taught me to take care of my feet.) I did, however, step in a hole on a run and sprained my knee—which instantly started to swell. I didn't report it or let it slow me down, and anyway, everything else hurt too.

The rest of the week only got worse. There was one arduous task after another, including the 'dog run'. This is a simulated operational job where our team had to chase an armed offender (an instructor dressed up and firing blanks) through the bush, while providing protection to the police dog and his handler. We ran for hours with our full kit and rifle, all the while wearing a respirator. A respirator only allows a limited amount of air in through the filter. In times of physical exertion, you sweat into the mask and the lenses fog up. Panic naturally sets in when you can't get enough oxygen. It was my moment of greatest challenge. I was struggling and some of the instructional staff noticed. At one stage, I had four of them on me. They yelled and abused me constantly before realising I was holding up. Then they changed their tactics.

"Come on man, we can see that you're struggling.

Seriously, just tap out and hey, it'll all be over. You can get a good feed. What about a nice juicy burger and chips? And I'll even get you a cold beer. Seriously, this isn't for you, but that's fine. No shame. You've done well. And let's be honest, even if you finish, you won't be picked. This whole group is dogshit anyway. From what we've seen, honestly, no one here is anywhere near good enough to work with us, especially you." After that, there was no way I was going to give up, even with tear gas sprayed on us as we crawled through a tunnel in one of the few instances where we could remove our masks. My lungs felt like they were going to explode. I just kept putting one foot in front of the other. I dug deep. I wanted this.

One morning at 4.00 a.m., our group were thrown on a bus and taken to the public swimming pool in ▇▇▇▇▇▇. It had been a rough night with one of the instructors throwing a sound and flash grenade, or 'stunnie' as we call them, into our tent while we slept. There was a heavy frost on the side of the pool. We were instructed to strip. Everyone lined up in nothing but our mandatory 'budgie smugglers', Speedo-style swimmers. "Righto you pansy arses—jump in," the instructor yelled, his voice echoing in the still clear morning. As I resurfaced, it felt as if my lungs had collapsed. "You okay princess? You look like you might be a little cold or something?" the instructor taunted me.

"I'm fine staff."

"All righty then, let's have a little fun," he sniggered.

We were divided into pairs. Our challenge was to push a pig iron weight across the bottom of the pool, with one person under water at all times. I was teamed up with my mate from the army reserve. Shorter and leaner than most, but very fit, he loved adventure racing, mountain biking and endurance kayaking. The bloke did everything at a million miles an hour.

He had dirty blonde hair and dark wide-set eyes. Gus called him 'Luke Perry's inbred second cousin'. Everyone called him 'Atts'. We commenced, holding our breath in the arctic-like cold water, while diving down, before trying to stay on the bottom, pushing the heavy weight with our hands. It hardly budged. This was a competition, and I didn't want to finish last. At one stage, I couldn't recover enough breath in the short time above water. I fought through oxygen deprivation and completed the task. The instructors let us jump out of the pool for a few seconds—not to recover—but to observe for signs of panic. Then, they lined us up so that they could direct highly individualised insults about our 'shrinkage'. My entire body shook. "How was that then?" an instructor goaded us. "Fun?"

"Yes staff."

"I can't hear you guys?"

"YES STAFF!"

"Oh good. I'm glad. Hmmm? So then, seeing as you're enjoying it that much, you can all jump back in, and you can do it again tomorrow and then the next day too." (I never did work out which response the instructors wanted. Both answers resulted in further punishment. It was just another way they were mind-fucking us.)

After the first four days, the instructors were content that everybody was sufficiently fatigued. We were then exposed to a different sort of test. Our group was required to run to a rifle range where we were issued with an MP5 sub-machine gun with deliberately basic instructions on how to aim, fire, reload and conduct stoppage drills. Most of us had never seen one, let alone fired one. Our group were then taken for another exhausting run with our gas masks on before returning to the range where we were expected to apply our brief lesson and reload and fire, shooting targets at varying distances. This included handgun shooting with our police-issued Glocks. I wasn't the best, but I wasn't the worst either. In between serials we were ordered to do push-ups in a group. I heard one of the instructors explode with pure rage. "WHAT!" Everyone froze. "What did you just say to me recruit?"

"Nothing staff," he answered.

"That's not what I heard. I heard you say, 'fuck you' under your breath."

"No, I didn't staff."

"Are you calling me a liar?"

"No staff."

"So, what's it going to be recruit?"

"Sorry staff."

From that moment there were at least four instructors on the man the entire time. If they sensed a weakness or an attitude problem, they'd go after him until he cracked. Even after we ran back from the range to ███████████, they were still relentlessly baiting him. "So, are you going to tell me to fuck off again?"

"No staff."

"I don't like you. You have an attitude problem. You're not a team player. I've been watching you. You only ever look after yourself."

"No staff."

"Are you calling me a liar again?" the instructor shrieked with an unnatural ferocity. The recruit had had enough. It was his tipping point. He got to his feet.

"You guys can all get fucked. This is bullshit. I'm too good for this and I'm too good for you losers." With that, he stormed off. It was the last we saw of him. He was, as one of the instructors said, 'an A-grade cock'.

I had copped it earlier too. A fellow recruit (the redhead) had fallen over and was pinned under a tractor tyre during an exercise that involved rolling them through the bush. I pulled it off him before helping him up. "Bloody hell man, stay on your feet," I said with an encouraging smile. But this wasn't the way the instructors interpreted it.

"███████, are you turning on your mates?"

"No staff."

"We've got eyes on you." A group of instructors then followed me for hours abusing and baiting me until they were satisfied it wasn't an issue.

After a controlled aggression exercise where I had to slug it out in boxing gloves with a man-mountain Māori recruit, we were taken to the 'Kill House' training facility. Our group were put through close-quarters room clearance scenarios using Simunition rounds (a normal cartridge with a plastic tip containing paint). There were both 'shoot' and 'non-shoot targets'. Pressure was applied under extreme fatigue. Hitting a 'non-shoot' target was an instant failure.

Late one night, everyone was taken into a demountable building with the air-conditioning turned up to maximum heat. A long, deliberately dull lecture was given on the chemical make-up of tear gas and its effects on the human body. As hard as I tried, I couldn't stay awake; none of us could. We were then instructed to write a three-page essay on what we had just learnt.

Another test exposed us to heights. The activity began by scaling the side of the three-storey training facility using rock climbing holds. Once at the top, each recruit was attached to a rope and had to walk to the side of the building and lean out so that we faced the ground. This was my introduction to 'Perro'. He was from an Australian-Italian family, a big bloke, tanned with receding light-brown shaved hair, a distinctive Roman nose, tiny ears, and beady eyes. Always the funniest man in the room, and happily the butt of the joke, Perro was born *not* to play poker. You could always tell exactly what he was thinking—incapable of hiding his emotions. Raised on Rambo, he could pretty much rattle off any line from the movie series— which, come to think of it, probably wasn't that difficult. He led us in marches because he was ex-regular army. As Perro was lowered forward, he was shaking at the knees, clearly petrified of heights. And as he faced the ground, out it came—a 'man yelp'.

The instructors suspected, incorrectly, that Perro was a 'grey man'. In all special forces and SWAT training, instructors are on the look-out for a recruit who doesn't excel, but doesn't fail either. To identify this during selection, tests are designed to plumb the extremes of physical and psychological endurance. In one such assessment, a tent was filled with a high concentration of tear gas. Our group were taken on a hill run causing profuse sweating. (CS gas attacks your sweat glands.) As we went into the tent with our respirators on the gas was so thick that I couldn't see a thing. "Righto recruit, when I say so, remove your mask and run me through the alphabet before I see you take a breath. Then, and only once I've said so, reapply the mask and blow out, clearing it. Do you understand?"

"Yes staff."

"Don't run out or panic. You must work through it, or you can go home. Got it?"

"Yes staff."

"Let's go!"

I removed the mask and was instantly hit with severe pain to my eyes that were then forced shut. The exposed skin on my face was burning. I recited the alphabet and got to the letter 't' before I was needed to take a breath. My lungs felt as if they were on fire. A natural panic set in but I fought through it; I had to. I slowly and methodically reapplied my respirator before blowing out with what little air I had left in my lungs. "Well, that was easy enough, wasn't it recruit?" I heard the instructor say. I just nodded; I still couldn't see him. "Let's try and get all the way to 'z' and then I'll let you walk out of here."

"Yes staff."

"Remove the mask recruit."

The pain hit me again. I began reciting the alphabet. It was intense, but I kept forcing myself to continue. I made it through to 'z' but then started coughing and choking and nearly threw up before being let out. Snot was streaming uncontrollably from my nose and saliva dribbling from my mouth. I held out my arms to ventilate as directed and my burning eyes eventually opened. Other recruits vomited; some couldn't handle it and ran out of the tent in a panic—an instant fail.

On separate occasions during the week, each of us was pulled from the group, sat down with instructors, and interviewed—an opportunity for them to play mind games with us. I found it impossible not to be affected by what they said. They repeatedly told me that I was 'arrogant'. Throughout the week instructors referred to personal information in my application—especially what I identified as my strengths and attributes: 'highly motivated, focused, works well both in a team environment and independently, served in the army reserve' and so on. "You turned on your mate ████, you dirty jack son of a bitch, and you think you're a team player; do you? Bullshit you are."

"Yes staff."

And at every opportunity, they reinforced that even if I finished the week I wouldn't be selected because they didn't want to work with someone like me. Some of the guys had written huge reports promoting themselves, listing every weapon they'd fired in the military. This was also referred to by instructors. "What you're telling us recruit is that you're competent enough to fire a rocket launcher in the army, but you can't even fire your Glock."

"Yes staff."

"You know what you are recruit?"

"No staff."

"You're fucking Jason Bourne on paper and Dad's Army in reality."

Then there were tests of loyalty. Each recruit was entrusted with certain information and told not to let anyone know. The instructors asked questions about your opinion of fellow recruits, to see if you'd turn on them. You were even asked if you liked them or if you thought they'd make a good operator. Throughout the week, instructors stood around with folders and notepads. Everything you did was watched and scrutinised and recorded. It was especially hard when they looked at you and started frantically writing something down.

There were many times, day and night, when you were stood in front of your stretcher and assessed for the state of your equipment. The instructor's way of doing this was to throw all your belongings out of the tent screaming, "I've seen homeless winos with more pride." It didn't matter how tidy you were, they'd find something and then you'd be berated for it.

By this stage, we were completely exhausted, and our numbers had diminished significantly. I noticed that most of the ripped guys with 'show muscles' had pulled out. Their bodies obviously required constant energy replacement to perform. A lot of recruits also withdrew because of injury. Your time spent with the paramedics was monitored, ensuring that you weren't using it as a chance to take a break. I suspected some guys exaggerated their injuries looking for a face-saving out. I was also mindful that, if you voluntarily removed yourself from the course, you wouldn't be asked back to attend selection again.

We all lined up in our full kit. "Righto recruits, we haven't managed to get rid of all of you yet, so I reckon this next exercise should do it. I have to say I'm going to really enjoy this: the stretcher carry." There were two stretchers, both containing a life-sized dummy. To make it harder, metal weights were added. Each took four recruits to carry. If you weren't carrying the stretcher, there were jerrycans full of water to lug or tyres to roll, all with your 20-kilogram backpack on. It was already late afternoon and we had been run for most of the day. I took up my position at the front.

As the four of us lifted it above our chests in unison, I realised how heavy it was. My right shoulder hurt with every step. This test was a way of determining whether you were a team player and truly a person who would never give up. I tried to be on the stretcher as much as I could. I was told to rotate out, but I'd always get myself back on it. However, after the first hour, I noticed there were some recruits who avoided the stretcher for lighter activities. The instructors noticed too. We continued well into the night. I lost track of time. It was pitch black with Cyalume glow sticks placed on the ground indicating a path. Together each man pushed on, hour after hour. The instructors didn't let up. I was so fatigued that I barely noticed their screams anymore. I've never been in such a state of pain and exhaustion.

Then the guy beside me on the stretcher stumbled and collapsed. He managed to roll out and was replaced by someone a lot shorter than me, which meant I had to carry the entire weight. I completely withdrew into my own mind, shutting out the pain and exhaustion. The instructor's comments kept repeating over and over in my mind, 'even if you finish, you won't be picked. So, what's the point?' There were times when I did ask the question, 'Is this really what I want to do?' It was impossible not to.

After another guy collapsed, the instructors let us have

a drink. I looked up into the blazing stars through clouds of coffee steam as my hot breath hit the cold night air. I realised that this was just a moment in time and that I could, and would, get through it. Then it was back to it. Sometime after midnight one of the instructors surprised us. "Righto limp dicks, listen up. As some of you soft serves keep falling over, we'll pull the pin for tonight." We'd been going for seven hours. As I frantically loaded the equipment onto the truck, I noticed that the glowsticks were placed around a track. In my near delirious state, I hadn't realised that for the last few hours, we'd been walking around in circles.

At 6.00 a.m. the next morning, everyone was back at it—instructed to run around the Kill House carrying dummies while wearing our gas masks. We were then ordered to lie on our backs with our hands and feet moving around in the air like dying cockroaches—the ultimate dehumanising ordeal. By this point in the course, I would have done anything the instructors told me to do, regardless of how degrading or demoralising. It was the last day, and I was spent. "Okay you bunch of disgusting disease-spreading roaches, put your dummies down and grab your backpacks. No one was impressed by your piss-weak last effort, so we'll do it again."

"Yes staff."

Night was setting in. We lined up. "Righto, you pea-hearted girl's blouses, follow me at my pace," the instructor hollered, as we ran down the path after him.

"Yes staff."

"Are you bunch of human shitstains serious? You know it's the last day and you've already switched off."

"NO staff."

"I didn't hear you."

"NO STAFF."

In my fatigued state of mind, I hadn't noticed that we'd

looped back around before bursting into a clearing where the instructional staff were clapping us in. We'd finished selection. The instructors put on a big BBQ and even supplied cold beer. It was surreal. These men had been beasting us all week and now they were talking to us like human beings. In turn, each instructor congratulated me for finishing the course. It was overwhelming. At first, I couldn't believe that it was over and then I felt sheer relief and later a sense of accomplishment. What we didn't know was that we were still being assessed and that a final decision hadn't been made. They were observing us to see what sort of blokes we were when our guards were down. But then, there was one last task to be completed—a confidential peer vote. This is common to all special forces and SWAT selection courses so that instructors can tell what we think of each other.

Forty-four recruits had started and only 14 finished. The following morning, I was the fourth person called. Two guys before me returned absolutely devastated. The other recruit couldn't hide his excitement. I walked into the room. Every instructor looked up and stared at me at the same time with no emotion on their faces whatsoever. The inspector started, "Take a seat. So how do you think you went on this selection course ▮?"

"There are things that I could've done better," I said reluctantly.

"Yes, true," one of the instructors replied. I could feel the palms of my hands beginning to sweat and I was struggling to talk: my mouth was that dry.

One of them then leaned forward and looked me straight in the eye. "Before we go on, I want to tell you that anything said or done to you in selection wasn't personal; we just needed to know that we have the right person for the job. Do you understand that ▮?

"Yes, staff, of course, sticks and stones," I replied.

"Exactly," an instructor replied nodding in agreement. The suspense was killing me.

"Well, I won't leave you waiting any longer. After watching you all week our unanimous view is … we're happy to welcome you to the TOU."

"Thank you. Thank you so much," I said, nearly overwhelmed. Everyone at the table shook my hand.

"You did well son; you should be proud of yourself but, don't forget, this is only the beginning; you have a year of hard courses ahead of you, and this is going to cost the taxpayer more than a million bucks—just to train you. I'm sure you won't let them down."

"I won't let you … err … them down. Thank you, sir." Atts, Perro, 'Robbo', Smithy and Z were selected too.

SWAT

After selection, we returned to our LACs and were instructed to wait until a training course was scheduled. There was no indication of when it would commence, making the wait even harder. It was back to the streets of Bankstown for me, trying to avoid any complaint that could complicate a transfer. I was regularly asked about selection by my police mates and I struggled to respond with any real explanation. How do you describe something like what I'd just been through? Every time I spoke to Gus, I'd ask if he had an update. He warned me, "be careful what you wish for mate, selection is just a taste of what's to come." I wrote him off as being overly dramatic.

Months later, I received notification. My motivation to exercise quickly returned. A week out from the training course, I was on a late-night pack march with my staffie Josie. Headlights from an oncoming vehicle momentarily blinded me. I trod in a deep pothole, rolling my ankle before I hit the asphalt. The car just drove on. What was I to do? Was the dream over before it even began?

I arrived at the ████████████████, meeting up with other successful applicants. They all looked just as excited and nervous, although I still had to notify training staff of my injury and wait for an outcome. Finally, we were allowed in and marched through the office as TOU operators inspected us. Our group was told to go to the briefing room and wait for instructions. Everyone sat in silence, in our two-blues dress uniforms. After a friendly introduction from the boss, the instructional staff spoke with us in a very different tone. They quickly filled us in on 'how things were going to be.'

We were officially 'new operator trainees' or NOTs. We were *'not* TOU'—*not* to eat in the meal room and *not* to associate with trained operators. And I was even directed by a sergeant *not* to talk to Gus at work, ever, as he was from the course before me and was already trained (even though I'd been his best mate for years).

"Righto, our first activity is to run the sand dunes at Cronulla. I can already see that some of you wannabes have let yourselves go," an instructor said looking us up and down. I raised my hand sheepishly. "Excuse me staff."

"Yes, ███, what the fuck do you want?" he barked.

"Um, staff, I need to notify you that I, ah, rolled my ankle on a pack march."

"You're shitting me. What are you even doing here?" he yelled shaking his head before storming out of the room. A few of the boys looked over at me as though they were about to say something but they changed their minds. After a long wait, the instructor returned. The boss had obviously gone against instructional staff's wishes and I was given a week to recover or else be booted out of the Unit. I found the instructors incredibly creative in devising new ways to individually exercise me beyond exhaustion so that I didn't miss out.

However, selection was only a taste. The next 12 months were to be the most gruelling and challenging by far. The first six months consisted of SWAT courses where we were under constant scrutiny. Any mistake could result in being cut from advanced training and ultimately the TOU. The first weapons course was 'tactical handgun', effectively Glock retraining and combat shooting. This set the tone for the rest of the year. Our group was on the line of an underground shooting range, conducting stoppage drills, when I heard, "You've got to be kidding me. That's the second time you've done that. Don't do it again!" a huge instructor yelled at one of the NOTs. The instructor was over six feet tall and nearly as wide, with a shaven head and the intense look of a seriously annoyed silverback gorilla. The NOT was much smaller and slighter. Out of the corner of my eye, I watched as the instructor whacked the unfortunate man across the back of the head, sending him face first onto the ground. We all stood silently, not daring to move.

During my long train ride home in the evenings, despite being exhausted, I went over everything: weapons nomenclature, cycle of operation, strip and assembly and firing positions; I knew the consequences of getting it wrong. As NOTs, we had to know everything about the M16 and M4 assault rifles, the UMP40 and MP5 sub-machine guns and the Remington 870 pump-action and Benelli semi-automatic shotguns.

Each course had a hard qualification shoot, then a physical demonstration of weapon knowledge, followed by a written assessment. There were also 'stress shoots' for each weapon platform. This involved being exposed to a series of intimate lifelike gunfight scenarios. We were exercised to the point of physical exhaustion with our gas masks on, before running onto a 'lights out' firing range to shoot designated targets while instructors ceaselessly yelled at us. To increase the stress level to tipping point, they discharged their rifles and shotguns over our heads or next to us and even deployed sound and flash grenades—all to the sound of throbbing death metal music, strobing white lights and even smoke on some shoots. At this point, each NOT was ordered to complete a strip and assemble of his weapon, proving fine motor ability under duress. If we shot an 'incorrect target' it was an immediate fail. We needed to be level-headed in the most extreme situations because, in an operational situation, this was the difference between shooting a 'hostage' and a 'terrorist'.

Part of our SWAT training also involved a 'vehicle operations' course—effectively high-speed, high-risk, vehicle stop training that included ramming a vehicle or vehicles off the road. The most memorable part was 'motorcade training', which is part of protecting high priority dignitaries (such as visiting heads of state). One of the sergeants repeatedly rammed my car at high speed as I was reversing out of a simulated hostile situation. It really was 'next level'. I loved it.

Despite comprehensive training in the best ways and means to take a person's life, we were also trained in every option available to ensure that this is the last resort. The 'less lethal course' was where we were trained in hand-to-hand combat and the use of 'less than lethal tactics' such as Tasers, ▮▮▮▮▮▮ shotgun rounds, tear gas and police dogs. Being chased down by a snarling, determined German shepherd, hoping that it was going to latch onto my protective sleeve and not my groin, was quite an experience and a rite of passage. The ultimate test. Man versus canine.

There were also courses for the use of the ballistic shield and armoured vehicles, shooting and operating under night vision, reconnaissance, operational planning and the critical 'method of entry' course or 'MOE'. This involved advanced training in various ways of getting into any stronghold through manual means such as rams, entry tools, chainsaws or other power tools, as well as specialised shotgun rounds for firing through door locks, hinges, or glass. And then there was explosive entry, where a device or charge is placed against a door, wall or window—the closest thing to guaranteed access. On the completion of the course, we stood in our group as instructors detonated a huge fuel-air explosion just behind us, making for a dramatic photo backdrop. (A fuel-air explosion is used tactically as a very effective ▮▮▮▮▮▮ technique.)

All these courses led up to the big one—the 'close-quarter battle' or 'CQB' course. (Two NOT operators had already been culled by this stage.) CQB drew together all previous courses into one, featuring a live fire, short-duration, high-intensity conflict, characterised by sudden extreme violence at close range: 'Decisive entry into a stronghold, searching for and engaging or killing the threat(s) and evacuating hostages'.

We quickly learned that we had to stick together. It was us against the best efforts of the instructors to break us. As a group facing almost continuous adversity, we became very close. Psychological abuse, exercise punishment (penalties for mistakes), character beastings and the ever-present threat of removal from the TOU constantly hung over all of us. Each man struggled with separate courses or skill sets. However, one of the boys noticed Perro's terrified expression on the roping course and called out, "Hang in there mate. You'll get another $1.50 a day if you finish all your courses." Dangling off the side of the sandstone pylons of Sydney Harbour Bridge, Perro immediately called back, "I hate this course so much that when I get home, I stay awake as long as possible, so it feels longer before I have to be back up here again." Everyone laughed. We were all mates. We'd do anything for each other, without hesitation—an entirely necessary trait for a TOU operator. (And we even got to do the Harbour Bridge walk for free!)

We called ourselves 'the wolf pack'. The times away from the instructors were the best, especially the long drives on the bus to the Special Forces training facility at ███████ army base. Perro was a big fan of 1980s classic rock and regularly loaded up the PA system. His favourite was the soundtrack from *The Karate Kid*, "You're the best around." Belting out the words was something that made us feel normal, if only for a short time.

The counterterrorism courses went for another six months and extended beyond the professional standard of other international SWAT teams. This included: the 'linear assault' course onto buses and trains; the 'aircraft operations' course, involving assaults onto large commercial aircraft; the 'tactical roping' course, involving abseiling down high-rise buildings, smashing through windows, swinging in and clearing rooms; the 'active threat' course for urban terrain combat-like streetscapes and large strongholds such as shopping malls, especially confronting multiple active shooters; the 'bushcraft' course that honed remote navigation, survival and rural combat skills; the 'helicopter operations' course involving fast roping from choppers and the 'water operations' course or deployment from water or a vessel onto a passenger liner, large commercial vessel or land-based target, before clearing the area and freeing hostages.

There was one last test to prove ourselves—the 'survival swim'. This was conducted at night and based on the scenario of your chopper going down at sea. It entailed swimming from Balmoral to Manly in Sydney Harbour, a breeding ground for bull sharks. What made it worse was that a navy clearance diver had been attacked in the same area only days before. He lost an arm and leg while wearing the same equipment as we were: a long black wetsuit and black fins—to all intents and purposes a fur seal—a shark's favourite food.

As we jumped from the wharf, right on dusk, I was sure I'd be taken although, as exhaustion set in, the thought of being bitten in half seemed to disappear from my mind. We weren't allowed to slow down to release the cramps brought on by the cold water and constant finning—even for a few seconds—swimming like this for six hours. Waves constantly crashed over us. This caused me to swallow gulps of sea water. All the while I fought through exhaustion with my cast iron replica rifle held fast to my chest. (A navy guy in the previous course took in so much salt water that his entire body blew up like the Michelin man and he had to be hospitalised.) I momentarily turned my attention to the distant headland and the twinkle of lights from people's houses. They'd all be fast asleep in their warm Posturepedic beds.

Near the end, my legs kept buckling. I struggled through the waves and onto the beach. "What the hell do you wankers think you're doing?" barked the instructor. "Get back into that water. You thought this was over? Swim back! As in right now!" I was nauseated with fatigue, but I wasn't going to give up. We finned out a couple of hundred metres before finally being allowed to return to the beach.

And that was that. I had completed my courses. What started with over 200 recruits was now just six fully trained operators, including my mates Atts, Perro, Robbo, Smithy and Z. We now qualified for the prestigious 'blacks ceremony' where the boss of the TOU officially handed us our new uniforms—black fire-retardant overalls—and issued our personal operator number. In my case, it was #■■ embroidered on a black uniform patch. As TOU operators our identities are suppressed and court appearances only require the use of our ID number. We're also entitled to have our addresses deleted from external police databases and allowed to remove our details from the electoral roll. We arrest the most dangerous criminals including, of course, terrorists, so anonymity is important to alleviate the risk of reprisal. We were no longer NOTs but now among the 'boys in black', with our names in gold lettering on the TOU honour board, proudly up there with past and present qualified operators. That night, I was celebrating in a pub in Surry Hills with the other guys and I met Lisa. She was working in the local Emergency Department. We 'clicked' immediately. I was 29 years old.

*****

On the surface, Lisa and I seemed to be from parallel universes. She was from Ireland, and I wasn't. She was a tall, blonde, striking 'alternative'—and completely at home in the city—

surrounded by everything weird and wonderful that goes with that. I was from the country. I'd never really lived outside the Hawkesbury or the neighbouring Hills Shire, but we were both strong-willed, adventurous and determined. And above all, Lisa was as dedicated to her career in emergency nursing as I was to mine in policing.

As a young woman, Lisa travelled to Australia with nothing but the promise of a job through an agency. A recruitment representative met her at Sydney airport, before shouting at her for arriving alone. (Her friend had been held up in customs in Dublin.) Without so much as an explanation, Lisa was driven to the only available accommodation. (The place was condemned a few years later.) She was then shown to her small room in the nurses' quarters, containing nothing but a single bed. The next morning, after walking into her first giant flying cockroach and then an introduction to a red-bellied black snake in the garden, she made a commitment to herself to make it work—no matter what.

By the time we met in that Surry Hills bar, Lisa was enjoying the life she'd created for herself. Challenging me on so many levels, she loved music, especially indie and rock, and took me to festivals. Always the life of the party, Lisa was full of energy and addictive to be around. Then there were her friends. I thought SWAT operators were a unique bunch but they pale in comparison to emergency doctors and nurses. They really knew how to party and have a good time. They were free with their opinions and had a dark sense of humour that rivalled that of most cops.

A lot of her best friends were flamboyant gay men. They really were fun to be around. Lisa often told me that I was different from anyone she'd ever dated. I noticed that she deliberately kept me at a distance, because at the back of her mind she planned to return home to Ireland and the last thing she wanted was to get stuck on the other side of the world.

Our make-or-break moment came soon enough. I asked her to go on holiday with me. My mother loaned us her motorhome. The plan was to drive from Sydney (via the town of Glenrowan, where Ned Kelly made his last stand) to Port Melbourne, Victoria. We boarded the *Spirit of Tasmania* (a large roll-on/ roll-off car ferry-cruise ship) and explored our way around the 'Apple Isle' together. It wasn't the sort of holiday Lisa would've chosen for herself, although she'd once backpacked with a friend up the east coast of Australia. It was just she and I, for three weeks, with no escape from each other.

Soon after our return, we moved in together. We lived in the inner west Sydney suburbs of Surry Hills and Redfern before finding a cute single-storey terrace in the inner-city cultural hub of Newtown. I'd lived in more places in those first 18 months with Lisa than I had in my entire life. Our two years there were some of our happiest times. We travelled to Ireland to meet her family and friends and got engaged on a snowy Christmas morning.

The two of us bought our first place together in Cronulla in Sydney's south. (Lisa wanted to stay in the city.) It was a run-down red-brick building with rising damp that needed to be completely gutted. The place was 'a renovator', right on the beach. (The truth was that she saw me as a renovation project as well.) After I'd finished making the place liveable, we brought our first baby girl home.

*****

It was a month later and my first big job. I was excited but trying my best to hide it. We rushed to our vehicles. Undercover officers reported that three men were on their way to commit an armed robbery. A high-risk vehicle stop was urgently requested. We scrambled into our equipment and gathered everything necessary. I was allocated the rear passenger seat and given the shotgun—a Remington 870 pump-action, with 12-gauge ▮▮▮▮▮▮▮ rounds. (This a specialised cartridge designed to impact with glass and then release ▮ gas into the cabin).

I was in an unmarked V8 LandCruiser as part of a TOU convoy. The lights and sirens were activated as we attempted to catch up with the known criminals before they reached their next heist—a petrol station. The police chopper was in the air and surveillance vehicles were in the field providing location intelligence. My team leader in the front passenger seat spotted the offenders. Lights and sirens were cut. We needed the advantage of surprise. Ours was the blocking vehicle, with another 4WD crew behind us and the fast-car team, in a Falcon XR6 turbo, backing up. We waited for the three-word activation code.

The target vehicle was travelling at over 100 kilometres/hour on the busy Great North Road. I checked my shotgun again; it was ready to go. I grabbed hold of the brace handle and prepared for impact. This was it, the moment I'd been trained for. Our driver sped up beside the offenders' vehicle, a stolen dark-blue turbo-charged Subaru WRX. Our heavy bull bar slammed into the front driver's side wheel, buckling it with precision and crashing the car at speed into the kerb.

I quickly recovered from the collision and jumped out. The other 4WD was positioned beside the target car, with the fast-car team at the rear. As I ran to the offenders' car, I saw the driver glance towards me. His eyes were as dilated as dinner plates, with a terrified expression that said, 'I'm about to be shot in the face'. I racked the pump-action shotgun—*Chung-chung*—and deliberately aimed it downwards into the rear passenger-side window. *Boom* and then *Boom* again.

Another operator also fired from the rear. The front window was surgically smashed in before a Taser was deployed. The same thing was happening on the other side of the car.

The driver was screaming with fear. I reefed the door open and instantly copped a face full of tear gas. I started choking but fought through it, grabbing the driver in a headlock, as my partner cut his seatbelt with a hook knife. I ripped the man out, before throwing him to the ground, and into handcuffs. Another of the offenders literally wet himself. On the front seat, there were two loaded 9mm semi-automatic handguns and, in the back, a sawn-off shotgun. It was a perfectly executed operation, seizing the initiative, and overwhelming the threat through the 'violence of action' namely, 'speed, strength, surprise and aggression to achieve total dominance'. This put the armed and dangerous criminals instantly on the back foot, resulting in neither us nor them being injured. We were given authority to do what we were trained to do, took the initiative, acted decisively and prevailed.

I smiled to myself. The barrier testing, selection, and a year of back-to-back-cutting-edge courses were all worth it. I was where I wanted to be—a fully qualified operator—a state asset in one of the toughest and best-trained tactical operations units in the world. And then I reflected on the chief inspector's words at the information day in what seemed a lifetime ago. "The TOU are looking for a person who will not be rattled or overwhelmed in any situation. The TOU require individuals who will overcome extreme adversity with the highest level of skill and resilience." However, there was something that was never explained—in selection, in advanced training or in the many thousands of operations that followed: there are actually two types of resilience: operational and psychological. Because eventually every one of us would pay a personal price for our service. 'Suck it up' was the unspoken rule—'it's the Australian way'.

Near Misses, Close Calls And Injuries

Near misses, close calls and injuries are common in TOU training and in our everyday operations. Taken on an individual basis, we learn from every one of them. Being able to manage potentially life-ending risks in the line of duty is essential. It's what's expected of a highly trained state asset. It was what was required at Lindt. However, over time, the physical and psychological damage accumulates. At first you laugh it off. Then you just shrug your shoulders. At some point you find you're not laughing as much anymore; and then you don't laugh at all.

As part of our water operations course, we were required to undertake 'covert swim-up assaults' on a decommissioned Royal Australian Navy ship. A method we use is to deploy a ▮▮▮▮▮▮ wire caving ladder. This is a narrow steel-cabled device that's deployed using an ▮▮▮▮▮▮▮▮▮▮. It requires several operators to hold the ▮▮▮▮▮▮▮▮▮▮▮▮▮ in the water and then hook it over the side of the ship. The pole is then extracted leaving the ladder in place. On this day, the task was completed effectively. It was my turn to pull the ladder down as tightly as possible, securing it in place, allowing Perro to begin the long climb to the top.

Perro was 25 metres above me. It was his first attempt. The ladder flipped and he was caught against the ship's steel hull. He tried to rectify this situation at the top—and nearly managed it—before he lost his footing. Then I heard it again—a 'man yelp'. I looked up and saw him fall, straight towards me, with no way for me to move in time, crashing only millimetres from where I was treading water. The impact of a heavy man, strapped with equipment, landing on top of me from that height, would've broken my neck. Fortunately, I was unharmed.

Perro, however, wasn't so lucky. His rifle—or rather a cast iron training replica—hit him in the face.

"Bloody hell man, that was a pearler of a stack, you nearly killed me," I laughed—not so much in relief for myself—but at how flustered my mate was.

"Sorry ▓▓▓▓, trust me, I didn't mean it. You know how freaked out I am of heights."

I looked more closely. "You're okay, aren't you?"

"Yeah. What do you mean?" Perro replied, clearly not understanding my question.

"Man, your top lip is pissing out blood."

"Ahh, yeah, I know. The gun smashed me square in the gob when I hit the water. Don't tell the instructors," he said, as he wiped the blood away with the sleeve of his wetsuit.

"You sure? It looks pretty bad," I continued, pressing him out of concern.

"Yeah, seriously, she's cool. I'm already embarrassed enough about falling," Perro grinned strangely as he held up his 'weapon' to show that he somehow still had it. He adjusted his overvest, checked that both the HEED emergency oxygen bottle and compact personal flotation device were in place, spat out a squelch of blood and, smiled again—as if nothing had happened.

"What are you two dumb arses talking about? Get up that bloody ladder," came the barking response from one of the instructors.

With a little shake of the head Perro then muttered, in his best John Rambo *First Blood Part II* impersonation, "Do we get to win this time, Sir?"

I've had plenty of close calls in TOU water operations training, especially in ship under way vessel boarding. One such time, we were conducting the boarding of a Sydney Harbour ferry as part of a counterterrorism exercise. I was a member of an assault team on a rigid-hulled inflatable boat or RHIB (pronounced 'rib'). This is a specialised fast craft operated by water police and special forces all around the world. It can carry up to eight operators, plus a driver and support officer. Another team was entering from the far side of the ferry and a third crew were fast roping onto the roof from the police chopper. All were to conduct the assault simultaneously. As the most senior operator I was assigned as first to board the distinctive single-hulled commuter craft. Permission to engage was given—"Go! Go! Go!"

As our RHIB approached, it bounced on the waves like a rodeo bull. We all held on. The sea swell was particularly powerful that day. The ferry was also moving at speed, creating its own wake. We needed to get aboard as quickly as possible as the simulation involved a terrorist hijacking with hostages. I jumped up, readied my feet, and started running between the seats and the inflatable hull, anticipating that as the RHIB made contact I'd land on the deck of the ferry. Unfortunately, as I launched myself off the rubber bow, a swell interrupted our approach and the RHIB violently bumped back. But it was too late for me. I was already committed.

Airborne, I became acutely aware that there was no RHIB below me—just ocean and swell. Somehow, I managed to grab hold of the ferry's guard rail in time to save myself, pulling up hard and fast, just high enough to miss being crushed between the RHIB and ferry. Then, there was the real threat, if I fell, of being sucked under the water and cut to pieces by the ferry's massive bronze propeller. There had been incidents of this nature in the past. I shrugged it off.

It might sound as if all we do in the TOU are water operations when, in fact, most of our deployments are land-based and urban. We were conducting the method of entry (MOE) course as part of my initial training. On this occasion, it was a drive-up assault on a stronghold at the Australian Special Forces ▇▇▇▇▇▇▇▇ at ▇▇▇▇▇▇ army base in South-Western Sydney. This course is both brutal and dangerous and includes shooting out door handles and hinges as well as windows with shotguns. It also includes crashing through glass doors and windows at a full sprint and cutting through doors and garages with power tools, including chainsaws. Window entries are especially hazardous. A huge ladder is placed as quickly as possible below a windowsill, often at second-storey level. The first operator then smashes out the glass with a 'reamer' (a long, hardened steel pole). Inevitably, shards fall onto the rest of the team. Then stunnies are lobbed through the window by other operators, effectively distracting anyone inside.

At the top of the huge ladder, on a small platform, you quickly set yourself, reaching your free arm through to the inside windowsill while holding your rifle at the ready with the other arm, before swinging through the opening. Many windows are tiny and banging off the bottom windowsill is unavoidable. (My left butt cheek was bruised black and blue for weeks after the course.) (For some reason, all my injuries have been on my left side.)

However, the fastest and most effective way of entering a stronghold—or any secure area for that matter, is through the expert use of an explosive charge. Explosives can be fashioned into different shapes and sizes depending on the requirement. The TOU are well trained in this field. Some charges are designed for windows, some for doors or brick walls and even steel roller doors. On this occasion, the breacher selected a 'fold-up charge' or, as the Americans call it, a 'folding silhouette charge' placed against a door and stuck in place with dollops of axle grease. (We now use stick-on 'toilet ducks' that create a unique smell after an explosion—a mixture of gunpowder smoke and citrus.) Once positioned, the 'breacher' returns to his place in the stack behind the front man holding a Perspex riot shield, protecting the entire group from blast residue. He then detonates the charge. The huge explosion shakes you to your core, even at a stand-off distance. It blows a clean rectangular hole in whatever obstacle is targeted, allowing operators to pass. A breacher requires a special skill set. Breachers are experts in all types of access, especially explosive entry. There's a long-standing, friendly rivalry between breachers and snipers, as there is, for instance, between Australians and New Zealanders in sport. We snipers say that all breachers are brain-dead from traumatic brain injury caused by repeated exposure to explosions. (Although we're all exposed to the same damage and snipers have the added exposure from the repeated firing of large calibre rifles.)

I was allocated as 'cover man'. Our team approached quickly in our special-purpose vehicle or SPV. This is a beast of a four-wheel drive with a steel platform on the back and sides that allows operators to hold onto the outside and then make a quick exit. I was at the back-right drivers' side with the breacher in the middle and another cover man to my left. In this operation, the breacher faced backwards holding the explosive charge. It was my job to physically secure him in place along with the other cover man. This can be very dangerous. It needs to be done precisely. In a fast-moving and unpredictable live-fire operation, these skills can make the difference between life and death, for hostages—and for us.

We were directed to assault the building. I banged on the roof twice to let the driver know that I was ready. I stood with my right arm holding my rifle upwards ready to engage. My left arm locked the breacher into position. Speed is essential to minimise vulnerable time in the open; however on this occasion the vehicle was going unusually fast. Suddenly and unexpectedly, the driver swerved to the left on an off-camber corner. I held on as tightly as I could with my left arm. I nearly managed the situation but the breacher couldn't hold and he bumped me. I fell from the back of the Special Purpose Vehicle (SPV) at 60 kilometres per hour, smashing into the asphalt and tumbling over and over in a sort of controlled recovery. This falling technique, together with my bullet-resistant vest and my ballistic helmet, saved me from serious injury. Still, I'd whacked my head and was unsteady on my feet. I could see stars. Taking a knee, I looked up, saw the team near our entry point, and stumbled towards them. "Stop, Stop! End ex (for 'end exercise') I repeat. End ex!" the senior instructor yelled. "Come over here ▆▆▆."

"Yes staff."

"Firstly, are you okay ▆▆▆?"

"Yes, of course staff," I answered. (I knew that I wasn't.)

"Are you sure? So, you're ready to continue?"

"Definitely, staff."

"Take a look at your weapon ▆▆▆."

I looked down and saw that that my MP5 sub-machine gun no longer had the magazine in the magazine well. "Seriously mate, take a few seconds to set yourself," the instructor continued, now with a less confronting tone. That's when I noticed how painful my foot was. It was killing me, especially my toes. I gathered myself before fronting the instructors again. "▆▆▆, I have to say that you're a useless prick for falling off the SPV, but you somewhat redeemed yourself when you rejoined the fight," growled the instructor.

"Yes staff."

"Go and see the medics."

"Seriously, staff. I'm fine."

"▆▆▆. Do it!'

The specialist ambulance officers had a good look at me. They attend all our dangerous training involving firearms and explosives. "You all right? I saw the whole thing. I was sure you wouldn't be getting back up again," one of the paramedics commented. They checked my vital signs: heart rate, respiratory rate and blood pressure, before shining a penlight torch into both my pupils. They even had a look at the grazes on my arms and knees—but thankfully they didn't make me take my boots off.

"Seriously fellas, I feel fine. I reckon I just got the wind knocked out of me," I again reassured them.

"Righto you bunch of useless numpties, get your heads in the game, that was a monumental cluster fuck. Let's switch the fuck on and not screw this one up."

"Yes staff," we all responded.

I was aware that, if I pulled out because of injury, I'd have to abandon all my courses. This would mean waiting another two years to start with the next group. I wasn't going to let that happen. For the rest of the day, I was under the constant suspicious gaze of instructors. They could see that I was limping, despite my very best efforts to cover it up.

"You going to be able to manage this ▮▮▮," the instructor asked several times.

"All good staff," I replied with the thumbs up signal.

When I got home, I could barely manage to get my boot off. My left big toe and the one next to it were broken. As a kid, I'd broken the same toes in motocross and had to stay off my feet for weeks. The next morning, I strapped my broken toes together with electrical tape and forced my boot back on. I somehow finished the week and the course but, just as importantly, I gained a reputation for toughness, particularly under pressure.

It was another training exercise involving the water police, PolAir (the police air wing) and the TOU. I wasn't scheduled to join but found myself in the right place at the right time. The training was being conducted at North Cronulla, well away from the main beach. The exercise was called 'helocasting'. This was part of our extensive helicopter-based training.

Another TOU capability is fast roping. This is a dynamic method of deploying operators from a chopper to various locations, for instance, onto the top of buildings, large boats or hard-to-reach locations. This dangerous activity requires complete focus, with any lapse in concentration potentially resulting in a tragedy (like the famous scene in the Hollywood movie, *Black Hawk Down*, where a special forces soldier falls to his death).

After the chopper's rapid approach to the drop area, it conducts a quick stop manoeuvre by pulling up with the helicopter nearly facing vertically, then dropping its tail before levelling off. A long rope is thrown out over the target drop zone. While you lean out to take hold, pulsing bursts of wind and the roar from the rotors add to the overall experience. (If you miss you die.) As you slide downwards, you must wrap your legs around it to help you slow down.

Once, on a course, the end of the rope had blown off the side of a three-storey building that two of us were fast roping onto. If I hadn't been aware of this and the operator above me hadn't noticed either, it might have ended in catastrophe. With all my heavy tactical equipment on board, it was extremely difficult for me to stop completely—only slow down. But for the quick thinking of the helicopter crew directing the pilot back onto the top of the building, we would both have plummeted to the asphalt below. There are no safety harnesses or safety measures. Fast roping must be conducted at speed to minimise exposure time to potential threats. An instructor on our course repeatedly screamed the same comment. "It's fast roping you bunch of gumbies not medium-fucking-paced roping."

In contrast, helocasting essentially involves jumping from the police chopper into the ocean. The TOU are responsible for high-risk vessel boarding and water operations for the State of NSW. The use of this tactical skill involves rapid deployment into the sea or any body of water. This allows operators to complete a covert swim-up assault onto a vessel or land-based target.

We all readied our water operations equipment. A safety briefing was conducted with all the units involved—a run-through of how our deployments were to occur. We were cast into the water about 300 metres offshore before being picked up by the water police.

The chopper, a twin-engine Bell 412EPI, fired up and we were ready to go. I was on the 'second stick' (or second group). After dropping the first stick, the chopper looped back to get us. It flew with open doors. There was no need for straps or harnesses; we had to be ready to jump at short notice. I climbed out onto the chopper's skids as the backdraft from the chopper's rotor was whipping my face. Far below, I could see white caps forming on the surface of the water. The only thing I had to hold onto was a small green nylon strop. It was a rush. A crew member, or 'crewy' as we call them, gave us the signal—a downward chop of the hand. It was time to go. I jumped the five metres from the skids and into the ocean—while the chopper was still flying forward, not hovering. A perfect deployment.

We completed a couple more jumps before we had a break to let the chopper refuel. "You're taking it a bit easy out there aren't ya mate?" one of the TOU boys unexpectedly said to the pilot.

"Sorry, what do you mean?" he replied.

"Could you go any lower?" the operator continued

sarcastically, clearly baiting him.

"Are you serious?" the pilot continued.

I joined in. "Just bloody send it. What do you think we are, the riot squad or something?" Everyone laughed. It was a long-standing 'in joke'.

"All right, but don't say I didn't warn you," the pilot replied, with an 'I'll show you' expression on his face. The boys just couldn't help themselves. We wanted to go higher and faster. This wasn't just about cockiness. Often live fire deployments require great risks taken at a second's notice. Hesitation can potentially jeopardise an operation—or spell disaster in a hostage situation.

The chopper fired up as we got our gear back on. I noticed one of the straps that secured my vest containing the HEED emergency oxygen bottle had broken, but as it was one of two, I wasn't concerned. This unfortunately was an accident waiting to happen. We boarded the chopper. I waited in anticipation. The crewy again gave us the signal and I climbed out onto the skids. This time we were a long way up, perhaps over 100 metres, and still flying at speed. I clung onto the strop as tightly as I could.

For a TOU operator, this was challenging and dangerous but also exciting. I thought to myself, 'I can't believe we're actually getting paid to do this.' The chopper continued its descent and began easing in speed, somewhat. We were about 15 metres above the water. It felt like over 20 knots or about 35 kilometres per hour as the wind lashed my face. The crewy gave me the drop signal. I looked at him and shook my head thinking, 'Are you seeing what I'm seeing? No one had committed. He again gave me the signal. I didn't want to look soft in front of my senior operators, so I mustered up my courage and without further hesitation—jumped.

I was in the air for a long-time, toppling forward towards

the water. I wouldn't have done this if I hadn't jumped from so high. Then I felt a massive impact. Something was wrong. I resurfaced after a few seconds, but I was struggling to stay conscious. It took all my focus to not pass out because I knew the consequences. I spat out a large amount of blood. Even in my dazed state, my concern was sharks. Deciding against doing it again, I just swallowed. The other boys in the water weren't aware of my injury and, like Perro and the caving ladder incident, I didn't want them to know either. The water police boat finally arrived and we were pulled on board as the speedboat was still moving. One of the water police guys looked at me. "Holy crap. You all right mate? You've got blood pissing down your chin."

"Yeah, all good. I think I just bit my tongue. Nothing to worry about." But he continued to stare at me, so I turned away, wiping my face with the arm of my wetsuit. The boat dropped us in the water just beyond the breakers so we could swim the short distance to shore. As I stood up in the shallows, I called out to one of my colleagues. He turned to face me as I said, "I think I might've knocked out some tee … ."

Two of my front teeth then projected out landing in my hand. As I looked down in shock, a wave knocked me over and washed my teeth away. This was too much for the other operator. He fell to the ground in a fit of nervous laughter and began rolling around on the sand.

"I'm sorry mate, but that was one of the funniest things I've ever seen."

"I suppose you're right." I said with a newly developed lisp, which set him off again.

As I walked up the beach, the other two operators came to find out what my colleague found so funny. The sergeant changed his tune when I opened my mouth. "Shit ████, you've knocked out two teeth."

"Really? Two?"

"And put all the others through your tongue. Uggh! Are you okay?"

"I'll live. The missus will be stoked with the new look," I said, attempting to be humorous. It didn't work. And I knew Lisa wouldn't find it funny either.

"We're going to need that checked out right away," the sergeant said.

I immediately replied, "I need to get back on the horse sarge. I have to go up again. If I don't, I may never want to do it again."

"You can't be serious. You're banged up pretty bad."

"Seriously, I need to do this."

"All right then, but it's on you."

"Thanks. It's my decision." He just shook his head.

We moved into position as the chopper touched down. I turned away so the crewy couldn't see my face. (I'm sure that they wouldn't have let me go up again if they knew.) We looped around. It was the last jump of the day—a clear blue sky and a soft sea breeze. It took a concerted effort to control my nerves. I made my way onto the skids. We were high and coming in fast. I had to do this. I stared at the crewy just waiting for the signal. There it was. Flexing every muscle in my body I jumped without hesitation. This time I leant back so I didn't topple forward. I braced for impact and hit the water. It was a lot better this time but my mouth was still tender from the previous impact. I'd done it. Now I felt confident enough to do it again in the future. Mission accomplished.

The sergeant organised a lift for me to the emergency dentist. "Oh my God, this is horrific. How did you say this happened again?" the dentist asked me, looking a little unwell himself.

"Jumping out of a helicopter."

"Are you joking?"

"Deadly serious."

"Well, I don't see something like this walk in every day."

"I can imagine."

"You've lost two teeth at the top front and the two next to them are so badly damaged they will need veneers. I can see 11, 12 … 13 piercings of your tongue. You're lucky you didn't bite it off entirely," he continued, thinking out loud, making notes on a laptop.

"I'd have been luckier not to do it at all," I said with a pronounced lisp. The comment just went over his head.

"Hmmm, challenging," the dentist mumbled, again obviously thinking out loud. He shook his head and rubbed his brow. "How high did you jump from again?" he questioned me.

I replied, "I hit the water from 15 metres and, on impact, my oxygen bottle slammed me under my chin."

"Are you mad?" he asked, in a way that meant that he thought I was.

The next morning, Lisa realised that I wasn't quite right. I was struggling to remember who the prime minister was—although, in Australia, that's a challenge for everyone—we've had so many of them lately. More importantly, however, I was having trouble recalling details about the previous day. Lisa took me straight to the ED at Royal Prince Alfred Hospital where I was admitted. Over the next 12 months I had a ridiculous number of surgical procedures to fix my mouth. Every morning for six months, my routine was: car keys, phone, wallet, teeth—from a glass of water beside the bed. "It's like living with a pensioner," Lisa remarked with more than a hint of Irish sarcasm. But Gus went one further after I got my new teeth. "Mate, you now have Nicole Kidman's smile on Danny DeVito's head."

*****

It was an emergency call-out to a housing commission block in the inner Sydney suburb of Redfern. "Tactics only?" I enquired. (Permission to use special weapons and tactics (SWAT) needs to be approved by a regional commander.) On this occasion, we were only given permission to use 'less lethal tactics' such as OC (pepper spray), CS (tear gas), ▊▊▊▊ shotguns and Tasers. If a lethal option was required, we still had our sidearms—a Glock 40-calibre semi-automatic pistol with a 15-round magazine.

We kitted up in our black bullet-resistant vests, complete with ceramic plates front and back that will stop most rounds. Then it was helmets and personal gear followed by any extra equipment required for protection from knife attacks, together with manual breaching equipment such as a tactical ram. I had the Perspex riot shield and a Taser. The operator behind me had a CS fogger, a large canister of tear gas that can be deployed manually. It serves a similar purpose to the pepper spray GDs officers carry but is more effective with a far greater available volume. Another operator had selected a Remington 870 shotgun—a pump-action weapon that uses a special ▊▊ ▊ round. When fired, it shoots a cartridge with an exterior material pouch filled with ▊▊▊▊▊▊▊— a very effective method of subduing violent offenders without killing them. We also have a ▊▊▊▊▊▊ round that can be deployed through a 40-millimetre grenade launcher, but this was decided against because the POI was holed up in a confined space.

One essential item for knife jobs was a pair of chain-mail gloves that extend to the shoulders (as worn by medieval knights). This is ideal for safely grabbing a blade from an offender. I held the riot shield up to my face and peered into the open doorway, rechecking that the strap was secured to my left arm. I was positioned at the front of the stack, providing protection for the rest of the team—a common role for a newly-qualified operator eager to prove himself to his seniors. At the far end of the poorly lit room was a large, muscular, shirtless, tattooed man who was pacing back and forth in a methamphetamine-induced rage. He was holding two large knives with the blades facing downwards, the sharp edges to the front—as a skilled knife fighter would. This allows for both downward stabbing and slashing. It was initially a domestic violence incident with the POI pulling the knives when GDs police arrived.

The man pointed his blades menacingly at me. "Get my fuck'en mate Johnno down here or I'll stab as many of youse motherfuckers as I can before youse kill me," he roared. He then feigned a lunge before withdrawing, becoming further enraged, swirling the knives acrobatically in a boxer's stance. I had my Taser, drawn but not activated. The light source and laser pointer would've further aggravated him, and, at that point, we just wanted to de-escalate the situation.

"Righto boys, let's go get him," the team leader further back in the stack called out. I gritted my teeth. It was my time to shine. I felt my adrenalin levels surge as I pulled the shield higher and activated the Taser safety catch. I took a step into the room. The man's bulging, bloodshot eyes opened wider, and his nostrils flared like an angry bull's. He charged towards me with both knives held up above his head so that he could stab me with a downward thrust. I took aim. *Crack*. The Taser discharged with the barbs hitting home. A stream of tear gas deployed by another operator simultaneously passed over my head hitting the POI in the face. It didn't slow him down in the least; he was already committed. I dropped my weight as low as I could, pushing my shoulder forward and flexing every muscle, bracing for impact. This was a technique I learnt in junior rugby league, which was especially useful when a 120-kilogram, six-foot-tall, 14-year-old Pacific Islander kid was running straight at you.

The man began to topple forward. I could see him coming right at me. I watched in what seemed to be slow motion as the knife blades struck the shield with mere millimetres of clear Perspex between me and an urgent trip to a packed ED waiting room. Just as the man's full weight hit, I shoulder charged. His forward momentum bumped me back. I felt the weight of the operator directly behind me but the stack held firm. I pushed forward again, knocking him onto his back, landing on top of him. "Die you fuck'en cop dog," he bellowed, as the air went out of him like a deflating party balloon. I was still conscious of the blades, naturally hoping that they wouldn't pierce me (or him for that matter). The operator with chainmail gloves engaged and, after a violent struggle, we got the POI into handcuffs.

In the job debrief, the sergeant commented, "Good work by the new bloke," to the nodding approval of other senior operators. I couldn't help smiling. And so began my love affair with the Taser. From that day on I seemed to be mentioned in most jobs as 'the operator deploying a Taser'. (I still hold the record for the most TOU Taser deployments, although my mates would be chasing it.)

There was another close call at an outlaw motorcycle clubhouse in Western Sydney. The 'war on bikies' had been a big part of the NSW Police Force's 'war on organised crime'. This was in response to the highly publicised brawl in Sydney Airport between two rival gangs, which resulted in a man being beaten to death with a steel bollard in front of terrified travellers.

I was part of a four-man squad including 'Old Dig' (short for 'old digger'). At 52 years of age, he was the oldest operational SWAT cop in Australia—and maybe the world. The aim was for the 'bikies' not to know that we'd entered. It was a particularly dark night. Our job was to escort specialist police so they could secretly install ▮▮▮▮▮▮▮▮▮▮▮▮▮ devices under the terms of a court-issued warrant. It was about 3.00 a.m. when we got the all-clear to go in. The clubhouse was located inside a three-storey factory complex framed with high fences and topped with razor wire. The only way we could enter without activating their CCTV and alarms was across the roof. We got onto the ridge with large extendable ladders and carefully crossed the gable using night-vision goggles.

Old Dig and I were leading. The two of us walked slowly to avoid making a noise on the corrugated-iron sheeting. Suddenly, the roof below us creaked and buckled. We both froze and looked at each other. Our night-vision goggles masked the terror in each other's eyes. The two of us has inadvertently trodden on a large, clear skylight panel. This was impossible to see with night-vision equipment. After a brief pause and a tense whispered conversation, we slowly eased our feet back, half a step at a time. Somehow the panel stayed intact. A fall from that height—three stories onto concrete—would have been fatal. It was just one of hundreds of 'what if?' moments I had in the TOU. Fortunately, we managed to gain entry undetected—and unharmed.

While ▮▮▮▮▮▮▮▮▮▮▮▮▮ was being installed, I had a good look round. The club had a seedy-looking, fully stocked, stale alcohol-smelling bar area and a raised stage with a stripper pole for private shows. There was also an enormous 'Stars and Bars' Confederate battle flag backdrop. It was a glimpse into the dark world of outlaw motorcycle gang crime: illicit drug dealing, illegal weapons sales, money laundering, people smuggling and sex trafficking. This was one of many operations where the TOU were at the centre of a highly successful policing strategy that ultimately crushed what was a serious law-and-order issue—but also an operation that could easily have ended in tragedy.

*****

One morning as I was getting ready for work, I pulled my teeth from the glass on the bedside table and copped the usual eyeroll from Lisa.

"You do know I can't help it don't you?" I said returning the eye roll.

"Yes of course, but you really have had some injuries from that beloved job of yours, haven't you?" she responded, still in bed, and secretly hoping for a sleep-in; as was the cat.

"Yep, true, comes with the territory," I replied, considering the question.

Lisa yawned and said, "I think the answer is too many."

"Do you really want to know?" I continued, hoping she would.

"Yes, of course," she said, appearing to be interested. It was something we rarely talked about. Like most TOU operators our work and our home lives are kept very separate. Most of the guys are family men with only daughters (for some reason) and we want our partners and 'little princesses' to be as sheltered from our violent professional world as possible.

"Well," I said to Lisa, "I've been punched in the face—plenty of times—and then smacked over the head with an old man's walking stick in a full-on community brawl while assisting detectives to repossess a car used in an armed robbery. I've been bitten, kicked, and scratched breaking up a fight outside a nightclub … by girls mind you. I was set on by drug house guard dogs and a getaway car rammed me against a fence. In the part-time riot squad, I was grabbed, punched and strangled while arresting a radical university student during an APEC (that's Asia-Pacific Economic Cooperation) protest."

"Okay. Interesting," Lisa said. (It takes a lot to shock an ED nurse.)

"This doesn't tell the full story. At the 2007 APEC Summit, some hard-core anarchists, wearing all black with their faces covered, held up a 'pink battle flag' and we knew it was on. A storm of darts was thrown at us. The only thing I could do was tilt the brim of my police cap to protect my eyes. I saw one dart lodge itself in the old school sergeant's head right beside me. I said, "Ah sarge, there's a dart hanging out of your head."

"Dirty fucking hippy bastards," was his matter-of-fact reply as he ripped the dart from his head.

I still had Lisa's attention.

"One of my mates had his head split open to the skull with a metal pole wrapped in cardboard to disguise it. Marbles were thrown under the hooves of police horses, forcing them to stumble and fall. The poor creatures were then stabbed with ID pins ripped from our uniforms. It was very ugly."

"Poor horses," Lisa said, genuinely upset, as I continued with my stories.

"I've been blown up and I have permanent hearing loss and tinnitus. I've broken knuckles and fingers from smashing out glass doors and windows. I cut my hands jumping fences chasing a home invader who turned out to be HIV and hepatitis C positive. He punched me in the face before I returned the favour. Blood to blood contact. Then I had that stressful six months of testing to make sure I didn't have it." Lisa nodded.

"And of course, I've had teeth knocked out and now I have no feeling in my bottom lip and chin." I drew a breath. I was enjoying the debriefing. Lisa had clearly given away the idea of a sleep-in and the cat was never really interested in what I had to say anyway.

"And then, there's Gus. He's got the same 'TOU bad back'

that all of us eventually get, with our bulging disks and early-onset arthritis from the 25-kilogram vests and equipment crushing our spines. But did I tell you about the time that he had scalding hot water and boiling oil thrown on him and then was stabbed by a batshit-crazy Cambodian ex-soldier? Luckily, his vest saved him. And then there was the time on a counterterrorism search warrant when a brick wall fell on top of him, pinning him to the ground, knocking him out cold." I paused to see if Lisa was still awake. She was. "Remember the Qantas meat-grinder bomb job?" Lisa nodded. "So," I continued. "Would you like me to tell you about the time I was shot at by a man hanging himself?"

"Okay, why not? You seem to be on a roll," Lisa replied.

It was an urgent job on the North Coast of NSW. A man had taken his wife and child hostage. He had a shotgun and was threatening to kill himself and his family. I was assigned to drive the armoured vehicle under lights and sirens all the way from our headquarters in ▇▇▇—a road trip of nearly 400 kilometres. My offsider for the journey was 'Houso'—a professional operator who looked more like a bricklayer than a police officer. (He wore the badge of a long footy career—a nose broken so many times that it made your eyes water.) Houso was one of those blokes who could fall asleep anywhere. Even with loud sirens and after a jumbo can of Red Bull, I could hear him snoring within five minutes of leaving.

We arrived on site—a single storey, run-down fibro weatherboard home in an otherwise quiet country town. I picked up the rest of the operators and drove into position on the man's front lawn. The negotiators were then engaged. On jobs like this, there is always an Alpha arrest team, and perimeter teams (often with a tactical dog) who surround the property to prevent the offender escaping. The armoured vehicle's headlights lit up the front of the house and, with the aid of the powerful spotlight mounted on top, we were able to see inside. The POI was now faced with the reality of TOU operators with assault rifles right outside his house. He agreed to release his wife and child. The wife painted a grim picture of her husband's disturbed mental state.

From the driver's seat, I had a good view of him. He was wearing black tracksuit pants and a polo shirt with the top button done up; he was of average height and build with short dark hair and beard stubble. I immediately noticed his brand-new white running shoes as they reflected the light. The rest of the team were positioned at the back of the armoured vehicle and a sniper was covering from the turret. The man was pacing back and forth with an old single-barrelled shotgun in his right hand. There were definitely 'a few roos loose in his top paddock'. Then he momentarily disappeared out of sight before returning with a dining room chair and a length of rope—positioning himself below a ceiling fan. He then climbed up on the chair, fashioned a knot around the fan and made a hangman's noose with the other end of the rope. "He's tying a rope off to the fan sarge," I said with trepidation.

"You sure it's a rope ▮▮▮▮? It looks like string from here," the sergeant replied, requesting clear conformation.

"I'm positive. It's nylon Parramatta rope like the tradies use. One hundred per cent."

"Righto boys, this isn't looking good, ready yourselves."

I jumped out of the driver's seat and took my position in the stack behind the operator holding the ballistic shield. The sergeant relayed the development back to the command post over police radio. I watched as the man took his time to finish tying the noose. He then placed it around his neck and stared straight at us still holding the shotgun. He momentarily paused before jumping off the chair. "He's hanging himself," I yelled.

"Okay boys? Go! Go! Go!"

We ran to the front door as operators on another entry point smashed a window with a reamer and positioned the ladder. The operator on the tactical ram bashed at the door. It gave way with one blow. I followed Houso through the door and the two of us ran towards the living room. On entry, I could see the man hanging, but even more alarming was that he levelled his shotgun at us. *Bang.* Smoke filled the air from the close-quarters gunshot. My ears were ringing.

I looked up. The man was violently thrashing and choking. His face was plum purple. It was a disturbing sight—even for us. Houso grabbed his legs and lifted him slightly. I ripped my tactical knife from its scabbard and cut the rope above his head in one swift motion. He dropped into Houso's arms. Both of us went to our hands and knees. The man's eyes were rolling back in his head and his tongue was hanging out.

"Shit, the rope is still strangling him," I yelled to Houso. The braided light-blue and yellow nylon had dug deep into the flesh on his neck. His veins were bulging, and his eyes were bloodshot and protruding. I ripped off a glove and, with Houso's help, managed to lever my fingers under the rope and slowly ease the tension. I felt for a pulse. I watched for his chest to rise and listened for a breath—nothing. The paramedics rushed in. I stayed to assist. The unconscious man was rushed to hospital.

I took a deep breath, got back to my feet, and walked over to the chair the POI had used to hang himself. The old shotgun was on the floor and had blown itself in half. "Bloody hell Houso, have you seen *this*?"

"Yeah, which explains *that*," he said pointing at a large hole in the wall right next to our entry point.

I swallowed hard. *Gulp.* "Old mate managed to get a shot off at us even though he was hanging himself," I said to Houso, who had a shocked look on his face.

"That was next-level crazy," he replied.

All I could say was, "Bloody oath! That was a close call."

"It sure was," Lisa suddenly piped in, breaking the spell. "Do you think you could make me a coffee now?"

The Hunt For Malcom Naden
Australia's Most Wanted

Policing is essentially a war against crime that never ends. There is no peace and no truce. It's different from a regular war that's either won or lost. Of course, war and policing are very different but one thing they have in common is that the violence associated with service is hardly ever talked about, at least not in public.

One ANZAC Day, I overheard a digger talking to his mate about killing an enemy soldier. His recollections were a brew of disgust, guilt, horror, revulsion, remorse and self-loathing. Clearly, he'd paid a high price for his service. All who serve on the front line eventually do. And, like soldiers in wartime, state assets trained for peacetime, like the TOU, also pay a price when operations threaten to take a lethal turn, as they did in the hunt for Malcolm Naden and then, later, when they did become lethal, at Lindt.

Malcolm Naden was Australia's 'most wanted' fugitive and the subject of a seven-year manhunt, (June 2005 to March 2012) one of the largest and longest in Australian history. Initially, he evaded police after the aggravated indecent assault of a 12-year-old girl. Police attended his grandparents' house in Dubbo, in North-Western NSW, where his cousin's girlfriend, Kristy Scholes, a young mother, was discovered brutally strangled and repeatedly raped post-mortem (while her children were in the next room). Her body was found where Naden had been living and hiding. Police also found peepholes drilled in the ceiling above the bathroom and bedrooms. Chillingly, Naden had left notes: 'I watch you getting dressed', 'I watch what you do', and 'You and I could have sex together'. Detectives then made the connection that this was the last known address of another young woman, Lateesha Nolan, Naden's cousin, who had disappeared six months earlier. Her empty car was discovered on the bank of the Macquarie River, just south of Dubbo, where Naden later confessed to killing and dismembering her. (Her remains were found by a bushwalker at nearby Butlers Falls, 12 years after she was murdered.)

Because of saturation media coverage and a high degree of public paranoia, there were reported sightings of the former abattoir skinner and boner all over the country—from Sydney to Broome and from Adelaide to Darwin. There was even a report of Naden in disguise, wearing a dress, in Redfern, an inner-city suburb of Sydney.

Naden's first confirmed sighting was in Western Plains Zoo, Dubbo. He'd been living in the roof space above one of the animal enclosures. But, despite a police lockdown, he somehow managed to evade capture. A bounty was issued for $50,000 and later raised to $250,000. Strike Force Durkin was the first time since the days of the colonial bushranger Ned Kelly that such a reward had been offered for the capture of a wanted fugitive.

Then, 14 months later, confirmation through fingerprint testing from the scene of a break-in at Stewarts Brook near Barrington Tops, NSW—but again there was no sign of Malcolm Naden himself. (Incredibly, Naden had trekked over 340 kilometres through the bush from Dubbo.) The next sighting was in October 2008 at the Misty Mountain Wilderness Retreat north-west of the town of Kempsey. Naden had been stalking a female caretaker there for weeks—secretly watching her through her bedroom window and while she was swimming naked in a local creek. One night, Naden attempted to break in. The caretaker started to scream and he ran off. The next day Naden left a handwritten note on her bedside table: 'nice moles'. This proved that he'd been in her bedroom, but also confirmed that he'd been spying on her without her clothes on, as he had Kristy Scholes before strangling her.

Naden's history of violent and predatory behaviour had police concerned that he was planning to make the caretaker his next victim. But, once again, he managed to escape, vanishing into the wilderness. Police later identified a trend, working out that Naden was constantly on the move, breaking into houses and stealing food and other items, including rifles and ammunition.

In November 2011, police received reports of several break-ins in the small township of Nowendoc, north of Gloucester NSW. Nowendoc is a four-and-a-half-hour drive from Sydney. The area is made up of rural farms and uncleared bushland, bordering mountainous rainforest. Police devised a plan. They hid trackers in items they hoped Naden would eventually steal. There was evidence that he'd targeted remote farmhouses, huts and sheds including many that hadn't been occupied or used for a long time. An █████ tracking device had been stitched into a sleeping bag that was then stolen from a local farmstead. It was time to call the TOU.

The TOU's initial response was for an inspector to run the operation, with two TOU operators and a specialist tactical dog handler. The idea was that a small team would make less noise trekking through the bush than the usual six operators. (The ████ tracker was primitive compared to the equipment we use now.) Our operator, 'Brad', held up an antenna connected to a headset, much like the ones used to locate animals in David Attenborough documentaries. Brad was shorter than most of us but muscular, with a chiselled jawline and a close-cropped flat top haircut. He spoke with a slight lisp. (He'd been a gymnast as a young man. I once saw him walk the entire length of a basketball court on his hands.)

The tracker indicated that they were getting closer. The

team located food scraps, empty baked bean cans and plastic white bread wrappers near a cold campfire site. A cache of high-powered weapons believed to belong to Naden was also found hidden in a PVC pipe. After days of stalking, right on dusk, the crew of three operators were getting close to the source of the activated ▮▮▮▮▮ tracker. However, given that he was armed, it was deemed by the bosses too dangerous to continue in the dark, so they withdrew.

*****

Malcolm Naden was a tough man, surviving for years in the harsh Australian wilderness, evading police capture. But so was a tungsten-hardened career criminal I encountered around the same time from 'the Block' in Redfern, in the heart of Sydney. I veered onto the wrong side of the road and floored the accelerator. The unmarked Falcon XR8's engine roared as it accelerated aggressively. I quickly swerved back to the left, avoiding a collision with an oncoming truck. I then pulled in behind the second of two TOU teams in their Toyota V8 LandCruiser driving at maximum speed. Our vehicles were under lights and sirens as we raced through Kingsford in Sydney's Eastern Suburbs, attempting to catch up with a stolen BMW M3.

Three men had just committed an armed robbery on a jewellery store in the wealthy harbourside suburb of Double Bay. They'd smashed their way through the display window using a chainsaw and a sledgehammer. Once inside, they terrorised employees before making off with over $600,000-worth of jewellery. The robbery and serious crime squad had already set up a task force targeting this gang—monitoring them for weeks. These men were career criminals and prone to extreme violence. "Target vehicle sighted, kill the lights and sirens and form a stack," came the call from the sergeant in the lead car. Unexpectedly, the BMW pulled into the kerb before we were in position and all three offenders jumped out and ran. TOU operators gave chase.

"Let's cut them off," yelled our team leader. I punched the accelerator and turned at the first side street. I sped down the alleyway looking for somewhere to intercept them.

"One target in custody. Two still outstanding," came the call over the police radio before vague descriptions were broadcast. "POI 1: male, tall, muscular build, Aboriginal in appearance, wearing a black backpack, dark pants and hoodie. POI 2 male, average height and build, Aboriginal in appearance, wearing a light-grey hoodie." (The cops now use the term 'First Nations People' or 'FNPs'.)

We hammered through the surrounding streets with the police chopper circling overhead assisting in the search. "Bullshit, that's him," my mate 'Bruiser' in the back seat yelled, noticing someone in a dark hoodie casually walking up the road. As we got closer, the man spotted us and quickly disappeared over a wooden paling fence. My team leader was 'Browny', one of my good mates. He was relieving in the role of sergeant. He was tall, with dark hair and intense eyes that reflected his personality. He and Bruiser gave chase. I accelerated up an adjacent street before slamming on the brakes and screeching to a halt. Springing from the car, I jumped over a high metal barrier in the hope of cutting the offender off. After running through several backyards, I met up with Browny but there was no sign of the POI anywhere.

"He must have gone to ground," Brownie said, "Because he didn't get past me."

"Dog 45 on location. Where do you need me?" the handler called over the police radio. I didn't know the handler or the dog—Odie—as it was a general-purpose dog and not one tactically trained to work around TOU operators. Despite this, Odie performed well. A startled elderly man came rushing from the front of his house, waving his arms, signalling for us to come quickly.

"A big guy just came running through my garden only 30 seconds ago," he reported. The dog then tracked the POI's scent through a series of suburban backyards. First, there was the concreted garden with white pebbles and an ornate alabaster 'little boy urinating' water fountain; then there were shady grapevines, flourishing tomato plants and mismatched plastic tables and chairs and a family of perhaps 20 people having lunch together; then an unkempt property with a lawn partially invaded by bamboo, a small clearing strewn with cigarette butts next to a goldfish pond and an amazing vegetable patch and, finally, a teak-oiled wooden outdoor deck and gas barbecue area where men were drinking beer from stubby holders, sitting on bean bags and watching the footy on an enormous flat screen TV while their kids ran wild under a garden hose. They were all equally startled by three balaclava-clad men suddenly appearing, dressed in black with assault rifles and an enormous wolf-like German shepherd. Eventually the dog pulled up in an open space before momentarily appearing to lose the scent. It was then that I noticed a garden shed in the far corner of the yard. I held my UMP sub-machine gun in the firing position and moved quickly and quietly to the corner of the green Colorbond structure and peered behind it.

Then, our gazes met. The man was staring straight at me, without a hint of fear in his piercing dark eyes. A pile of gardening tools was stacked in front of him. He reached for something. I dropped my sub-machine gun, letting it sling, and took a deliberate step towards him. We were face to face, standing between the shed and the fence. As he menacingly lifted a large garden mattock, I swung my right fist with full force, hitting him in the left side of his face so hard that I broke one of my knuckles. But he still wouldn't release his grip. This came as a surprise to me because during my boxing days whenever I punched someone that hard, they went down. Rather, he gave his head a little shake and shot me a look that said, 'Really, is that the best you can do?' I took a step back and drew my Taser. I switched the safety catch to 'fire', which activated the laser pointer and light source. I moved the small red dot onto his torso, ensuring a clean shot, as he lifted the mattock above his head ready to strike, still looking into my eyes.

Crack. The probes tracked towards him before the steel barbs pierced his skin. He dropped to his knees as 50,000 volts entered his body. *Tick. Tick. Tick* as the Taser completed its five second cycle. I thought I was on my own but, unexpectedly, Odie the German shepherd appeared from the other side of the shed. The powerful canine lunged forward, attempting to grab the offender's flailing hands that still had hold of the mattock handle. But, glancing off, the dog bit down hard on the man's open mouth, pulling him to the ground, violently shaking the poor fella's head. Odie, the general-purpose dog, planted his feet and tried to drag the man backwards. It was hard to watch. "Dog on, dog on," I yelled. It reminded me of my Staffy at home playing tug of war with a knotted rope. The handler then put his dog in a headlock, inducing the choke reflex—the only way to get a determined animal off its prize.

I reholstered my Taser. Amazingly, the POI was still struggling. It took three of us to zip tie his hands behind his back. As he was lifted to his feet, I got a better look at the extent of his injuries. I could see his teeth through a large gash in his cheek and his tongue was protruding through a laceration under his chin. "Bloody hell, are you okay?" I said with genuine concern.

"Youse fuck'en, dirty, fuck'en pigs can all fuck off!" he slurred and spluttered as he tried to spit blood in my face. I'd come across some genuinely tough criminals in my policing career—bikies were mostly all show (a lot of them didn't even own a Harley, or any sort of motorbike for that matter); terrorists 'went to water' as soon as we arrested them but this man was bloody tough—'old school' one of the boys called him. In the bush north-west of Kempsey, we were facing someone old school in Malcolm Naden too.

*****

Due to the discovery of high-powered weapons in the search for Malcolm Naden, the decision was made to send in a further six TOU operators, myself included. Our team arrived at the makeshift headquarters in the early evening. The boys were filthy and looked completely exhausted. We all shook hands. "Fuck me dead fellas, you look stuffed. What have you all been up to out here in the bush, mud wrestling?" I said.

"Yeah, sure man, not quite, you've got no idea how thick the bush is out here. It's like a bloody jungle," said Houso. He had his trousers down around his ankles and was adjusting his underwear in front of us.

"What's that on your legs mate? You're bleeding," I said, concerned.

"Black leeches. The bastards. I thought I got 'em all." (Leeches, once attached, pump an anticoagulant into your tissue to increase blood flow, then they feast. When removed, the wound continues to ooze for hours.) Houso was attempting to remove an engorged leech the size of a man's thumb from his groin using his razor-sharp combat knife.

"Christ. There's one of the buggers on my ball sack," Houso exclaimed with a hint of genuine panic in his voice.

"Aren't you supposed to burn them off with a cigarette lighter or use salt?" I said, more worried about him using a knife on his inner upper thigh than he appeared to be himself.

"Yeah, but you got any?"

"Good point," I replied. (And perhaps a lighter wasn't such a good idea down there after all.)

"Takes too long anyway," Houso continued. "We've been getting smashed with them, and then there's the ticks. I'm covered in the little bastards."

Everyone was up early. The other boys set off on the same path. For some unknown reason they'd been told to leave before us, against previous operational orders. The plan was for our team of four to come in from the other side to prevent Naden's possible escape, with the remaining two operators in the chopper ready to respond. There was no way to know if Naden would be there, or if he'd ditched the sleeping bag with the ▮▮▮▮▮ device and moved on. We scrambled, grabbing our bush kit, jumping into the 4WD and speeding off along a series of remote fire trails.

The area was beautiful, with wild creeks and rivers surrounded by steep rugged mountains. All of us were kitted up in camouflage—army style—with bullet-resistant vests containing spare magazines, a first aid kit, a police radio and CamelBaks full of water. We had camouflage cream on our faces—light green, dark green and brown, and carried our M4 assault rifles at the ready, with our usual Glock sidearms secured in a holster at our sides. A sniper oversaw navigation. Our group pushed on through the dense vegetation.

Then—*Bang*. The unmistakable sound of a rifle being fired in bushland echoed up through the gully. Everybody froze. Who had fired? Moments passed. We still hadn't heard anything. Brad's muffled but surprisingly composed voice then came over police radio. "Contact, contact. I've been hit." My heart sank. Our team leader 'Baboon', so named because of his hulk-like physique and his ape-like thatch of hair and melon-sized head, got on the police radio.

"What's your location and current status?" There was another long pause before Brad whispered over the police radio. "I need urgent medical attention ... require immediate evac. I've been shot in the neck."

"Your location?" Baboon said, requesting clarification. He was the big silent type who never seemed to get flustered. This time was no different.

"Offender's location unknown. We have taken cover not far from where we were yesterday."

"We'll be there ASAP. Out."

"Shit just got real," Baboon gravely said. Everyone nodded. This is an expression used in the TOU for describing a potentially lethal situation. I looked around at my mates. Their faces told the same story—deep concern for Brad and the boys.

The circumstances were far from ideal. The bush was so thick that it was impossible to walk through it quietly. There was a gunman ahead ready to shoot us and he had the advantage of both cover and local knowledge. Our group spread out, but this just created another problem—we were losing sight of each other. At one stage it was just Robbo and I with the others to our right. The two of us had been on the same training courses. Robbo had played rugby league at a high level and, although as fit and strong as other operators, he had the misfortune of carrying an unmistakeable beer gut. (Gus called him 'Rhubarb' although no one seemed to know why.)

I heard a rustling in the bushes about 30 metres ahead. I took a knee and lifted my rifle to take a sight picture. My peripheral vision told me that Robbo had done the same thing. Moments passed. My heart was pounding. I could hear the close quarters sound of leaves and sticks crunching under foot. I flicked the safety catch to fire. My finger was on the trigger. The sound was getting closer, moving right towards us. It had to be Naden.

A pulse was thumping in my ears. I strained my eyes, willing them to make out his shape. This was it. I eased slightly on the trigger ready to release the shot. Then, three metres in front of me, a wallaby burst out of a low wattle bush. It got just as much of a fright as I did. I took my finger off the trigger and engaged the safety catch. *Click*. Robbo and I walked towards each other. "Fuck me ▇▇▇▇, I was sure that was him; nearly had a heart attack," he whispered.

"Skippy's bloody lucky—that's all I can say," I smiled back. We regrouped. I pictured Brad bleeding to death with the other two covering him. They had no idea where the shot had come from nor whether they would be engaged again.

As quietly as he could, Baboon again got on the police radio. "We think we're at your location, but don't have eyes on you."

"I can hear you, but we can't move. He has us pinned down," came the equally subdued reply.

"Brad's situation?"

"Stable, but we've got to get him out."

It was one of the most desperate and frustrating moments of my life. We continued searching but just couldn't find them. (It was later discovered that we'd been supplied with the wrong map datum coordinates for our GPS—much like the fire brigade turning the water off as we were about to be incinerated during a later job in Sydney's east and the frontline frustrations we experienced at Lindt).

Then, the rain came. It absolutely bucketed down. I was saturated within minutes before a rolling fog completely overwhelmed our vision. We could've walked on top of Brad and the boys without seeing them. Of course, that also went for Naden. Baboon took charge and called us together. We were all shaking from the cold. This didn't concern me. I needed to get to my mates and that was all I could focus on. The desperation on the faces of the other three told me they felt the same.

"Bravo one. This is Bravo two. We've located the boys" suddenly came over the police radio.

"Brad's condition?" replied a clearly relieved Baboon.

"Appears stable, bugging out."

New coordinates were provided, and everyone regrouped. The special casualty access team, or SCAT, ambulance officers, were on hand and they rushed Brad to hospital.

"Righto, let's go and get this prick!" the sergeant from the chopper team said with determination in his voice.

The situation had changed. I was angry. This was personal. Naden had shot my friend. I wanted him captured; we all did. Everyone headed back out with renewed purpose and quickly located the site where he had been hiding. It was only metres from where Brad was shot. There was a small blue tarpaulin in the shape of a basic tent. It was close to the ground and well hidden. I had a look around ensuring not to disturb anything before sighting the sleeping bag. Naden had been living rough. The forensic unit later located a spent bullet cartridge. This proved that he had cocked the bolt action weapon with the intention of firing again. There were two bush tracks leading away from his secret campsite, one down to a creek and one up and out of the gully. We followed this until it opened into a clearing. Our teams divided. I hoped at least to locate a footprint in the mud but, again, there was no sign of him.

Our team continued like this for hours. Night fell. The freezing rain kept belting down. It was hopeless trying to navigate the dense bush like this, even with our night-vision goggles on. There was a remote farmer's hut nearby and the decision was made to place it under surveillance. I lay in position behind a fallen gum tree, in the dark, willing Naden to appear. Then, I became acutely aware of how cold it was. My lower jaw wouldn't stop chattering. I also noticed patches of blood seeping through my battle fatigues—bloody leeches. I hadn't eaten all day but there was nothing to be done about it. I'd been so whipped up in the moment, brimming with adrenalin, that food wasn't a consideration. I made an effort to take a sip of water. As I lay there, I reflected on my time in the army reserve.

*****

Our unit was deployed out bush for two weeks as part of infantry training and we were rained on continuously. The entire day was spent digging defensive bunkers. The night was endured in a drenched sleeping bag in equally saturated clothing. Sleep was impossible. Our position was located on a downhill slope and water was running right through my army Hoochie. (This is a small, camouflaged tarpaulin erected just above the ground and used as a basic shelter.)

Pickets, or guard duty, were required throughout the night with our position constantly 'attacked' at hourly intervals. When 'assaulted', everyone was required to sprint to a bunker and jump in behind the machine gun. The defensive pit was half-full of water that came up to my waist—not unlike the state I was in now. A call from Baboon snapped me out of my daydream. We were finally allowed to leave our position and get to the vehicle before driving back to the command post.

*****

The two blokes with Brad when he was shot were clearly rattled. We were all exhausted and lost in our individual thoughts. I broke the silence. "So, boys, you all good?"

The dog handler 'Seany' responded. "That was bullshit ay?" He obviously wanted to talk. Houso just nodded silently. Seany was a tall guy of average build with a dark 'big M for Maccas' receding hairline—a good-hearted Aussie bloke from the mountains who'd been working with us on jobs for over a decade. He was tough and reliable, and we all trusted him. Some years earlier, just before Christmas, his beloved German shepherd Titan was stabbed to death on a TOU job by a drug-crazed methamphetamine user brandishing two large knives. He took it hard. We all did.

Seany filled me in on how Brad was shot. Houso had been in the lead as cover man. Brad was next with his headset on, holding the antenna. Seany followed with Ranger, his tactical dog. As they passed their position from the previous night, the signal grew stronger. Then Houso noticed something ahead. He gave the hand signal, and they all took a knee. Brad peered through his aimpoint to get a better look, turning his head slightly to the left, whispering to Seany what had been discovered. That was when the shot rang out. Brad dropped to the ground holding his neck, blood streaming from the wound. Houso yelled, "Contact," before moving in front of Brad. "Malcolm, Malcolm, it's the police. Don't shoot,"—not that this would've made a difference.

Houso and Seany located a slight undulation in the ground, not cover but the best they had under the circumstances, and dragged Brad into it. Ranger was kept low with his leash pulled tight. They had no idea where the shot had come from as they were in a deep gully and the sound echoed up through the gorge and off the surrounding mountains. It was far from ideal, attempting to cover all angles from further attack—while putting manual pressure on Brad's wound. The boys bravely positioned their bodies in front of Brad, shielding him from further gunfire. Houso located the projectile that had passed through Brad's shoulder and neck. It was still lodged in the webbing of his vest. He stashed it safely away for later evidence. Brad's decision to turn his head had saved his life. As Brad looked through his holographic sight, Naden had taken aim. The bullet's intended trajectory was likely between Brad's eyes. Later, the surgeon said, if the bullet had impacted his body one centimetre lower, he would have died.

I needed to call Lisa and let her know that I was okay. We'd just moved into our rundown unit in Cronulla and most of our things hadn't been unpacked. I had to drop everything to deploy urgently, leaving her to cope as best she could. Lisa hadn't heard the news until a friend called her asking if I was safe. As I was out bush with no mobile phone reception, there was no way for her to contact me. I called her late that evening from the command post. "You heard the news?"

"Yeah, so obviously it wasn't you?" Lisa said in her typically broad southern Irish accent.

"No. Were you worried?"

"I was, but when I heard the officer was in a stable condition, I wasn't too concerned after that."

"Really?"

"Yep."

"You really are a typical ED nurse, aren't you?"

"Yes, I suppose I am," she replied.

Naden shooting a TOU operator was breaking news nationwide. Cameramen and reporters in helicopters descended on the small town like a plague of locusts. As I walked back to our makeshift base of operations at the local town hall, a crime reporter from one of the networks called out from under an umbrella. "Excuse me, hey officer, can you give us something?" At first, I ignored her, but then a craving for nicotine made me walk back. (Tobacco was my occasional 'go to' when I was stressed, even though at that point, I'd long 'given up'.)

"Tell your cameraman that filming isn't an option," I said in a serious tone with my balaclava pulled high up over my nose to disguise my identity.

"Okay, sure, of course," she replied, signalling this to her offsider with a dismissive swat of her hand.

"I've been out bush for days without a cigarette. Bring me back some smokes and I'll give you something to report on," I said.

"I'm on to it," she replied. I watched her trot off through the mud in her high heels like a brolga in the wet season, before returning in remarkably quick time. She handed me five individual cigarettes with a look that conveyed she'd met her end of the bargain.

"Thank you," I said, turning back, not entirely impressed as the cigarettes were menthol.

"Excuse me officer, you said that … ," she persisted, with a hint of desperation in her voice.

"Oh yes, that's right I did, didn't I?" I had her full attention. She looked like a seagull waiting for someone to throw it a chip.

"The media are falsely reporting that the army are out here looking for Naden," I said.

"Okay," she replied, "I'll sort that."

"Also, you guys *always* report *this* incorrectly … ." The reporter held out her notepad and pen ready to scribble, eagerly anticipating a scoop. "We're the Tactical Operations Unit—the trained specialists in this type of police operation. We aren't the 'heavily armed' riot squad. I'll see if the boss wants to come out and update the media with anything new in an organised press conference. You know how it works." I could feel her eyes boring into the back of my head. I just kept walking.

The NSW Police Force responded by launching a large-scale operation with the TOU at the centre of it. This required a lot of manpower and involved working constant seven-day rotations—often patrolling in hazardous terrain. Most of the time the weather was horrendous, giving Naden an even greater advantage. The creeks and rivers then flooded, leading to dramatic water crossings. We held our rifles above our heads with the water lapping up to our necks. The immense amount of rain was accompanied by thick fog. This made everything slippery and visibility a nightmare. I did, however, become an expert at removing leeches and ticks.

Not all of it was bad though. I loved being in the bush. There was plenty of off-road driving through all types of terrain and many a ration pack was eaten on car bonnet or sitting around in a group having a good chat. There were constant interactions with wildlife—mostly snakes, but also a young koala that had fallen from a tree, which we reunited with its grateful mother. Another day, an emu followed us in line for hours just like he was a member of the patrol. I even got a couple of days up in the chopper with the side door open, legs hanging out with my M4 aimed up and at the ready like a scene from a Vietnam war movie. We searched from the air for any signs of Naden and landed at numerous abandoned huts. A small team of us cleared farmsteads one at a time and even searched an abandoned dairy before returning to the air and resuming our quest.

The terrain was perfect for someone to hide in, with over 10,000 square kilometres of dense old-growth forest. Reports started to come in that some locals had sided with Naden. (One local fish and chip shop even advertised 'The Malcolm Burger: Eat here or on the run'.) They had clearly fallen for the media's bullshit narrative that he was a 'modern-day bushranger' and a 'freakishly gifted master bushman', promoting the idea that police would never find him. Some even left food out for him, possibly unaware of how dangerous he was, although his brutal crimes were widely known at the time.

Live CCTV footage of a man fitting Naden's description was captured on a home security camera and reported to police. Inexplicably, GDs officers were dispatched by the bosses to investigate—not immediately, but the following day. The TOU were deployed to another location nearly 100 kilometres in the opposite direction. "Try explaining that one," I said to Gus.

When GDs officers arrived at the remote farmhouse, they saw a rifle resting against the front door. Naden suddenly appeared. He reached for the weapon but changed his mind. Perhaps it was because police were pointing their firearms at him. He then ran back into the bush. The GDs police were only armed with handguns and not equipped to chase him. This was disheartening. We just couldn't understand why we hadn't been sent there in the first place and neither did the public who, in frustration, were calling for the army to be sent in. It was the same old story for the TOU. If we had been given operational independence and allowed to do what we were trained for, then the manhunt would have been over far quicker.

For the TOU to be deployed, permission must come from someone of the rank of assistant commissioner or above. Once deployed, we're placed under the control of the superintendent of the local area command. In this process, our inspector merely acts as a tactical adviser. Some operational decisions are passed up to the assistant commissioner for consideration and approval. Unfortunately, the local superintendent is usually not tactically trained and so he or she nearly always errs on the side of extreme caution. Superintendents know that decisions will be heavily scrutinised and that their careers will be on the line if things go pear-shaped. This produces management paralysis where 'no decision is better than a wrong decision'.

The TOU are the trained experts in this field, but it is the pen-pushers and the corridor creepers who make the decisions. (This was later to play out at Lindt.) And then there are the cost-saving measures. Within weeks of the operation commencing, our shifts were cut back to save on overtime. The truth was that we needed to be allowed to do our job, as most SWAT units around the world are. One thing we knew for sure was that Malcolm Naden wasn't actively evading capture on a nine-to-five timetable with sleep-ins and late starts on the weekends.

However, there was some positive news as well. First, the rifle Naden left behind was matched to the one used to shoot Brad. Then some intriguing intelligence. Naden had gained access to a computer. His entire online search history was related to pornography, including bestiality and incest. He hadn't attempted to search for his name or look for details about the operation to capture him. His priorities were obvious. "No wonder poor bloody Skippy was a bit nervous," Robbo smiled.

Having missed a clear opportunity, our search continued for months. Trail cameras were set up on bush tracks that he may have used. One managed to get a photograph of him. The image was confronting. It showed Naden walking through the bush in a large khaki trench coat and matching beanie, carrying a canvas bag with a rifle slung over his shoulder. It was a stark reminder that he was out there, armed and dangerous—and that we must be vigilant. If our patrol came across him in the bush, everyone expected that one of us would be shot before confirming his location—but this time we had the numbers on him.

The bosses informed us that we were going to be joined in the search for Malcolm Naden by 'somebody special'. Command had engaged an 'expert bush tracker', brought all the way from the Northern Territory. I expected someone like David Gulpilil. Instead, what we got was a short, stumpy, sweaty, red-headed white fella.

The local superintendent proudly explained, "Gentlemen, the tracker will be of great assistance in our mission."

"This is going be interesting," Gus whispered in my direction.

We headed out with our new man in the lead, kitted up in army camouflage, patrolling across a grassy field towards dense bushland. Then, unexpectedly, his right hand dramatically shot up into a fist (the 'freeze' hand signal) before he waved for us to get down. I immediately dropped and crawled into a position of cover. The tracker then tapped the front of his forehead with his open palm, signalling the team leader to approach. I was close enough to hear the conversation.

"Someone has been through here. Look, a broken stick and over there, that fern has been bent over."

"Yeah, okay?" the team leader replied with a quizzical look.

"Let's follow this trail here," he insisted.

The tracker gave the signal to move on, but before long he found some grass that had been flattened and again stopped the patrol. I'd spent a lot of time in the bush myself and we'd all been out here for months. Clearly the path had been used by many people and not just a single man conscious of not leaving tracks. "But what would I know?" I said to Gus. It was later confirmed that the other patrol—of part-timers from the New South Wales State Protection Support Unit (SPSU) had passed through the area that same morning. As it turned out, our 'specialist' was in the army reserve and had only just completed a two-week course in bush survival. I looked to Gus, crossing my hands above my head with the signal for 'disregard previous command'. We couldn't contain ourselves any longer and had a well overdue belly laugh. It was either that or cry.

Everyone anticipated that Naden would never surrender, and that the manhunt would end in a shoot-out. Motion detectors were being triggered repeatedly in a shelter known as Ken's Hut in the Moppy Valley. The boys kitted up. It was a clear, freezing-cold winter's night, without a cloud in the sky. The team advanced through the thick bush in the pitch black under night vision. In the distance, they could see a hut in an open space illuminated from within. Naden had the fire on and was completely unaware of TOU operators approaching.

There was just one last obstacle to overcome. An enormous black bull suddenly appeared out of the darkness. It snorted, with clouds of steam pulsing from its nostrils, stomping its hooves and waving its massive horns; then it charged. Gus pointed his rifle straight at the bull with the safety catch off, bracing to fire. Fortunately, the bull deviated from its course just short of impact, before crashing through a barbed wire fence and eventually coming to a stop. Being gored and trampled in the middle of nowhere would have had huge repercussions, but Gus knew the importance of the operation. He was well trained and kept his cool. Gus is one of those people who everyone loves from the moment they meet him. The bull too, it seemed. (My auntie and old nan only met him once but still ask about him.) The beast clearly had second thoughts as well and just looked passively on, as the boys slowly walked towards the hut. A seven-year operation to arrest Australia's most wanted fugitive was nearly compromised by an unforeseen threat in the form of an angry bovine.

The boys regrouped. They managed to surround the hut quietly and without detection. On the team there was also a police dog squad officer with his German shepherd, ensuring that there was no escape for Naden. Unfortunately, due to the immense workload on the dog squad officers (and their dogs for that matter) the boys only had the use of a non-tactically-trained dog and handler who was just filling in. Suddenly, the man himself appeared from the back door of the hut peering out into the darkness, sensing that something was wrong. TOU operators were only 30 metres from him. "Police, get on the ground."

Naden turned and ran straight back into the hut and then right out the front door to where our team were waiting for him. Luckily, he didn't pick up the rifle or it might well have ended very differently. Naden frantically ran as operators lit him up with torches from their rifles. Smithy crash-tackled him to the ground with Gus and Z coming to his assistance. In the heat of the moment, the police dog, Chuck, latched onto one of Naden's legs. Gus remembers that although Naden was struggling to get away, he showed no sign of pain as the dog ripped into his flesh. We've been involved in many arrests using a police dog. There had never been an occasion, that we could recall, where an offender hadn't screamed in agony whilst being dogged. This surprised Gus who was only just realising how tough Naden was.

Confirmation of his identity was required. "What's your name?"

"Malcolm."

"Malcolm who?" Atts the team leader continued.

"Malcolm Naden." (*The Daily Telegraph* reported on

their front page, that after seven years on the run his first words were 'Yes, I'm Malcolm Naden'.) So ended the largest manhunt in modern Australian history. Z got directly onto a satellite phone and rang Brad notifying him of the arrest.

Naden squatted in silence on the freezing ground in handcuffs wearing only light clothing. He looked dishevelled and gaunt, sporting a huge full black beard. He'd obviously tried to shave his head in the hut but had done a terrible job—a shadow of the man who had gone on the run seven years earlier. Gus's teeth were chattering from the cold, even in his long-sleeved uniform and insulating bullet-resistant vest. Naden, on the other hand, appeared to be completely unfazed. It was as if he didn't feel the cold or the pain. The injuries the police dog inflicted on his leg would've buckled the hardest of men. He didn't complain once. After ambulance treatment, Naden walked to the car as if nothing was wrong.

During the hunt for Malcolm Naden, police had consulted a high-profile psychiatrist. His professional opinion was that, because Naden had spent so many years in the bush on his own, he would have lost the ability to communicate. On the contrary, while Gus and Z waited for backup, they couldn't shut Naden up. (On a positive note, the psychiatric profile did identify that Naden had changed the way he operated and was becoming 'sloppy' in his efforts to evade us.)

In the back of the police vehicle 'Australia's most wanted' was securely seated between two tactical officers. Z had his Taser on Naden the entire time. He suddenly became concerned and said, "What da fuck ya doing mate?"

Z replied, "It's a Taser."

"What da fuck's a Taser bruz?" Naden fired back. (Naden had clearly been in the bush a long time.)

"It's for ... ," Z started to explain but, then gave the idea away.

Gus was intrigued and just had to ask, "So what did you actually live on out there?"

"Wasn't that hard bruz. I'd just seen a bird, shoot it, cook it, and eat the bastard. That's about it," Naden explained to Gus in a matter-of-fact tone.

"Any animals?" Gus enquired.

"Yeah, goannas and wallabies—grubs and worms—anything mate." (Little wonder Naden had earned the nickname 'the bad bush tucker man'.) There were also reports that he'd torn the head off a critically endangered giant Galapagos tortoise and eaten it raw whilst hiding out at Western Plains Zoo. He'd also stolen bananas from the gibbons' enclosure.

"Where'd you sleep?' Gus continued.

"Anwhere, even in da rain in winter. I just got used to it." Naden said, looking down at the ground, avoiding eye contact.

"Weren't you freezing?" Z asked.

"Nah, not really, but one time I woke up with a snake biting me arm."

"Holy shit man, you're lucky you didn't cark it," Gus chimed in.

"Yep, s'pose so. It made me crook for a couple of days, but I just kept goin'," Naden replied.

"Where'd you get your water?" Gus the city boy continued, captivated by Naden's explanations.

"Creeks or rivers—puddles if it were real dry. I got sick in the guts tons of times."

"That's insane man. When we were out there looking for you, I had to drink from the river. I got paranoid that I was going to catch giardia or something." Naden just nodded with a vague expression on his face. (Giardia would've been the least of his concerns.)

"Did you know that we were out here?" Gus continued.

"Yeah, I knew youse were after me."

"You never saw us?" Z added.

"I saw youse in a 4WD and I seen your chopper too. I figured you were. I just walked under a tree and waited for youse to go."

Naden gave Gus a humourless grin before adding, "I was sure there was no way youse fellas were going to take me alive," he said, looking Gus directly in the eyes.

"That's not how we work, mate," Gus reassured him.

Naden seemed to be relieved that it was all over. Gus and Z then filled him in on what'd been happening in the world since he'd removed himself from it. "You're shitting me. There's a black President?"

"Yes, his name is Barack Obama."

"Jesus. What? A Muslim?"

"No mate."

"Fuck me. I didn't think that'd ever happen," Naden said shaking his head in disbelief.

"And we have a female prime minister now too. Her name is Julia Gillard," Gus explained. Naden didn't seem remotely interested in that.

"What happened to old mate Johnny Howard?" Naden continued.

"Gone. Lost the election. Lost his seat too, the poor bugger—to some boring ABC chick. We've had another one after him too—Kevin Rudd," Gus replied.

Naden shook his head again and said, "Fuck me. Who's Kev fuck'en Rudd anyway?" But before Gus could explain, Naden interrupted him. "A black President ay. Da world really has changed."

Gus and Z found Naden to be tough, but they were also aware that he'd brutally murdered two women and shot their mate. Detectives interviewed him following his arrest. For weeks he refused to answer questions but then, unexpectedly, he wrote a 25-page handwritten confession, including details about his murders. He later led police to where he'd hacked up the body of his cousin by a riverbank. He also confessed to trying to kill Brad. Naden was sentenced to life in prison—without parole.

Brad survived his physical injuries but was never the same again. He developed a twitch that got worse over time. I remember sitting beside him one day, in the office, and his head was bumping up and down so badly that I just had to ask, "Are you okay man?"

"Yeah, no problem. What'd you mean?"

"Mate, I dead set thought your head was about to fall off."

"███████, I don't know what you're talking about."

Brad had little idea of how much psychological damage he'd sustained in the hunt for Malcolm Naden and in countless other high-risk TOU operations, although he confided in me that he'd started to drink heavily. He retired from the police force shortly after that.

And, as for 'Chuck the wonder dog', the media flew him at their expense, by helicopter, together with his police handler, into the ANZ stadium in June 2012 to deliver the rugby league ball for the NSW versus Queensland State of Origin clash.

Thornleigh

It was Good Friday morning. I was at home with our little girl, keeping her entertained. Lisa worked most weekends, so it was another daddy–daughter day. Our plan was to go to the local park. A picnic lunch was prepared and packed into her Peppa Pig backpack. We were just about to walk out the front door when my work phone rang. There was a 'situation' in Thornleigh, an upper-middle-class suburb on the North Shore of Sydney. As part of my job, I was often on call, and this included weekends. All available operators were required. However, my immediate concern was what to do about my 18-month-old daughter. Fortunately, we had a great neighbour who offered to look after her until Lisa got home. I quickly got changed into my uniform, grabbed my kitbag and took off with lights and sirens. My little girl waved and smiled as I sped away.

When I arrived on site, after a long, high-speed drive, I felt a little exasperated. Even with the warning devices activated, some drivers wouldn't move over in the traffic. When I did get to the location, I was let into the command post by a GDs officer who had cordoned off the area with some blue and white police tape. Our inspector was already in discussions with the boss from the local precinct and the police negotiator coordinator. Another job came in; an armed robbery in progress, and I was tasked to pick up the armoured vehicle. By the time I got back to the office, the job up north had been resolved, so I hurried back to Thornleigh.

The inspector gave me a quick rundown. There was a man on the premises with a long history of psychiatric illness. A mobile mental health team had attempted to check up on him but he refused to speak to them. In fact, he threatened to shoot them if they didn't leave. There was also a woman inside—the POI's sister—and he was refusing to let her go. I was directed to approach the Alpha team, who were stacked up at the front door. The team leader was my mate Browny. The complex was made up of several large, well-maintained 'cookie cutter' townhouses. The split-level dwelling was locked up with all the curtains drawn.

The boys seemed happy to see me. The usual familiar heads were there including 'Mad Dog Pauly'. Pauly was a larrikin country boy from Alice Springs in the Northern Territory. He was a bit older than me, about six feet tall, with a solid build and a rough head set off by contrasting short, neatly cropped light-brown hair and unevenly matched footy player cauliflower ears. He especially loved a drink at the pub and a good time with his mates. Pauly specialised in being 'loud and inappropriate' but had a huge heart. We seemed to be involved in most of the big jobs together, although neither of us believed that Thornleigh would be anything more than a run-of-the-mill assignment. We were wrong.

Browny told me to stay with Alpha. They'd been on-site for five hours by that stage and had only just been given permission to smash in the rear glass door to gain entry, make observations and place the loudhailer in position so that negotiators could communicate. Browny walked me around to where the other team was located. The Bravo team consisted of three operators, an experienced veteran in 'Wildcat', with 'Baby-faced Guesty' and 'Little Mick', who was holding the ballistic shield.

Little Mick was a 'CIA' a Chinese-Indonesian Australian. Most of our guys were big burly blokes, over six feet tall; we towered over Little Mick in physical presence. Plus, English wasn't his first language, so he sometimes struggled with communicating over the police radio. Still, he had a lot of drive and completed the same gruelling TOU training that all operators had. In fact, Little Mick worked harder than any of us—because he had to. Still, I struggled with Little Mick's size. Stature and strength matter in our role. If I was injured—blown up or bludgeoned, shot or stabbed—I wanted to know that one of my fellow operators could drag me to safety. We also had to lug heavy equipment, sometimes for hours, and this included the polyethylene-plate ballistic shield.

As Bravo entered a small downstairs foyer, they reported being shot at with something. The boys showed me the small hole that the projectile made in the Gyprock. The bosses devised a plan to enter the adjoining duplex, after getting keys from evacuated occupants. Browny's job, with my assistance, was to gain an understanding of the layout based on the floor plan of the neighbour's adjoining unit that we anticipated would be the same, but in reverse. At the front there was a double garage attached to each brick dwelling, with the front door to the far left or far right.

On entry, we observed a small hallway with a laundry off to the left. Walking forward, this opened into a double-height floor-to-ceiling mezzanine with a staircase leading from the ground floor to our right. The main living areas were located downstairs, with the bedrooms in front of us. It was a bizarre layout and hard to draw and report on. There were only three potential entry points—the front door, the bottom-storey back entrance where Bravo was positioned and, potentially, the garage. Browny returned to the command post to devise a plan. I went back to the boys and we continued with our usual banter. Everyone was in good spirits, especially as we were all on public holiday overtime pay rates. I had a friendly crack at 'Hipster', a beanie-wearing, scooter-mad, skateboard-riding, weekend surfer, with an upper-class Sydney Northern Beaches accent, blue eyes, and long blonde hair tied up for operations in a tight man bun (much to the fury of the old school operators and the ex-military guys).

The NSW Police Force's policy of 'surround, contain and negotiate' hadn't de-escalated the situation. The offender was still on the premises with the hostage and refusing to speak with any of the negotiators. It was starting to get dark. After nearly an entire day, we were at a stalemate and something had to be done.

The decision was made to extract the POI and rescue the hostage. The plan was to go in using two entry teams: Bravo at the bottom consisting of three members and Alpha with eight, being the main arrest team. Everything still appeared straightforward. I checked my equipment, including my X-26 Taser holstered on my ballistic vest. As I took hold of the black Bakelite handle (GDs Tasers are yellow), I smiled to myself and thought of how I got the nickname 'Sparky'.

*****

It was an extortion job. Two reportedly armed men were returning to a suburban address demanding money from the occupant. The Alpha team were positioned in an unmarked van parked close by. I was the driver of a four-wheel drive cut-off team propped in a backstreet. My team leader was Z and we had a dog squad officer with his German shepherd on the back seat. As the POIs pulled up, they looked in the direction of the unmarked van containing Alpha. Pauly was in the driver's seat dressed in civilian clothes. One of the men screamed at him to move on, whilst giving him hand signals that he was about to shoot him. The decision was made for Alpha to leave. Pauly drove on.

The two male POIs then walked to the front of the house and knocked on the door before they rang the occupant's phone. One was bearded and overweight. The other looked like he enjoyed a regular brew of steroids; both wore a manbag.

Both were of Middle Eastern appearance. The phone call was our cue to arrest them. The big V8 motor roared under full acceleration before I swerved onto the other side of the road and came to a screeching halt right next to them. The two men just stared at me in confusion. I jumped out and ran towards them. One appeared to reach behind his back for a gun. *Crack*. My Taser discharged with the probes striking him in the chest and stomach. The device ticked over with 50,000 volts of immobilising electricity entering his body. The second POI turned and started running up the driveway as he reached down the front of his pants. After a short sprint, I grabbed his shirt with my left hand and, in one motion, forced the Taser hard up against his upper back—'drive stunning' him as the device sparked over and over. He fell to the ground screaming and moaning with me on top of him. I glanced to my left. The first POI was still immobilised, with the probes discharged in him, and now the second offender was also being zapped. I was effectively tasering two men at the same time with the one Taser. Z came to my aid as the tactical dog barked ferociously, desperate to get involved as the handler struggled to hold him back. Pauly and the boys in the van backed us up. Both men were disarmed, searched, arrested and handcuffed. I commented to Z, "Some standover men. They screamed louder than some of the toddlers at my daughter's day-care."

Later Z said, "█████ I have to say, in all my years of policing, that's probably the coolest thing I've ever seen mate. You're a bloody legend!"

*****

Back at Thornleigh, our agreed entry point was the front door. A hand-held battering ram and a backup petrol chainsaw were prepped for when we got the go ahead. Our alternative entry point was through the laundry window, although this would be difficult as it was up high and very small. A ladder was set and a reaming tool readied. A reamer is a metre-long hardened-steel pole with a pointed end. It has a hand guard and is generally used with protective gloves. Our team stacked up, waiting for initiation from the inspector. Our operator 'Jet' was positioned with the ram and 'Armies' was ready with the chainsaw. As was his usual practice, Jet had a perfectly shaven head to disguise his red hair and distract attention from his freckles. Armies was so named by Gus because he loved to talk and talk and talk about his army reserve commando unit and his tours of Afghanistan. I had my Taser drawn in position towards the end of the stack. We were ready. "All teams, Go! Go! Go!"

Jet swung the tactical ram hitting the front door—nothing. He swung at it again and again. The door barely budged. Browny instructed Armies to start the chainsaw and the other boys readied themselves to smash out the window. Jet repeatedly swung the big ram, but it just kept bouncing off. I heard the chainsaw getting pulled over. It spluttered but wouldn't start. Things weren't going to plan.

Pauly took over the ram as the window was smashed out at the alternative entry point. A washing machine and some cupboards were stacked against the window—so there was no way in. This wasn't identified in our reconnaissance, as the glass was frosted. Then, the unmistakable sound of stun grenades going off inside. *Boom. Boom. Boom.* The Bravo team had obviously encountered a problem. As a stunnie deploys, it explodes nine separate times. Each explosion is designed to debilitate the target through deafening explosions and blinding flashes of light.

Browny was getting concerned and said so. "Armies, get that fucking saw going!" He then tapped the other operator on the shoulder and yelled, "You have a go at the door!" Browny attempted to raise Bravo on the police radio—but no response. As instructed, the other operator started smashing the door, this time with 'extreme prejudice', as our American SWAT counterparts like to say. Something budged. The entire façade began to give way as another stun grenade went off inside and then another. *Boom. Boom.* We needed to get in there—and quickly.

The door finally started to crumble under repeated blows and then the entire jamb collapsed inwards, dislodging some of the bricks. The operator on the ram stepped aside and I followed Hipster into the unit. It was dark and smelt of rotting wet carpet. Hipster peeled right into the laundry. I continued forward with my Taser drawn and light source on, activated and ready to deploy. That was when I noticed the smoke. The air was thick with it. The smell reminded me of Cracker Night. The visibility was like driving in heavy fog. Gathering my thoughts, I tried to remember the layout from next door. Coming to the end of a partition wall I turned left into where the room opened up, navigating the smoke. Then—*Whack*. Something hit my right shoulder. The force spun me around, knocking me backwards. Pain momentary immobilised me. I took a deep breath as I retreated behind the partition to regroup. That's when I saw it. An arrow sticking out of the wall just behind me. I yelled, "He's firing at us, he's firing at us. Stay back!"

"With what?"

"I just copped an arrow, stay behind cover," I shouted.

"Copy," someone yelled in return. You can bring a wild boar down with a bow while it takes a large calibre bullet to do the same thing.

Thwack. Another arrow came flying past me, embedding deep into the plasterboard wall close to my head. Shit just got real. I rubbed my painful shoulder and attempted to self-diagnose my injury. The arrow had hit the braided nylon strap that connects the front and back plates of my bullet-resistant vest and deflected off. 'Bloody lucky', I thought to myself. But there was no time to count my blessings. *Boom. Boom. Boom.* More stun grenades were going off. The Bravo team were copping a pizzling. I momentarily paused to contain myself, glancing sideways at Hipster who was advancing out of the laundry to my right. Another arrow suddenly appeared out of the smoke before lodging in the hardwood lintel, just as he was about to come through the door. It missed him by centimetres.

Hipster tried again—but *Thwack* and *Thwack* again, another two arrows embedded in the wall right next to the first one, this time perhaps millimetres away from him. He was pinned down. Our whole team were.

I yelled, "Just stay in there. Maintain position. You're going to get fucking shot."

Thankfully, "Yeah, copy that," was Hipster's response after three close calls.

I couldn't see two metres in front of me through the thick acrid smoke and had no idea how the offender was managing to shoot so quickly—or accurately. This guy was ready for us; he was clearly prepared but I was too. This was one of those exact moments I'd been trained for. I put my Taser away and pulled out my Glock. I stepped up to the corner of the partition, activated the weapon's light source, held my breath, and poked my head out from behind cover. I scanned as quickly as I could—right to left. Perhaps it was my subconscious but, without thinking, I ducked back behind the wall a mere second before another arrow flashed past my face, this time right in front of me. *Thwack.* 'That was close. Too close', I thought to myself, shaking my head, regaining composure.

I called for the shield to come forward. Pauly backed me up yelling "I'm covering you 'Insane-o', get that fucking shield up to those blokes." (Insane-o was actually a very sensible person—Gus just liked the way it sounded) pushed forward to my right. Pauly was cover man with his M4 over Insane-o's right shoulder. Another arrow struck, this time glancing off the shield with near point-blank force. *Thwack* again.

'Immo', ex-army, great bloke, came forward and positioned himself behind Insane-o, next to Pauly. The shield was only 80 centimetres in height and 40 centimetres wide, which just covers an operator's torso, not including the head. Three guys behind one is a stretch, let alone a whole team. Suddenly, out of my peripheral vision I saw Immo's head violently jolt backwards. He looked stunned. An arrow had struck his Kevlar helmet just above the eyebrow ridge, also glancing off. He tactically withdrew behind me.

"We're going to have to push forward," Browny said. We needed to get to the offender, but this would leave us dangerously exposed. He had the better of us—for now. Then, another distinctive sound. *Bang. Bang. Bang.* This time it wasn't a stun grenade, but gunfire.

Browny tried to radio Bravo again but no response. Pauly yelled out from behind the ballistic shield, "Was that you guys firing?"

There was a moment's silence before the affirmative reply, "Yep that was us."

I looked over and called out to Insane-o, "I can't see shit. Can you see anything?"

Insane-o coughed and replied, "Nah, nothing. Too much smoke." There is a bullet resistant glass viewing port in the ballistic shield. I was hoping that he would be able to see something through it. I knew what I had to do. Pausing, I calmed myself and panned out. I scoured the room with my light source, again recalling the layout compared to next door. For the entire time I was exposed, I pictured a hardened steel-tipped hunting arrow appearing from the darkness and striking me in the face. I pulled myself back behind cover just as another arrow whizzed past my nose. All those years of motocross, honing my reflexes, didn't let me down. The arrow travelled through the open laundry door and smashed out a window. Again, it must have just missed Hipster and it showed. He was now clearly content to stay where he was.

I was confident that the POI wasn't in the rooms across from us. He must be in the last room at the very end. We needed confirmation. I told Insane-o that I'd light it up with my sidearm's light source. 'Here we go again,' I thought. I set my feet and panned out with my Glock, shining the light in the direction of the end room. My finger was on the trigger ready to take the man's life if the opportunity arose. I strained my eyes, willing him to appear. I saw the shadow outline of what might be the man but I wasn't 100 per cent sure. I applied gentle pressure on the trigger. I'd been vulnerable for some time, just waiting to be hit. Then, *Bang*. The unmistakable sound of another gunshot. I ducked back behind cover. A man's voice groaned in agony.

Little Mick was holding the shield in the stairwell with the other two operators behind him. Bravo had copped a barrage of arrows and in response had been lobbing stun grenades to create a distraction which explained all the smoke. One of the boys had been shot, taking a chunk out of his right cheek. He'd returned fire at what he believed was the offender but hadn't managed to hit him. Little Mick had observed my torchlight above him. He pivoted, following the stream of light to see where I was pointing. As he swung back, he glanced up. The POI was right above him, leaning over the balustrade from the mezzanine, a natural sniper's nest, with a compound bow pulled right back ready to shoot Little Mick in the face at point blank range. Little Mick instinctively swung the heavy ballistic shield upwards, just as another arrow was released striking the shield. *Thwack*. Calmly, he raised his Glock, drew a bead, and fired—*Bang*—shooting the man in the hip.

There was a slight pause in the barrage of arrows after the gunshot, followed by loud groaning. At first, I was worried it was one of our boys who was hit. Browny managed to raise Bravo on the police radio who informed us that it was the POI who'd been shot. I hoped that this was going to be it. I'd started to think this was the case when—*Whoosh*—another arrow flew past me and struck the shield. *Thwack*. Browny again moved up and said, "We need to advance boys—there's still a hostage in here." This was going to be risky. There were more arrows bouncing off the shield in rapid fire succession—*Thwack. Thwack. Thwack*—and there were new holes appearing in the Gyprock. It was pure mayhem.

I told Browny I was confident our target was in the end room. The offender couldn't have planned it better. Browny's plan was to push forward as a team behind the shield. As we did, I was to throw a stun grenade into the end room. At the same time, Jet's job was to run to the back of the house and lob in another stunnie, smashing it through the second storey window and also into the room. The plan was to distract the POI long enough to cross the landing, get down the stairs and face him. We stacked up behind the partition wall. Insane-o was point, Pauly next, then me, with the rest of the team behind us. Browny drew a long audible breath in and out and then coolly said, "Righto boys, let's get this done!" Insane-o stepped off.

Convinced I was about to be shot, I could feel the unmistakable cold hand of fear on me. I could taste the adrenaline. I passed the partition and the point of no return. "Stunnie" I yelled, throwing a grenade as hard as I could towards the room. But then it hit something and bounced away, deflected by one of the many *Home Alone*-style barricades set up inside the house. Another operator tossed his onto the landing near the door. *Boom.* As our stack moved forward, I was again intensely aware of how exposed I felt—and was. My left side was completely vulnerable. If a barbed hunting arrow were to hit me, nothing would stop it. I flexed every muscle in my body, focusing on the left side of my abdomen. I held up my arm in an effort to shield my face. This wouldn't have stopped anything, let alone an arrow, but it steadied me. I grimaced, waiting for impact.

Then I noticed how slippery the floor was. Stumbling here, at this moment, would spell disaster. We continued our advance towards the stairs, before slowly and methodically making our way down, under the constant threat of being shot. It felt like an eternity. I couldn't believe I hadn't been hit—yet. Every second that I was exposed was an opportunity for the offender to kill me. I willed Pauly to speed up but knew that he couldn't. Our stack reached the base of the stairs before turning left to face the offender. I took a breath and relaxed my now aching core. We were now at least behind the shield, although visibility was still poor. The boys at the back of the stack cleared rooms as our main group pushed on. Armies yelled, "Hostage secure."

"Copy," came the reply echoing from several quarters. That was a relief. The man's sister was found hiding in the bathtub, petrified with fear, curled up in the foetal position, holding her hands over her ears, rocking and moaning. Armies put a reassuring hand on her shoulder, "It's okay, you're safe now."

I could just make out the room at the end of the hallway. Our stack moved towards it slowly but deliberately, navigating our way through barricades, traps and trip ropes. Now only metres away, I saw smoke billowing from the doorway. Jet's stun grenade had set a mattress alight. We pushed forward into the room as Pauly peeled left, leaving me behind Insane-o. I couldn't see a thing. The fire was well ablaze. Then, to our right, appearing out of the darkness and smoke, I saw a terrifying sight.

The man suddenly emerged, swinging a large-bladed tomahawk straight towards Insane-o's head with the ferocity of a Viking berserker. *Swoosh*. Insane-o swivelled the shield just in time, blocking the blow. *Smash*. The force pushed him back and onto me, nearly knocking us both over. With a blood-curdling scream, the offender then pulled his arm back, winding up for another hammer blow. I pulled my Taser and pointed it past Insane-o and the shield. Incredibly, the POI was wearing a face mask of sorts. I carefully aimed and fired. The probes lodged in the man's neck just below the mask—an amazing shot. Fifty thousand volts now entered his body. He dropped the tomahawk, convulsing from the electric current, as Insane-o and I pushed forward. Together we wrestled him to the ground with Pauly assisting. The Taser continued ticking over as we rolled him onto his front. Even after being shot, tasered and tackled, and now with two big men on top of him, the offender continued to fight like a Tassie devil. Immo and Hipster came to our assistance and we managed to handcuff him. The fire was extinguished. Thornleigh was over.

As the lights came on, I began to better appreciate the situation. I reached down and removed the barbed probes from the man's neck. He was an enormous, heavy-set giant, with large steel plates on his front and back, attached by leather straps, effectively creating a Ned Kelly-style suit of armour. He was also wearing a flip-down industrial grinding mask. A large amount of blood was gushing from a gaping bullet wound in the man's side. We rolled him over so that Insane-o could apply manual pressure with a field bandage. A bullet had hardly slowed him down. His drive to kill us even overshadowed his pain. He was one extremely determined individual.

I scanned the room. There was a large camo-coloured, carbon-fibre hunting bow on the floor with a stack of arrows. I counted four homemade rifles with custom-made bullets strewn across the bed, together with the wooden-handled tomahawk. Some of the bullets had obviously been more effective than others. The chunk out of 'Wildcat's' face was evidence of that. It also explained what else had been hitting the shield and punching through the Gyprock.

Armies escorted some ambulance officers in to care for the man. The entire house was now an active crime scene, so we were careful not to disturb anything. In the stairwell where Bravo team had been holed up, there were arrows sticking out of the wall and another embedded into the solid hardwood timber balustrade, punching more than half the way through it. Remnants of furniture and white goods were also stacked across the hallway. Canola oil was poured over the floor and stairs, explaining why it had been so slippery underfoot. "What sort of a lunatic would think to do that?" I said to Pauly.

"One like old mate just over there I reckon," came Pauly's not-so-philosophical reply. I found myself shaking my head as I examined the arrows sticking out of the wall where we'd been sheltering. There were more on the floor where Insane-o had been positioned with the shield. I called to Browny, "Take a look at this, man!" The front door had been secured with scores of heavy-duty baton lugs.

Browny replied, "I know, he did the same with the internal garage door." It had also been fastened shut with huge industrial-strength screws. It wouldn't have mattered if we had used the garage as our entry point, we would've faced the same issues. The place looked like a war zone and we were lucky not to have lost somebody. This man had clearly been preparing for us and his strategy was becoming obvious.

The POI's intention was for police to make entry on the ground floor through an easily accessible sliding glass door. This would have funnelled us into a narrow hallway before even attempting to navigate the steep flight of stairs. From his elevated position, it would've been as easy as shooting fish in a barrel. (Just ask the Bravo team.) But he also made extensive contingency plans if we managed to get through the front door. I was amazed at the lengths this seriously determined and motivated individual was willing to go to to inflict maximum carnage. It was also sobering to think of the potential loss of life should everything have been allowed to go according to his plan.

I exited through where the front door once was. I was back in the clear, still night air, finally free of smoke. I took a big deep breath and looked up at the stars. 'That was intense,' I thought to myself, much like I did during selection on the stretcher carry. Everyone stood in a group before Browny returned with the inspector.

"Well, that was a big one ay boys?" There was unanimous nodding. No one was thinking about public holiday penalty rates now.

Pauly then called out in his typically loud and often inappropriate way, "That fat arse Ned Kelly must have swallowed Robin Hood. Mad as a cut snake? He really had us goin' ay boys!" I laughed out loud, as did the others. It was a nervous laugh that momentarily relieved the mood. The inspector directed us to head straight to Hornsby police station where the critical incident team would speak with us. We arrived in minutes and were shown to a muster room where everyone sat in silence, each reflecting on the night's mayhem. I was lucky, bloody lucky. We all were.

I looked over in the direction of little Mick, then I sat with him. He told me of the moment when he was nearly killed before asking me if I thought he had done the right thing in shooting the man. "Yes mate. Definitely. It was him or us." I put my arm around him, looked him in the eye and said, "You did a bloody good job mate. You should be proud of yourself." This was the beginning of a long friendship. After that, I respected him for his abilities under extreme pressure. He'd held that heavy ballistic shield for hours, refusing to hand it over. I never had an issue with his size again. He was a tough little bastard and he'd more than proved himself. All the boys agreed.

Thornleigh left its mark on everyone involved. One of the crew was so rattled that he accepted a promotion and left the TOU. Not long after that, another officer left the police force entirely. It changed me too, but for a different reason. It was the first time I'd faced death. Thanks to my training and the backup of great mates I prevailed. Strangely, media attention was confined to very brief snippets of incorrect reporting across all the major news networks, as well as the local free newspaper. And stranger still, to date, there have never been bravery commendations awarded—not even to Little Mick, who was most deserving. Years later, his bravery was recognised as a mere commendation, essentially a certificate. The problem is, the cake eaters on the awards panel believe that's what we're trained for. But above all, Thornleigh taught me that I should never be complacent and that, in the TOU, there was no such thing as a 'straightforward job'. I wouldn't make the same mistake again.

Lindt

The day started like many others. I had been on call for the weekend and had given my mate 'Stevey' a Monday morning lift to work. Stevey would be lucky to be 5 feet 6 inches tall (on a good day), made worse by other TOU operators pointing this out to him at every opportunity. As a result, he spent a lot of time in the gym and was nearly as wide as he was tall. He had shaved salt and pepper hair, with more salt these days than pepper. (Gus reckoned it wasn't real hair at all but steel wool.) He was best mates with Browny who was tall and they fought constantly like brothers. Gus called this 'the Bert and Ernie show'. Stevey was a solid operator and an experienced sniper. The two of us burst through the front door of our office on ████████████████████ at 6.30 a.m., still chatting about politics.

We call our headquarters building 'the bunker'. The back of the building looks like reconstructed Stalingrad—bleak and functional. The front looks much the same but, with some huge plane trees, and an excessively large, bold, and silver-coloured capitalised sign that reads ████████████████████ (a favourite media backdrop for television talking heads).

After the usual exchange of 'G'days' and 'How ya goings', I started stirring up some of the guys over their latest protein 'paleo' (or 'keto') fad diets. One operator was eating a rare lean steak, another a cold braised chicken breast coated in peanut butter—for breakfast. "Briefing!" Baboon the sergeant called out. Everyone appeared to be in high spirits. During roll call, I was notified that it was my turn to attend a 'well check'. This is a mandatory interview with a police psychologist for officers who work in high-risk areas. I copped the usual barrage reserved for anyone unlucky enough to be nominated.

"Poor bloody shrinks. Imagine having to listen to you with all your head noises," one of the boys called out to me with a good-hearted laugh.

Next on Baboon's morning agenda was a review of possible jobs in the pipeline, although nothing appeared imminent. He then outlined the day's training activities before asking, "Has anyone got anything constructive to add?" Pauly jumped to his feet like a coiled spring. "Bloody oath I do sarge!"

"Why'd I even ask?" Baboon replied, rubbing his eyes, and shaking his head with a low moan. Pauly excitedly gave us a rundown on the success of the TOU Christmas party held the previous Saturday night. He was *el presidente* of the TOU social club and exactly where he liked to be—the centre of attention. Everyone then headed downstairs for equipment checks before returning to the office; then it was out to the café, senior officers first, with the junior staff looking after the shop. After six years, I was considered a senior operator. Morning coffee is a big deal in the TOU. It is a long-standing ritual and one of the unit's best bonding and informal debriefing times.

My appointment with the psychologist couldn't be avoided any longer. Only this time I didn't have to complete the 397 multiple-choice questions that all TOU operators must endure annually. The questionnaire was always much the same, so we knew how to answer it. Likewise, the quarterly one-on-one session included the usual vague questions and so, like everyone else, I gave the usual vague answers. It was the worst sort of box-ticking, a token effort at best.

To add to the pointlessness of it all, if I was struggling with a mental health issue, ironically the 'well check' wasn't the time or place to talk about it. In general, police psychologists must report anything they believe could potentially affect our capabilities. An adverse assessment usually results in an operator being taken offline—at least until further psychological testing is conducted; but on this day, if I did have an issue, this guy was going to brush it off; it was all just too much trouble.

The psychologist was 40-something, overweight and balding, with a glowing red nose and pastey pale skin, contrasted by thick black-rimmed glasses that clashed with his candy-striped long-sleeved cotton shirt. The poor man was just so bored in his job that all he wanted was for me to tell him operational stories—and then he'd hang on my every word. "Any good jobs come in lately?" he'd eagerly ask. I could imagine him in some dimly lit, smoke-filled, gaming dungeon playing *Counter-Strike: Global Offensive* or *Left 4 Dead*. I resisted the urge to play my own mind games with him. I didn't want the ordeal to last any longer than it had to.

I walked back through the front door of the office and instantly felt that something was wrong. A police negotiator sprinted past me. I couldn't recall ever seeing a 'neg' moving quickly, let alone running. He was followed by 'Lucky', a sergeant, whose concerned expression told me more than words. "█████ no duff! There's a counterterrorism job at Martin Place. Grab your gear, we're going now!" (Martin Place is a broad, open-air pedestrian mall that runs between George and Macquarie Streets in the Sydney CBD.)

"Oh shit! So, it's finally happened?" I called back. Lucky just nodded. We all knew it was just a matter of time, especially since the 9/11 attacks in the US.

*****

After 2001, the TOU were regularly briefed by the Joint Counter Terrorism Team (JCTT). This was made up of NSW Police, the Australian Federal Police, the Australian Security Intelligence Organisation (ASIO) and the NSW Crime Commission. One of their many sources was the *al-Qaeda* online English-language magazine *Inspire*, as well as ISIS social media propaganda outlets with their increasingly strident calls for 'lone wolf' attacks.

Only three months earlier, I'd been part of the JCTT-run Operation Appleby, the largest job of its type in Australian history. Simultaneous pre-dawn search warrants were conducted by over 800 police officers across NSW and Queensland, resulting in 15 suspects being detained on terrorism-related offences. A cell comprising returned ISIS fighters—and many others—was planning attacks on the Australian Federal Police building in Sydney, the ███████ ███████, where we work, the Garden Island naval base and Parliament House in Canberra. Orders issued directly from the ISIS leadership inspired advanced plans to kidnap a random civilian off a Sydney street, before beheading him or her and live-streaming the brutal attack on social media. The Endeavour Hills stabbing of two police officers by a terrorist in Melbourne, only weeks before, was also on our minds. For these reasons, the threat level at the time was 'critical', meaning that another attack was considered imminent.

My direct involvement in Operation Appleby was a search warrant executed on an address in a run-down, redbrick, public housing apartment block in Sydney's north-west. Our team approached under the cover of darkness and entered the internal staircase undetected. Inside, there was a damp carpet smell and the overwhelming stench of cigarettes. Paint was peeling off the walls and iron balustrades. The landing on the top floor was only tiny, making it hard to stack up outside the door. The operator on the ballistic shield was up front with me just behind him and other operators positioned in a line down the narrow stairwell. The shield provided us with limited cover in case we were fired on, although, if there was a bomb, we were dangerously exposed. I advanced with the shield man covering me and banged on the front door. "Police. Search warrant!"

There was only permission for a 'knock and identify' operation and far from ideal. A 'no knock' warrant would have allowed us to ram the door without notice. We had to adapt. The door was slowly opened by a woman hastily adjusting a burqa which covered her entire face. "It's the police. Come out now!" our team leader Insane-o yelled.

"Sorry, sorry, please, what have we done?" the woman said. (I was at least grateful she didn't fall to the ground feigning a heart attack.)

"We're here to speak to your son," I continued.

"Yes, I tell my son; he come," she replied anxiously.

The figure of our suspect appeared. "It's the police. Come out and you won't be harmed," I yelled. Unexpectedly, the man made a run straight for us, aggressively pushing his mother aside. The operator on the shield hit him with it— *Whack*—while I brought him down with a swinging arm. The offender hit the ground but continued to struggle. I rolled him over with assistance before searching for a weapon, or, more concerningly, a suicide vest. All clear. A good result. The suspect was then handed over to the riot squad boys so they could parade him like a trophy in front of reporters and television cameras and claim credit for the arrest.

Our team was later interviewed by Internal Affairs, accused of using 'excessive force'. I couldn't work out who the complainant was. During the interview the investigating officer kept glancing down at a document that he was clearly shielding from me. I momentarily distracted him by asking for a glass of water. He was reading directly from an ABC news bulletin. There never was an official complaint. Internal Affairs obviously had so little to do that they were investigating anything and everything.

Back at the ███████████████, I followed the sergeant into the lift. Nothing was said. We ran to the TOU secure storeroom, where I quickly donned my full kit, before jumping into the back of the BearCat armoured vehicle. My mate 'Big Bernie' drove at speed under lights and sirens while I loaded my M4 assault rifle. The vehicle unexpectedly hit a speed bump, bouncing us around in the back. Because of this, I wasn't convinced that my rifle was loaded correctly, so I repeated the process, removing a round from the chamber—a TOU standard issue 5.56mm 'pointed soft-point' (chosen by the police hierarchy for penetration)—and placing it into my top pocket.

Screeching to a halt in Elizabeth Street, I jumped from the back of the BearCat and ran to the corner of Martin Place. There were cops everywhere—and even more television cameras. A large group of onlookers were already being moved on by GDs officers. Atts, the team leader, was talking with one of our inspectors and other operators. I received a brief version of events as more information was coming in by the second. Atts confirmed, "An unknown male has entered the Lindt Café with a shotgun and claiming to have a bomb. He's taken all occupants hostage."

The café was located on the ground floor of a 15-storey landmark Art Deco building with its distinctive honey-coloured polished marble façade. The main double glass-panel entrance door was on the corner of Phillip Street and Martin Place. The other entrance into the café was through a foyer that contained Manhattan-style heritage elevators. Atts put me straight into the role of cover man with Pauly on the shield. It was reassuring to have one of my best mates on the job despite our long history of operational 'shit fights'.

"Benny boy," Pauly yelled so that everyone could hear, "Atts says you're going to be my cover man?"

"That I am mate," I replied.

"Well thank fuck for that!" Pauly replied boisterously. I hoped that the nearby television cameras hadn't picked up his voice. (I was especially wary of the ABC as most police are.)

From our location in Martin Place, with Elizabeth Street just behind us, I could see uphill towards the café and beyond to the Cenotaph and the sandstone Sydney Hospital—the oldest in Australia. NSW Parliament House is right next door on Macquarie Street. Earlier that year I was on a job where a disgruntled taxi driver dowsed himself and the inside of his vehicle with petrol. He threatened to blow up Parliament if the Premier didn't agree to speak with him. Like Lindt, all the major media networks had it on live feed. Atts had been my team leader on that job too.

What was particularly concerning were numerous open containers of fuel on the back seat—more than enough to do the job. As negotiations broke down, the man tried to light himself up, clearly intending for the car to explode. As we engaged, sprinting towards the taxi from our positions of cover, he was flicking a cigarette lighter. It was tight. The operator in front of me smashed the vehicle's window with a reamer before I filled the cabin with tear gas from my hand-held fogger while another operator sprayed the vehicle with a fire hose. The POI was ripped from the car still flicking his lighter. It was a perfectly executed operation. No one was injured—despite the obvious risks.

*****

Back at Lindt, the highway patrol officer who responded to the initial 000 emergency call provided us with a clear description from his earlier observations through the glass foyer door: "A man of Middle Eastern appearance in dark clothing, holding a shotgun and wearing a bulky black backpack with wires hanging out."

The POI had chosen his location well. The Lindt Café is in the heart of Sydney, with the Reserve Bank of Australia and the Channel 7 media building directly opposite. The city was shut down. From that moment the siege was live-streamed around the world on all major national and international television networks.

Atts reported, "The POI ordered the manager of the café, a 34-year-old man, Tori Johnson, to contact emergency 000 and read out this message: 'Australia is under attack by Islamic State. There are three bombs in three different locations: Martin Place, Circular Quay, and George Street. Police should not come close to me or other brothers, otherwise they will explode the bombs. Some hostages have been taken.''

The inspector then added, "Our snipers have confirmed that there are hostages positioned across four windows. Two of them are holding black flags with white Arabic writing, blocking a clear view." There were three separate sniper teams embedded. The first was in the Channel 7 building opposite the Martin Place side of the café. The second was in the then Westpac Bank building opposite the front entrance door on the corner of Phillip Street and the third was in the Reserve Bank of Australia building. My mate Stevey was 'Sierra one' or lead sniper for the entire operation. (He wasn't the so-called 'chief sniper' that *60 Minutes* later carried on about.)

At this point, our position was considered too far away to respond quickly and so our team was relocated. We made our way through a series of fire escapes until we reached the neighbouring building on Phillip Street at the top of Martin Place. There was a truck loading dock behind us that was an ideal base for front-line operations. It was only 30 metres away with a fire escape directly in front. Beyond that, there were four large windows that framed access to the main café entrance door.

I was part of the primary arrest or Alpha team. Pauly was on the ballistic shield, and I was first cover man, with Atts behind me and the remainder of the eight-man squad stacked up in a row. The colonial spire of St James' Church was behind us in the near distance with the NSW Supreme Court just opposite. The entire area had been evacuated. An eerie silence ensued with pieces of rubbish blowing past and along the otherwise bustling but now empty streets, past Martin Place's prominent faux sandstone bollards, blocking vehicular access and on to the dark-grey pedestrian promenade. Abandoned cars lined the asphalt walkway to the side of our position. The only sounds were the monotonously regular beeping of a nearby pedestrian crossing and the distant wail of police sirens echoing off the surrounding skyscrapers.

Everyone was ordered to remain in position and like a great many other TOU jobs it was a case of 'hurry up and wait'. The time was now 12.30 p.m. and we'd been on site for nearly three hours. It was summer in South-Eastern Australia and the weather was typically hot and humid. An update was broadcast over police radio that the terrorist or 'Tango', had taken 18 hostages but was refusing to speak with negotiators. Beyond this, from our position on the front line, there was an immediate lack of operational intelligence on what was occurring inside the café. This was because every member of the TOU sniper team's vision was obscured by a combination of human shields holding up flags against the café's windows and heavily stencilled festive signwriting proclaiming: 'Lindt— Merry Christmas'.

I needed to know what was happening inside the café. Pauly and I discussed our concerns before I approached Atts. "There's been nothing come in for hours, sarge. Do you reckon me and Pauly could push forward to that first window and have a look in?" We were exasperated. We needed a plan.

"Righto ▓▓▓," Atts surprisingly agreed. "But keep your guns up and try not to be seen."

"Thanks sarge," I responded with relief. "Pauly, let's go. I'll cover you."

Pauly slowly eased forward with the shield held close to his face, peering through the distinctive rectangular bullet-resistant glass viewing port. I was on his left shoulder with my rifle up ready to respond. We pulled up to the first of the four windows and peered in.

The very first thing I noticed was an extravagant display of Lindt chocolate balls of all colours and types. It reminded me of the brightly decorated Christmas tree that Lisa and I had set up at home that very weekend. I looked beyond one of the imposing green marble columns to where two female hostages were holding flags up to the windows. (Only two of the four windows were visible from our vantage point.) This confirmed what had already been reported by our snipers. Some hostages were seated and visibly upset. No one was talking or looking at each other. I clearly observed one young woman in a Lindt Café uniform: a black long-sleeved collared shirt, long trousers, and a maroon-coloured apron with gold lettering. She seemed to be on autopilot, oblivious to what was happening around her, serving drinks from a tray to other hostages. It was surreal.

Then the terrorist suddenly appeared, before ducking behind a hostage. He was wearing a black bandana with white Arabic writing on it and holding a pump-action shotgun—a Manufrance La Salle, with both the stock and barrel crudely sawn off. What was more concerning, however, was the backpack he was wearing. I looked at it very, very closely. The black Camel Mountain bag was stretched by its contents and I could see two wires looping out of the bottom—one black and the other red. "Are you seeing what I'm seeing, Pauly?" I asked.

"Yeah, that backpack definitely looks like a bomb."

"Can you see the wires too?"

"Confirmed. Not good."

"Fuck no!"

Only weeks before, a specialist from the Australian Army's Special Operations Engineering Regiment had shown us how to identify improvised explosive devices or IEDs so this was fresh in our minds. The tutorial included the types of bombs terrorists were currently using around the world: pipe bombs, shoe bombs, underpants bombs, suicide vests and the sort of backpack bombs that started to appear in early 2005. The operator also showed us some physical examples. I had a sinking feeling in the pit of my stomach. What I was observing looked just like the CCTV images of the backpack bombs that detonated in three London Underground stations and on a double-decker bus in Tavistock Square, killing over 50 people.

I knew that a bomb comprising a backpack full of easily obtained explosive material could vaporise everyone in the immediate vicinity—including us—and potentially bring the entire building down. For this reason, every floor above the café had been evacuated, as well as surrounding buildings. Was it the terrorist's intention to draw us all in and then detonate the device? In the April 2013 Boston Marathon bombing, the second explosive device, packed with ball bearings and rusty carpenters' nails, (although detonating prematurely) was intended to kill first responders such as police and ambulance officers. The same strategy also caused unbelievable carnage in the 2002 and 2005 Bali bombings. I put the thought out of my mind.

I reported my intelligence precisely to Atts in person, who then relayed it to senior officers in the command post set up in the NSW Leagues' Club on Phillip Street. After consideration, the bosses requested further details. Pauly and I took turns staring through the ballistic shield viewing port at the terrorist prowling around the café for some 25 minutes—undetected, paying careful attention to both the shotgun and the backpack. We also counted how many hostages were in the room and then recorded both their descriptions and locations so that they could be individually identified.

Atts came forward. The three of us agreed that the shotgun was a pump-action 12 gauge—and likely to have a four to five round rapid-fire capacity—a formidable close-quarters killing machine. Atts looked at me with his eyes wide open and then nodded in silent agreement; he also confirmed seeing the backpack and wires.

I looked closer at the women holding the black banner with white Arabic script—the 'jihadist flag' used by Islamist groups like ISIS. It said, 'There is no God but Allah, and Muhammad is the messenger of God'. One of the women was shaking and sobbing. The Tango continued to pace around the café shouting at hostages. We noticed that whenever he left his base at the far corner of the café, he always had a hostage in front of him with the shotgun pushed into their backs. He was clearly conscious of being exposed to any of the windows and ducked when walking past them.

"Bloody hell Benny, old mate seems to have a bit of tactical nous about him ay," Pauly noted.

"I agree, he looks like he actually has some situational awareness and an idea of what he's doing."

"And not just walking around thinking he's John Rambo with a big arse gun," Pauly added.

"Yeah, he sure likes that far corner ay? He's put some planning into this," I continued.

The terrorist appeared to be directing most of his abuse towards a male hostage dressed in a sharp, black, long-sleeved shirt, long black pants, and black polished boots, contrasted by styled blonde hair. The man clearly displayed a sense of calm, dignified composure. I now know him to be the café manager, Tori Johnson.

The Tango's human shield of choice, however, was a middle-aged, heavy-set, kindly-looking woman with fair skin and short, light brown hair, who I now know to be Louisa Hope. All we could do was watch as he frog-marched her around the café. Although visibly upset, her self-control seemed to enrage him. My determination to protect the hostages and neutralise the threat was growing by the second.

I then observed a young man with a fop of dark hair, who I later knew to be 19-year-old Jarrod Morton-Hoffman. He was talking on a mobile phone with the terrorist standing over him yelling instructions. The poor guy seemed to be holding up well under pressure although he was visibly shaking. When it was Pauly's turn to observe the situation, the young man bravely pointed out where the terrorist was, even using a hand signal to confirm that the Tango had a gun. This impressed us.

The terrorist unfortunately noticed Jarrod and turned towards us. Our eyes met and the realisation of just who he was looking at hit him—two heavily armed and determined trained assets. He immediately crouched low, pointing his weapon in our direction, before lunging towards Louisa Hope, grabbing her by her blouse, violently manhandling her to her feet and pushing the barrel of the shotgun into the back of her head. I could see that his finger was on the trigger. The expressions on the face of every hostage screamed, 'Why won't you help us?' The truth was that we were just as desperate to go in. At that moment, the terrorist became incensed. Louisa Hope was in grave danger. Suddenly a hand appeared, placing a rough handwritten note against the window in front of us—an action obviously dictated under duress: 'Police move away now, or a hostage will be executed'. Pauly and I immediately withdrew from the window.

Everyone stood in formation in our full-length black uniforms and 25-kilogram kits, with polyester mesh balaclavas pulled up to conceal our identities from the nearby scrum of loitering, hungry journalists and, beyond them, a forest of television cameras. The midday sun was starting to take a toll on us. I felt beads of sweat running down my spine under my bullet resistant vest, all the way to my underpants. We'd been in position for hours with no further updates since Pauly and I had taken the initiative earlier.

Then, suddenly, an elderly hostage burst through the front door of the café. Clearly driven by raw self-preservation, the man turned to his right and stared in our direction like a rabbit in a spotlight. A younger man dressed in smart suit pants and a perfectly pressed long-sleeved white linen shirt followed closely behind him, flapping his hands in the air hysterically. The stack pushed forwards to provide cover. "It's the police. Come over here!" They both had a look of blind terror in their eyes.

As our stack regrouped, the fire door directly in front of us suddenly swung open, this time with a loud *crash*. A middle-aged man, with a dark receding hairline and manicured eyebrows wearing a Lindt Café uniform, abruptly appeared. He immediately tripped and stumbled before we pulled him to safety as well. The man seemed even more overwhelmed than the others, barely able to understand basic instructions, repeatedly shouting, "You need to get in there, you need to get in there, he's going to kill everyone!" In over 12 years of front-line policing, I'd never seen human beings in such a state of distress, panic or shock. Atts tried to calm the situation by engaging the three in conversation. Good intelligence was desperately needed on what was actually happening inside the café but most of what he got was panicked garble. "No point," Pauly said, "They've lost it." We returned to our position as the men were led away for medical attention, debriefing and questioning. Our focus remained on the café.

No water had been brought to us since our deployment and our position had been in the full summer sun for most of the day. Pauly was relieved from the shield by one of the younger operators and disappeared into the darkness of the loading bay. He was only gone a few minutes before returning. "Here you go fellas, look what your good mate Pauly has got for you." He held up an armful of water bottles and some individually wrapped café-style chocolate chip biscuits. Pauly was like a natural-born larrikin ANZAC trench scavenger, looking out for his mates, just like the Aussie soldiers my Grandpa told me about in the Great War. (I remember Grandpa was fond of saying, "On the Western Front, if the British Generals ever wanted an Australian division to capture a German position— all they had to do was declare it out of bounds.")

"Where the bloody hell did you get all that from man?" I said to Pauly with genuine admiration.

"An empty café, back through there," he grinned, pointing into the cave-like loading dock. "Whatcha ya reckon fellas, bloody legend ay?"

"Yeah, good work mate," I laughed.

"The café owners of Sydney doing their bit to help New South Wales's finest," Pauly grinned, obviously pleased with himself.

"Mate, you're nothing if not resourceful," I shot back with a smile.

"I'll be sure to notify the corridor creepers so the café owner gets reimbursed. Good work Pauly," Atts said, giving my mate a slap on the back.

Atts was managing our fatigue by allowing half the team to rest in the shade of the loading bay although we were all ready to respond at a moment's notice. As I enjoyed the ice-cold water, I checked my phone and saw the missed calls and messages from family and friends. I browsed quickly over some of them. Despite wearing a tactical helmet and balaclava, a lot of people had recognised my eyes from the close-up television footage. The reason I wasn't wearing my work sunglasses was that our two-year-old daughter had broken them. Lisa later told me that our little girl had also recognised me from the live-streamed footage. "That's my daddy," she said giggling, pointing at the flat screen television. That was enough for Lisa. She turned it off straight away.

More TOU operators were called in. Gus's distinctive voice came over the radio. It was the first good news I'd received all day. Although assigned to the other entry team, it was reassuring to have my best mate around. Gus was a competent operator who wouldn't hesitate to run in once the order was given. At different times throughout the day, the situation ramped up to the point where I believed we were about to go in, before being ordered to stand down again. It must have been what it was like for the Diggers waiting to go 'over the top' in Gallipoli or in France. In those moments of down time, we talked. "You guys realise that, when we storm in there, we're all going to be worm food, don't you?" Pauly blurted out.

"Mate, but can you imagine the TV ratings," I added.

"Well at least there'll be cold beers and medals for the families all round," Pauly continued in his typically unfiltered way.

"You've got a big rough head mate. I'll just stand behind you and I'll be just fine," I replied, getting one up on him.

"Ha, ha, ha, says you Benny boy, with one of the biggest

heads in the TOU." Everyone smiled.

"Mate, come on, seriously, it's nothing in comparison to Baboon's oversized melon," I replied.

"Fair enough," Pauly grinned. The exchange had lightened the mood—momentarily.

"I suppose that's what we're trained for anyway … isn't it?" I said, with deadly seriousness.

"That's why I'm sending you two dickheads in first," Atts replied with a forced half-smile.

"I'll be sure to give you a left hook as I'm flying back out on fire sarge," I said, only half-jokingly. But the brutal reality, as we saw it, was that as soon as we entered the café, everyone was going to die in a massive IED explosion. In that moment, this inevitability hit us all like the proverbial Mack truck. Our training had incorporated strategies for deliberately putting away distracting feelings about being killed, but now death seemed almost a certainty. No one spoke. We just stood there, our rifles at the ready, shoulder to shoulder, ready to go, waiting for the 'whistle to blow', deep in our own thoughts.

A bomb meant that there was only a slim chance of getting any of the hostages out alive and every front-line TOU operator would die too—Pauly first, then me and Atts, followed by the rest of our stack and, of course, the boys in Bravo team, including Gus. I momentarily imagined the ghastly spectacle of our eviscerated, dismembered and mutilated bodies in pools of blood, live-streamed in full colour to hundreds of millions of people around the world—and into my home too.

I texted Lisa, trying not to let her know what I was thinking, asking her to send me some recent photos of our little girl. I showed Pauly, who reciprocated by scrolling through photos of him playing with his boys. (Meanwhile, Gus texted his wife, "Jadey, don't forget to put the bins out.") As I gazed over my pictures, a feeling of deep sorrow washed over me. I was resigned to the idea that I was never going to see my wife and daughter again and I wasn't ever going to hold the unborn baby that Lisa was carrying, let alone see the rest of my family and good friends again. I said my goodbyes through text messages as best I could, without revealing our exact predicament. But I'm sure Lisa knew exactly what was going on. I encountered many brave women that day but none braver than the woman I loved. Later, I found that she was both angry and disappointed that I seemed so willing to sacrifice myself and sentence her and the girls to a life of heartache and struggle.

Then, one of the TOU guys in the stack suddenly went white; he obviously couldn't handle it. I could see it in his eyes. The harsh reality of the situation had clearly overwhelmed him. I watched and didn't say a thing. Everyone had done the same selection and training courses, but the truth is no one really knows how they will hold up until their big test comes. I heard Stevey's voice come over the police radio requesting another sniper. Even before he checked with Atts, the operator accepted the request via radio. "Sorry guys, they need me." And with that, he walked off. We all just looked at each other.

The terrorist was finally identified. Atts was sent an intelligence brief on his smartphone. The man was a self-proclaimed Islamic cleric, Man Haron Monis, a 50-year-old Iranian-born refugee, currently on bail as an accessory to the murder of his ex-wife by stabbing, together with 43 outstanding charges, including 22 counts of aggravated sexual assault and 14 counts of aggravated indecent assault. (In April 2001, the INTERPOL contact point in Canberra had alerted the Immigration Department that Monis was also wanted by the Iranian authorities.) Locally, he'd obtained notoriety in the media by sending hate mail to the families of Australian soldiers who had died serving their country in the war in Afghanistan. Only a month earlier, he'd pledged allegiance to Islamic State on his website and then again on social media. "That's him, right boys?" Atts questioned, holding up his phone to show Pauly and me a photograph.

"Yeah man, that's the grub," I confirmed. Pauly just nodded in disgust.

"Shit, what's he doing out on bail? Someone has seriously fucked this one up," Pauly added, stating the obvious.

We soon discovered that senior police had consulted a psychiatrist to provide a subject profile on the terrorist and advise them accordingly. (His identity was suppressed at the coronial inquest). I had a negative take on this, as did the other boys. I still hadn't been able to move on from a psychiatrist predicting that, after years in the bush, Malcolm Naden 'would have devolved to an animal-like state' and that he 'probably would only be able to communicate in grunts'. It became immediately apparent to us that senior command was taking this peanut's advice seriously. But, at that stage, maybe the bosses were just grateful for anyone putting their hand up to give any old opinion? And, in fairness, it was up to them to accept his advice or not.

It was later revealed that the shrink believed the terrorist was merely a 'grandstander' and that he wasn't really a terrorist at all but rather just someone with a 'narcissistic antisocial personality disorder', undertaking 'a grandiose act' and that 'he didn't really want to hurt anyone once he got what he wanted'. He even doubted that Monis 'represented ISIS' because he didn't have the 'correct flag'. (Experts in Islamic terrorism later confirmed that the flag Monis used was frequently used by ISIS.) But it seemed to us that he'd missed the point, probably because he wasn't qualified to comment. (This all came out in the coronial inquest.) Although some of the terrorist's actions 'didn't fit ISIS methodology,' he was clearly capable of terrible violence, and certainly had the hostages terrorised. Based on close observations, our view was that he was operating in a controlled, planned and methodical way. I wondered how much more evidence senior management needed. Pauly summoned it up so precisely—"What the fuck!"

I thought to myself, the terrorist has taken hostages, has a weapon and a backpack bomb. Do the bosses really believe this man is going to come out with his hands up when he gets what he wants (whatever that was) and then spend the rest of his life in solitary confinement in a supermax prison. At a tactical level, this just didn't make sense. The terrorist must have known that he was going to prison even before ever entering the café.

From the front line, there was still a disturbing lack of operational intelligence. There were, however, some details sent through Att's phone that he immediately relayed to us. As individual hostages were identified, he received basic profile information, including photographs. I still remember Katrina Dawson's image and description: 'a 38-year-old barrister and mother of three children'.

The terrorist was still refusing to speak with police negotiators, only ever communicating through hostages, demanding via the media that police and politicians acknowledge that his action was an attack by Islamic State. He even forced a hostage to call the broadcaster Ray Hadley who, to his credit, wouldn't allow him to talk on air. A report then came in that he was demanding an actual ISIS flag. He was also insisting on talking to Prime Minister Tony Abbott. Persistent postponing of his demands was clearly increasing his emotional temperature, or at least that was obvious to us.

Then two more female hostages suddenly escaped. They'd snuck out through the foyer. I had a growing concern that a humiliated terrorist would be forced into a decision and then, according to what we believed at the time, execute his final act—an internationally-televised extravaganza of death and mayhem that would have energised ISIS lone wolves all over the world for a generation.

Senior commanders were, however, sticking to the long-standing 'contain and negotiate' strategy that had served them well up to this point. It must have seemed to them that most of the hostages were eventually going to escape by their own means—and that time was on *their* side—but it wasn't on *our* side, it was not what was needed, not what we wanted and not what we were trained to do—which was to aggressively seize the initiative at an exact time and manner of our choosing and, in doing so, save the hostages.

Pauly said, "What the fuck is happening in there? Why won't the fuck'en cake eaters let us go in? Why has this gone on so fuck'en long? If this were back home in The Alice, mate, some big fuck'en tradie would've said, 'Enough of this shit' and knocked him the fuck out inside five fuck'en minutes; and then his blackfella mate would've finished the fucking bastard off." We both knew that this same conversation—minus the expletives—would be playing out that night in almost every office and pub, work site and private home across Australia.

"Have a look around mate. This isn't Alice Springs. And it sure isn't where I come from either," I said to Pauly. "It's Martin Place and it might as well be on another planet."

Pauly replied in the most philosophical way he knew. "Fuck! This isn't going to end well, is it Benny?"

"No mate. It's going to be messy."

*****

A Deliberate Action Plan or 'DA' was drawn up by the

sergeant on the other entry team and submitted for approval. It was a well-thought-out plan for entry using intelligence provided by our lead sniper, Stevey, combined with the operational experience of the entire unit right up to the tactical commander. Our inspectors pushed for it, but approval was never given. However, even if the big bosses had agreed to its implementation at that time, the final decision rested with them and not with us.

The Lindt DA remains confidential through public interest immunity. This is because it reveals restricted tactical methodology currently used by the TOU in dealing with terrorism incidents. Without mentioning specifics, in the Lindt DA all options were on the table. This included ▇▇▇▇ entry, ▇▇▇▇ explosions (effectively a huge, controlled ▇▇▇▇ outside the café to create a ▇▇▇▇), as well as 40-millimetre grenade launcher deployments utilising ▇▇▇▇▇▇▇ devices. The well-considered DA allowed for a surgical entry at our time of choosing, incapacitating the terrorist before he was able to execute hostages or detonate the bomb. In close-quarters battlespeak: 'The use of speed, strength, surprise and aggression to achieve total dominance against your enemy'.

There had been Australian Army Special Forces liaison officers in the police operations centre the entire day. All were combat veterans who had fought in Afghanistan, professionals who had proven that they were among the best in the world. However, the counterterrorism response for the State of New South Wales is the TOU, tasked with providing the first and main response. The Australian Army's Tactical Assault Group (TAG) Army Commandos are the military's response. There's a close working relationship between the TOU and the Australian Defence Force (ADF)—and great mutual respect. If our resources are stretched, they're deployed, a decision made by the Prime Minister. This decision involves the declaration of martial law and isn't taken lightly. If commandos are called in, say for a situation like the Mumbai massacre, involving multiple active shooters, they don't necessarily take over our response but rather work with us by bolstering our capacity. That's why we train together in large-scale counterterrorism training exercises.

The TAG guys had constructed a mock-up of the café at their base and trialled our DA. They agreed it was a good plan and confirmed that they would likely do it the same way. Tactical teams from other States were also primed to practise in preparation for replacing us, but the plan was still knocked back. The bosses were clearly going to wait this one out. They were obviously under pressure.

In the absence of a DA, there was the existing Emergency Action Plan or 'EA'. This was proposed by Atts and approved by the bosses not long after we arrived on the scene. On the other hand, the triggers that would initiate the EA were the death or serious injury (or the imminent death or serious injury) of a hostage. Under an EA, explosive entry wouldn't be used. However, once initiated, we had to get in as quickly as possible, through the front glass-panel doors that would be breached with a shotgun using specialised rounds. Our only distraction option was for the two guys at the back of the stack to shoot out the first window, with the other operator throwing stunnies inside, as we rushed forward.

Both the DA and EA incorporated similar tactical methodology in terms of multiple teams assaulting simultaneously using different entry points. This plan was adopted to ensure the internal café floor plan was covered as quickly as possible, minimising an opportunity for the terrorist to shoot hostages. Still, overall, going in under an EA wasn't what any of us wanted.

Just as this was starting to sink in, Big Bernie, who had driven me to Martin Place in the BearCat, turned up to bolster our numbers. Bernie was a good bloke and a mate—half-Lebanese, half-Irish, affectionately known to us by one of Gus's brilliant nickname creations—'The Lebrichaun'. He was a solid unit, tall in stature, with thatched short black hair and a fair complexion. He was an interesting character—as many TOU operators are. (He has since completed his law degree but, at the same time, he's a keen practitioner of mixed martial arts.) "Hey boys, have a look at this," he said, bending over to reveal where his overalls had burst open all the way up the seam.

"Bloody hell, that's a good effort, I can see your jocks," one of the boys replied.

"It's lucky I didn't do it at full sprint while being filmed by every television camera on earth. Oh no, wait, that's right, I did," he said with a big smile. "Hey where have you guys been pissing? I'm busting!" he continued, changing the subject to something much more urgent. "If I don't go, I'm going to wet myself." We all knew how he felt.

"Just up there in the truck loading bay, towards where the dog squad guy and the negs are. See the red bin over there, on its side, propped up on its lid," I said pointing to a place out of view of the prying television cameras.

"Oh yeah. Got it. You're a good mate Benny," he replied with gritted teeth.

"Just go in the bin, there's nowhere else," I reassured him.

Suddenly I noticed a strong smell of urine. I looked down at my feet. "Are you serious? I meant in the bin, dumb arse; that bloody stinks." The loading bay was on an incline so Big Bernie's stored-up rancid urine just meandered in a little river that ran all the way down to our position, forming a smelly yellow pool at our feet. "Jesus man, I don't know what you were thinking. I'll tell you what though, you need some water, badly. Mate, that has some serious stink."

"Sorry guys, had to go, you know how it is. Hey, got anything to drink?"

"I do, but I'll tell you what, I could really do with a feed," I answered, handing him a bottle of cold water.

"I probably shouldn't tell you what I just saw on the way over here then, should I?" Big Bernie continued with a sly smirk.

"No, probably not, but you're going to tell us anyway," I replied.

"I had to come through the police forward command post where there are bosses absolutely everywhere doing sweet fuck all and, honestly, there were foot-long Subways stacked up 'this high' on all their desks." Every boss within a hundred miles wanted to be there so that they could have it on their CVs. Even so, there wasn't one of them who could organise a bloody drink of water for the boys on the front line.

"You're shitting me. We've been here all day in the hot sun, actually doing something and, all we've had is one skanky six-inch!"

"Yeah, I know, us too," he said with a look of famished disgust. "But what can ya do ay? Some things never change do they?"

An announcement over police radio alerted us to prepare to initiate the EA. Negotiators were about to notify the terrorist, through a hostage, that his demands for an ISIS flag and a telephone audience with the Prime Minister, Tony Abbott, would be refused. Everybody braced up in their positions. I felt the adrenalin surge through my body. This could be the moment. "The message has been delivered to the Tango." Then nothing. Not a sound. No updates or observations from our snipers. Nothing changed.

About an hour later, some specialist police came to our location to install ▮▮▮▮ and listening ▮▮▮▮ secretly within the café. They attempted to insert them through the fire escape directly in front of us. We were required to provide cover. They were there for a long time, but it didn't seem like they'd been too successful, although we did hear later that the device picked up the terrorist saying that he would kill any hostage who tried to escape.

*****

Other States had flown in operators from their equivalent counterterrorism units to back us up. The Special Operations Group (SOG) guys had come from Melbourne; some of the Special Emergency Response Team (SERT) from Queensland and the Specialist Response Group (SRG) from Canberra as well. There was a plan unfolding for us to stand down for a couple of hours to have a rest before being raced out to ▮▮▮▮▮▮▮▮▮▮▮▮▮▮▮▮▮▮▮▮▮▮ training facility to practise the DA in the mock-up. Our units trained together on an annual police tactical group course with every State sending operators, team leaders and snipers. The purpose was to ensure interoperability, especially in a situation like this. For this reason, I was a special constable in both Queensland and Victoria, and we had completed counterterrorism jobs in both States together.

I said to Atts, "Don't you let anyone take my position as cover man."

"No risk of that, it's all yours. No one else wants the job," Atts replied to my relief. Pauly then boisterously said he would punch on with anyone who tried to relieve him.

Darkness fell and the situation became increasingly frustrating for us—and dire for the hostages. The street lights came on, casting their strange shadows across the concrete jungle. The night air suddenly assumed an unseasonable chill. As I was fixing my night-vision goggles to my helmet, I noticed a slight breeze meandering up through the Martin Place urban canyon, rustling the tops of the palms along the street behind us. There was an unsettling feeling that events were moving towards a final climax.

This was far from a usual job. Under so-called normal hostage-taking circumstances, if negotiators hadn't made contact, then a DA would be put in place as it had in Thornleigh. From the front line, we had no idea there hadn't been direct contact with the terrorist—and never would be. (At the time, police negotiators received little if any specialist training in how to deal with such events.) All we knew was this had gone on too long. Still, I wasn't concerned about the terrorist and his shotgun. I was confident in our abilities to deal with that threat. The big issue was always the bomb. Command, like us, believed that, if we did anything to provoke the terrorist, such as make entry or have our sniper take a shot, then he would more than likely detonate the device and every one of the remaining hostages in the café would die.

Despite many in Australia having an opinion on the matter, a sniper shot would have had huge repercussions. The terrorist was very careful not to expose himself to windows but, if he had to, he would always hold his shotgun to a hostage's head. When shot, the body's natural reaction is to spasm in a jerking reflex contraction. I was a trained sniper myself and aware of this happening in both hostage rescue and battlefield situations. The only way to counteract this is to shoot the 'apricot' (the medulla oblongata or brainstem), which immediately results in total nervous incapacitation. Under the circumstances, it was a near impossible shot—and then, of course, we later found out that the Lindt Café glass windows were bullet-resistant.

It was, however, the threat of a 'dead man's switch' that was foremost in my mind. This had become a common practice with suicide bombers—who often had a manual detonation controller wired into the bomb. If he, or she, as was often the case in the Middle East and Sri Lanka, was shot and wounded or killed, then their 'dead hand' automatically released the switch detonating the device. Our boys in Afghanistan encountered this and we had veterans with direct experience of it in our unit. Talking about this amongst the group, we realised that, under the circumstances, it would take a lot for the bosses to approve a DA entry. Like us, they only saw two probable outcomes—either everyone would perish in a massive IED explosion, or as many as a third of the hostages would die in a close-quarters firefight—the so-called 'one to three survival ratio', the cold, calculated but unofficial guide special forces all over the world use to measure the success or failure of a hostage rescue mission.

I again found myself thinking about the far-reaching impact my death would have. Lisa would suffer emotionally and financially, and my children would struggle for the rest of their lives. But, despite the way the bosses were running the operation, I was ready to sacrifice my life, even for the slim chance of saving some of the hostages, a group of people that I'd never met. But I was just as willing to die for my mates, the boys next to me in the stack. Men with nicknames like 'Big Tits' the body builder, 'Carrot' the redhead, 'Big Hands' the breacher, 'Big Bernie' the Lebrichaun, 'Atts' the sergeant and 'Mad Dog Pauly' holding the heavy shield trusting me to engage the terrorist without hesitation. And of course, there was 'Gus', and all my other mates including 'Baboon', 'Baby-faced Guesty' and 'Lucky' running in with the Bravo team. I put these thoughts out of my mind and concentrated on the job at hand—as I was trained to do.

Around 8.00 p.m., the lights inside the café were unexpectedly switched off—from the inside. This created greater visibility issues for our snipers and it immediately put us at a ▆▆▆▆disadvantage as the café was in darkness and our position outside was well lit. The terrorist would clearly see our team in silhouette, especially if we attempted an entry.

At 10.15 p.m. the terrorist forced a hostage to contact police negotiators. He demanded that the street lights on Phillips Street and the Christmas lights in Martin Place be turned off. This would obviously be to our advantage, but an hour passed and they were still on. "How fuck'en hard can it be to turn some fuck'en lights off? He wants it done and so do we," I said in an exasperated tone.

"Shit happens … but not when you want it to," Pauly cryptically replied. God knows what he meant but I somehow felt reassured by him saying it.

"I need to see this one out Benny. Don't you man?" Pauly continued with a determined look.

"Bloody oath I do. We've been here nearly 15 hours, but I could do another 15 if I had to." I'd clearly developed a protective attachment towards the hostages especially after observing them so closely earlier in the day. This was personal.

It was just past 1.00 a.m. on December the 16th and the street lights were still on. How would the terrorist interpret this? He must be infuriated—just another of his demands not being met, just another direct challenge to his ebbing control of the situation, just another humiliation.

As 2.00 a.m. approached, something came in over the police radio. It was senior command assuring us that 'things were settling down for the night'.

"Settling down for the night? Settling down for the night"? I said out loud twice because I couldn't believe hearing myself say it the first time.

"What the fuck do they think is happening in there? That he's slung a fucking hammock and is having a little fucking nap or something," Pauly said with genuine confusion in his eyes.

"How can they think that? So, he's just going to wake up all fresh in the morning and clock back on to his day job as a fucking terrorist?" I said shaking my head.

Our entire front-line team was frustrated beyond words. There was also a general feeling that we'd soon be swapped out with standby operators or the out-of-State boys. Then the battery in my police radio went flat. This added considerably to my frustrations. I couldn't see inside the café and now I wouldn't be receiving radio updates. But I thought to myself, it didn't matter anyway because senior command believed that the situation was 'settling down for the night'.

Then *Boom*. "What the fuck was that?" yelled one of the other operators from behind me in the stack.

Pauly called out, "Shot fired, shot fired."

"That was a fucking shotgun going off inside the café. Oh fuck, the hostages!" I yelled.

Tiger! Tiger! Tiger!

"Alpha team prepare to initiate the EA," Atts yelled. The lives of the hostages were now in the hands of the TOU alone. "Ready yourselves boys, we're about to go in."

Then the unexpected. "Bloody hell, take a look at that, fellas," Pauly gasped, pointing ahead of us. A male hostage was sprinting down Phillip Street, wildly flailing his arms in the air, all the way to the police barricade. He then threw himself face down on the road in front of GDs officers and battalions of massed television cameras. "Fuck me dead fellas. You don't see that every day," Pauly added. All the boys nodded in agreement.

Then, relaying a frantic police radio message, Atts called out, "Six hostages have escaped from the elevator foyer and the Tango fired on them." I felt a surge of adrenalin. I allowed it to fill my body without resistance. This was it. It had to happen. I began to rehearse the entry over and over in my mind, just like I did in motocross, waiting for the gate to drop, powering off the line and manoeuvring to be first into the corner. Our only hope was to get in quickly and shoot him before he set off the bomb.

Picture postcard images flashed before my eyes in a kaleidoscope of hugs, laughs and kisses—our daughter's first steps, her first tooth and the day she first called me 'daddy'. But then an imaginary blinding pulse of hot light invaded my brain like a tormenting spectre. The blast rolled like a crashing wave, leaving a shadow world of charred and dismembered bodies in its wake—Gus, Pauly, Atts, me, and the rest of my mates in both entry teams. I forced it out. I braced, ready to go. We just needed to hear those three words and we'd charge in without hesitation. But nothing happened.

"Sarge, why hasn't the EA been initiated?" I asked in complete disbelief. Pauly just looked at me. The situation was beyond the need for him to respond with mere words. Things would escalate rapidly. It was just a matter of time. There was no question in my mind of that. But then minutes went by in excruciating slow motion—like the drip of a tap.

Boom. Another shotgun round went off inside the café.

"What the fuck is happening in there?" I said out loud. "Is he executing hostages?"

It took every ounce of my strength and discipline not to break rank and run in. I was like an over-wound watch spring. "Just give us the order for Christ's sake," one of the younger boys in the stack yelled.

"Hold!" Atts roared.

Another hostage burst from the café—a young woman wearing a Lindt Café uniform. I recognised her as the one serving drinks earlier. She sprinted out onto the street before heading straight towards us. We pulled her to safety and again refocused on the front door. Pauly was rocking on the balls of his feet. And then I noticed that I was too.

"You've definitely got my back, don't ya Benny?" Pauly said turning to look directly at me.

"You know I do; I've got 'your six' man."

"Mate, I just needed to hear it from you before ...."

"It's been great knowing you Pauly you mad bastard."

"I love ya Bro," Pauly replied, pulling the ballistic shield hard into his chest.

"Me too mate."

Boom. A third shot went off inside the café. I felt the blood pulsing in my ears. Over Att's police radio, I could hear, "Hostage down, white window two. Repeat, hostage down, white window two." I checked my ▮▮▮ laser pointer and light source one final time. With a single sharp slap of my left palm I confirmed that the magazine of my M4 was firmly seated. I was completely focused. My breathing slowed. I stared at the entrance door just waiting for the code word.

Then it came. "Tiger! Tiger! Tiger!"

Pauly stepped off with me right behind him. He moved surprisingly quickly considering the weight of the shield. We sprinted as a team along the dimly lit, weathered concrete footpath towards the café's front doors. *Boom. Boom. Boom.* Three rapid-fire shotgun blasts cracked the still night air and echoed off the surrounding tall buildings. It was the boys shooting out the window closest to the loading bay as they prepared to create a diversion with their stun grenades. We came to the end of the wall, before a slight left turn, now facing the double glass entrance doors. Pauly had the shield up to his face, peering through the viewing port. I stepped off the footpath and onto the entrance landing to Pauly's left. I activated my light source and laser, before staring into the café.

At first it was pitch black and silent. I struggled to see through the glare bouncing back off the glass door. I strained my eyes, scanning the room with my light source in deliberate sweeping arcs. Then, in the far back corner, in his favoured position, I spotted him—his white shirt catching the light. I flicked the safety catch to fire.

The terrorist, still wearing his backpack, was looking across the café towards where the boys had unsuccessfully attempted to shoot out the first display window. The building manager wasn't aware the café had once been a bank and the external windows were all bullet-resistant. Noticing my light source, he turned to face me. Our eyes met for a second time. The dripping tap of time slowed to an almost complete stop. I was ready to take his life.

He swivelled his shotgun at the hip and angled the large-bore barrel straight towards my face. (Louisa Hope and her mother Robin were positioned on either side of him as human shields.) At that precise moment, I saw the red dot from my laser pointer on the upper left of his chest, just where I wanted to place my first 5.56mm round. I paused, calculating, restrained.

In my peripheral view, Big Hands the breacher carefully aimed his shotgun downwards towards the glass entrance door. I pushed myself up against Pauly's back and behind the shield to lessen the expected blast impact to both of us. The ballistic shield would afford little protection from a confined explosion—I knew that—and so did Pauly. I applied gentle pressure on the trigger, taking up the final millimetre of slack.

Boom. The breacher's specialised round shattered the safety glass into a million tiny pieces, cascading downwards in front of me like a slow-motion waterfall. I could now see without the glare, as my rifle's light source beam deflected in darting, dancing shafts around the room, refracting off the café's chandeliers. At that point, the terrorist was a mere 15 metres away but, in the dark, it felt a lot further. He had lured us in, but I was ready for him. Without looking away, we locked eyes for a third time. I squeezed the trigger. *Bang.*

As my rifle restabilised, I could see the laser on him again. I squeezed the trigger. *Bang.* Then, incredibly, with two rounds in his chest, *Boom,* a huge muzzle flash appeared as he fired on our position. Remarkably, I wasn't hit. Someone yelled, "Man Down. Man Down." Where was Pauly? He wasn't in front of me anymore. Was he dead? I had to block this out and focus entirely on the target. I continued my deliberate advance on the terrorist at a fast walk, now on my own, while rapid-firing on the move.

Bang, forward, then *Bang* and *Bang* again. He was the only threat. Again, *Bang, Bang, Bang* in controlled trigger squeezes reassessing as I was trained to do between every shot. Then my foot hit something. I stopped moving forward. It was the entrance barrier counter, but I couldn't take my eyes off the target, otherwise I'd have continued to walk right up to him. I knew I was hitting home because I allowed my rifle to stabilise between every shot and I clearly saw the laser pointer on his upper chest before pulling the trigger again. I couldn't see blood at that distance. His position hadn't changed. The bastard wasn't going down.

Suddenly, again, somehow, *Boom*, another huge muzzle flash from his end. In that split second, I became acutely aware of being alone and completely exposed. I flexed every muscle in my body and squinted in anticipation of the maelstrom of lead that I fully expected would tear me apart. I knew it was hard to miss with a shotgun at such close range. In an instant, I'd gone from adrenalin-soaked fight mode to being convinced I was about to have my face blown off. Somehow, he missed again, hitting the wall just above me. But where was Pauly? Where was Atts our sergeant? Were they hit? Who was the 'man down'? There was no time. I needed the threat neutralised. I needed him dead. I couldn't allow him to detonate the bomb.

I saw my laser on his upper sternum and squeezed the trigger again, *Bang*. Incredibly, he still didn't drop. I reassessed, tracking up with my laser pointer to his neck and then to the middle of his head, right between his black eyes. *Bang. Bang. Bang.* His legs appeared to buckle beneath him or was he just taking a knee to keep firing? I couldn't be sure. From just inside ten metres I followed him down with my laser pointer and continued to fire. *Bang*, assess the threat, *Bang*. He collapsed onto the large square floor tiles and lay motionless. I stared closely at his body waiting for any movement—a groan, a jerk, a writhing, the slightest twitch—anything that resembled a final attempt to detonate the bomb. My finger was still on the trigger ready to fire again. Was the 'dead man's switch' about to activate? Was this the last moment of my life? A single drip of the tap was suspended, motionless, hanging in mid-air.

Then I heard stun grenades going off behind and around

me. *Ka-boom. Boom. Boom.* One jumped off the ground and detonated right next to my left ear. My head spun and my ears were ringing, but the pain also snapped me out of my stare trance. Time resumed. "Stop throwing the fuck'en stunnies, the Tango is down, the Tango is down," I screamed. The explosions stopped. My full attention returned to the target.

Someone entering my peripheral vision. Thank God, it was Pauly. His shield had been struck by a shotgun blast on entry, the impact forcing him back and, with that, the other full-length glass door panel exploded, momentarily forcing my mate to crouch under the sheer weight of heavy glass shards that rained down on top of him. Still reluctant to take my eyes off the threat, even for a second, I turned and quickly moved to the left. There was a cash register and some furniture in my way. I hadn't noticed them before. I walked up behind Pauly who no longer had the shield. He yelled, "With me?" using the acknowledged tactical term that verbally confirms backup without taking your eyes off the threat.

Squeezing Pauly's shoulder, I replied, "With you!"

My light source and laser were still activated and now Pauly had his Glock torch on as well. I lit up the target as Pauly and I advanced the remaining metres, past the second marble column towards him—aggressively, decisively, deliberately. I was fully prepared to fire again.

I stood over the terrorist. He was lying on his side, his entire body in a pool of blood. Part of his head was missing with brain tissue splattered in an arc across the tiled floor. My mind was racing. How were we still alive? I hadn't expected to take more than two steps into the café before the whole place convulsed in a white-hot fireball. Mere seconds before, this man and I were engaged in a life-and-death firefight. His bullet-riddled body now lay at my feet. He was dead and I wasn't. If the 16 hours before the EA was activated felt like weeks, then the past 30 seconds seemed like a lifetime. I flicked the safety catch back to safe.

I now fixed my eyes on the backpack. It was still intact. And so were the wires. In that moment it looked even more like a bomb. Then Pauly yelled, "You have been saved!" I refocused. The hostages were now our priority. We needed to get them out, as many as possible, before the bomb went off. I quickly paced to join Pauly who was on his knees next to a hostage. It was Louisa Hope. She was slumped on the floor with her back up against a leather-covered bench that ran the length of the café.

"You have been saved!" I reassured her, using Pauly's words. The poor woman appeared to be in deep shock, struggling to comprehend our efforts to get her to her feet.

I put her arm around my neck as Pauly and I lifted her together dragging her towards the exit. I could see she was struggling. I glanced down. Her foot was only attached by some exposed white tendons, leaving behind a thick smudge of blood across the tile floor. "Ahhh shit your foot. Are you okay?" I asked as calmly as I could. Pauly asked her if she could hop. She obviously couldn't. Without so much as a whimper Louisa Hope just nodded. We lifted her into a two-person seat-carry and moved towards the front door and onto the street where paramedics were ready to commence emergency treatment.

I took a couple of deep breaths and collected myself before heading back towards the café. I was still expecting a blast at any moment. To the left of the doorway, paramedics were attempting to resuscitate someone. It was a man dressed entirely in black. Then it came flooding back, 'Man down, man down'. I felt like vomiting. I clamped my hand over my mouth, but it wasn't Atts as I expected, it was the café manager, Tori Johnson. He was the 'hostage down in white window two', murdered in cold blood by the terrorist. He was clearly already dead. Feelings of horror and regret started to overwhelm me. Then came the anger. It instantly cleared my mind as the shocking reality hit home. I hadn't been allowed to do my job as I was trained to do and save him. If only we'd been allowed to go in earlier—when the terrorist first fired on the hostages.

A TOU operator assisting a distraught hostage out of the café bumped into me as he passed, forcing me to refocus before I returned to the chaos. The air was thick with smoke. A fire alarm was blaring. The lights had been switched on and the café felt like a completely different place—much smaller, with the harsh light of the interior ceiling globes revealing the full horror of the scene. It was like a war zone, with crying, moaning, screaming hostages being hauled out by operators. There were spent bullet cartridges, stun grenade canisters and shattered glass littering the floor, and blood everywhere.

I returned to the back corner where the terrorist was still bleeding out, close to where I had found the injured Louisa Hope. The sergeant from the other team called out, "Hurry boys. Wrap it up. We need to get out of here. The bomb could go off at any second—check everywhere." I searched methodically. No one could be left behind. I panned the room. A jumble of café-style pedestal tables were stacked up against the back wall. I looked down and, in the darkness, I saw the top of someone's head.

"Oh fuck, no, there's another hostage. Help me, help me!" I shouted to my mate 'Stubbsy' (an ex-British Royal Marine) who was on my right. As we frantically began throwing the heavy, solid wood-topped tables out of the way, the figure of a young woman appeared. She was fair-skinned with blonde hair, tied back in a neat ponytail. The young woman was lying face down into her hands. I reefed more tables out of the way before taking a knee. A puddle of ▮▮▮▮ was on the floor. I looked closer. There were small rips in her black, well-fitting jacket. Were they entry wounds? Was I responsible? I dismissed the idea; the young woman's immediate welfare was my priority.

I needed to urgently assess her physical condition. Carefully, I took hold of her left shoulder and gently pulled her over onto her back. Her head was now resting on my forearm. I recognised her from the profile photograph sent to Atts. It was '38-year-old Katrina Dawson, barrister and mother of three'. Gus was now next to me, but I couldn't look away. Her eyes were open and she was gasping for air. With each forced breath her head lifted slightly, before resting back down again. She then turned her head towards me. I looked intensely into her blue eyes. They were filled with confusion and desperation, the very same look she would've seen in mine.

She was desperate to live, and I was desperate to save her. "Medic, Medic!" Big Bernie screamed from behind me. The young woman stared upwards towards the high, ornate art deco plaster ceiling. I felt completely hopeless. All I could do was will her to force in another breath. Pauly was ready with trauma pads but the situation was beyond that. Then I noticed each breath was getting weaker and further apart. She continued to struggle but the situation appeared beyond help.

The young woman again turned to face me. The look of fear had completely left her and she just gazed peacefully into my eyes. Neither of us looked away. She then strained to get one last tiny breath into her lungs before her head finally came to rest on my arm. The pressure was unbearable. It was the weight of an entire world. It was crushing me. My heart was being ripped out. "Please, please take a breath," I whispered. "Please don't die."

"Move, move over, it's the ambos," said someone behind me as I felt a firm touch on my right shoulder. I slid to my left before carefully placing her head down. I fought against a deep protective urge to return to her side as I watched CPR commence. I stared down into her face as a wave of intense emotion nearly overwhelmed me and the grim reality of the situation sank in. I prayed that the paramedics could perform a miracle, but deep down inside I knew that Katrina Dawson had taken her last breath in my arms.

The sergeant from Bravo screamed out the evacuation code word three times. "Volcano! Volcano! Volcano!" This was instantly repeated by all operators. We needed to get out. I stepped forward calling to the paramedics. "Sorry guys, but we have to go." But they were completely focused on the task at hand and either ignored me or didn't hear. "We need to go now!" I repeated, this time more forcibly. Katrina Dawson was carefully placed onto a white plastic spinal board. Gus and Stubbsy assisted in lifting her while the ambos kept working. I turned and walked out front, clearing a path. "Move. Hostage coming through," I shouted.

We burst from the front door of the café into a scene of utter chaos. There were people everywhere—TOU operators, negotiators, bomb disposal specialists and the Police Rescue Squad. Frantic, yet controlled in their efforts, ambulance officers swarmed around Katrina Dawson, continuing CPR, and setting up intravenous lines. I watched helplessly as she was lifted onto a stretcher and carefully moved down Martin Place and into a waiting intensive-care ambulance.

I felt claustrophobic. I couldn't breathe. I ripped off my tactical helmet and balaclava. I just stood staring at the ground. The evacuation code was called out again but I couldn't manage to acknowledge it or even take notice. Then I felt someone shake me by both shoulders. It was Gus. "You all right man? We've got to go. Ben. Ben, come with me." And with that, he directed me away from the blast zone. At a safe distance, we all stood together in a huddle. "Seriously ▮▮▮, you all good, man?" Gus continued, clearly concerned.

"Yeah, all good," I lied, slowly nodding to reassure him. Then I remembered, "Someone yelled 'Man down. Man down'. Who was hit?"

An operator behind me answered, "Atts copped some buckshot in the face. Got his hand too. He'll live, but he got thrown on his arse."

"Oh fuck, as long as he'll make it," I replied.

"Yes mate, he'll live. He's a tough bastard—like you."

"It was horrific in there Gussy," I continued, rubbing my forehead with both hands.

"Tell me about it. I nearly slipped arse up in fuckhead's brains."

"I can't think of anything else but the hostage, man. It isn't looking good for her, is it?" I said fighting back tears. It was something I'd never experienced before in the line of duty.

"To be honest, no," Gus replied. He was struggling too.

"How many times did you shoot him, you reckon?" A sergeant from the snipers cut in, breaking the spell.

"Couldn't tell you how many exactly, but enough to make sure he couldn't detonate the bomb."

"Good work," he replied.

"Righto fellas, we've all got to go back to the holding area and wait for the critical incident investigators," the sergeant from Bravo advised us.

Every operator on the Alpha team then had their equipment and weapons taken from them. The entire group was directed not to speak to each other about the operation. I sat at a table lost in my own mind, reliving every detail. I needed a cigarette. I hadn't smoked for years but I needed one now. I saw a girl from police media who I knew smoked. "You got a dart?"

"I'm so sorry. I quit but I can see you really need one. I'll get you a pack." The poor girl then had to sprint six blocks to a 7-Eleven and back again.

"You're the best," I said, lighting it up with trembling hands, nearly dropping the lighter. I dragged the hot, heavenly smoke into the farthest reaches of my lungs—and then I called Lisa.

"Hello," Lisa said cautiously, clearly hoping to hear my voice but, equally bracing herself for bad news.

"Hey," was all I could get out.

"So, you're alive then."

"To be honest, I didn't expect to be making this call."

"Yeah, but you're all right, thank God, and that's what matters most," Lisa said reassuringly.

"Yep, I'm alive but not everyone made it."

"Phoebe came around to support me and we've been watching the whole thing on TV," she continued.

"It was so bad in there Lisa," I said, close to breaking point.

"Just come home. I'll be here waiting for you and so will our little girl."

*****

And then I found myself in a parallel universe. Within 24 hours, I'd gone from the Lindt Café human slaughterhouse to my two-year-old daughter's day-care Christmas pageant. The local hall was brimming with festive decorations made by the children. I could see a Christmas tree in the far corner bursting with presents on the promise that Santa would soon arrive. The uncomplicated beaming pride I saw in the eyes of the other parents immediately contrasted with the events in Martin Place: Tori Johnson murdered, Katrina Dawson dying in my arms, Louisa Hope's foot almost amputated, other hostages deeply traumatised, Atts shot in the face and my mates shell-shocked by the extreme violence of the operation.

The children were seated in a semicircle around the teacher as she told stories about their individual exploits during the school year. "Bernie loves to do the hokey-pokey and Kristelle always helps." I was getting the most appallingly gruesome flashbacks. I pictured the terrorist's black eyes, locked with my own, and then suddenly his head exploding. I was losing the battle. "Justine is very good at counting to ten and Andres always shares his little red ball."

I tried focusing on our little girl. She was the epitome of cuteness, sitting with her best friend, holding each other's hands. She was in a frilly white dress with a big gold star, silver sparkly studded shoes and angel wings on her back, her blonde curls held in place with silver butterfly hair clips. By the time it came around for her dance, I was hopelessly lost in my own head: 'Hostage down, white window two', 'man down' and 'Tiger! Tiger! Tiger!'

I felt a gentle tugging at my sleeve. Our little girl was too scared to stand at the front with the other kids. I took a knee and held her close. "It's okay princess, you can stay at the back with Mummy and Daddy and dance here with us." The strain on her innocent little face was instantly replaced with a huge grin. I smiled back at her, looking into her big blue eyes. The Christmas carols started and she began to dance without a care in the world.

I glanced around the room at the other parents. One man was becoming increasingly frustrated that he couldn't get a good position to film his son. A young mother was complaining about the lack of parking and that she had to 'walk five minutes to get to the hall'. Then the music stopped.

As the three of us were returning to the car, I overheard the conversation a group of parents just ahead of us were having—they were all talking about 'The terrorist attack at the Lindt Café'. One of the men started to say, "If I was there, I would've ...."

The Human Fireball
'Man down! Man down! Man down!'

It was 18 months after Lindt; another emergency job—much like many other call-outs—the war on outlaw motorcycle gangs, a siege, the arrest of armed and dangerous offenders, high-risk search warrants (sometimes inside methamphetamine labs in full breathing apparatus) or drug busts (especially where firearms are involved) and increasingly, counterterrorism operations; but on this day, our assignment was a suicide intervention. The TOU were urgently requested to attend a multi-storey apartment block in suburban Botany. 'A suicidal knife-wielding male' had locked himself inside his campervan in an underground garage. The area had been doused with petrol and the POI was refusing to follow police directions.

Our resources were stretched because of other operational commitments. (The Israeli Prime Minister Benjamin Netanyahu was visiting, and the TOU were needed to provide dignitary protection.) Thankfully, we had some SPSU officers backing us up. The SPSU are part-timers based in country and regional areas outside Sydney. They can be GDs police, highway patrol officers and even detectives in their everyday jobs but they have all completed tactical training; when called on, they respond—as they did in the hunt for Malcolm Naden. It was my responsibility to instruct at SPSU training camps as part of my rank. Over the years, I also got to know a lot of them through operational deployments.

I drove our emergency response vehicle, an imposing black V8 RAM, under lights and sirens, with Z, who was our sergeant, Pauly and a new bloke in the back. When we arrived, there were already police cars, ambulances, and fire brigade trucks clustered around. This incident had clearly been running for a while before our services were requested. As usual, there seemed to be a sense of relief from the local bosses when we arrived.

Suicide interventions are on the lower end of the scale in terms of risk to us and, for that reason, we weren't too concerned. Our team had done many jobs like this before—where the operational circumstances were considered too dangerous for GDs officers. The TOU's role in these types of situations saves lives because we have capabilities—advanced training and specialised equipment—that regular police officers don't possess. In fact, most suicide interventions where the TOU are deployed end with no injury to the offender, hostages, civilian bystanders or police—and that's what the taxpayer gets for all the dollars they invest in training us. We casually got our kitbags out as Z gave us a brief rundown on the job. He was a competent and reliable operator, an experienced team leader—as well as a good friend.

"Righto boys, we've got old mate downstairs in a campervan. He's locked himself in someone else's garage and is refusing to leave. He's armed with a knife and there's a strong smell of petrol in the vicinity. Negotiators have been talking to him for a while, but nothing appears to be happening."

"Tactics only then?" I asked.

"Yep," he replied in his typically matter-of-fact way.

"Let's get this done quickly and get back to the gym," I smiled.

Some GDs officers were keeping a crowd of onlookers well back as we followed Z into the underground car park. I gave our inspector a nod as I passed him. The garage was positioned about 50 metres to the right of the front entrance driveway and was a lot darker than I'd anticipated. Police negotiators were standing with the riot squad guys about five metres from the closed steel-frame and security-mesh garage door. We took over their positions. The riot squad have limited capacity to deal with incidents like this; instead, their training equips them to expertly manage antisocial behaviour. They seem to be in the press a lot, whereas the TOU avoid it. Although the TOU manage high-risk jobs, the media insist on calling us the 'heavily armed riot squad'. (I suspect they do this to be patronising, as the riot squad's main piece of equipment is a Perspex riot shield; that and a baton.)

The campervan was parked in the first of three linked parking bays. There was a concrete block wall to the left and the spaces were divided by steel mesh with another block wall to the right. The sliding side door of an old white campervan was open and a man was sitting with his legs hanging out talking with one of the negotiators. The smell of petrol was thick in the air, with a large blanket soaked in fuel in front of the van staining the concrete. The man was smoking but as there hadn't been an ignition, I wasn't too worried. A more immediate concern was the 20-centimetre-long kitchen knife he was holding in his hand.

I positioned myself out of view to the left of the garage with the SPSU operators and the new guy. Z and Pauly went over to the negs. Pauly placed himself in front of them holding the riot shield. (It's the TOU's job to provide negs with protection.) I recognised them immediately. One was 'Sash', a friend of mine, attached to our unit as a full-time negotiator. (A permanent unit was established in the wake of the Lindt coronial inquest. Significantly, they're now not only better trained but also skilled in counterterrorism.) This was her first operational deployment as lead negotiator.

Sash was a country girl in her mid-40s with light-brown hair pulled back in a ponytail and a bubbly, friendly personality. Sash was unusual for a neg in that she trained regularly at the gym and was physically fit. The other negotiator assisting her was my mate 'Matt' from the NSW Police Association, who was also a cop. He was wearing the neg's standard uniform comprising the infamous oversized plain-coloured polo shirt with the strange operational logo, denim jeans and work boots. They were both wearing their bulky bullet-resistant vests. This was made even more ridiculous-looking by their oversized and ill-fitting ballistic helmets.

"You look a little nervous?" I said to Sash, breaking the ice.

"Get lost ▮▮▮▮, I'm all over it," she smiled.

"I'm sure you are," I replied, attempting to be supportive. She and Matt worked together. Their boss, a negotiator-coordinator, was in the field command post set up on the ramp about 50 metres from the garage, together with our inspector and the local area commander. At this point, the negs were stacked up behind Pauly and Z who were about 10 metres from the POI.

"Come on mate, come out of there and we can talk about it," Sash said in a calm and reassuring voice.

"Nah fuck off. You don't care. No one cares."

"You're wrong. I care. All the police here care. We just don't want you to hurt yourself. Please come out."

"Bullshit! Piss off! The boys in black just want to whack me, the fuck'en dirty fuck'en bastards and you don't care ya skanky bitch. There's no fuck'en point in liv'en anymore."

"Don't be silly," Sash continued. "We're all concerned about you, that's why we're here. Please, just open the garage door for us and come out. We'll get you the help you need."

"I don't want *any* help. I'm *not* leaving so go fuck yourself ya mole."

"You can't stay here," Sash continued patiently. "It's not your garage and the owners want you to leave. We can help you, but you need to work with us by coming out."

"I'm not going back to gaol or the nuthouse. No fuck'en

way. So, you might as well just fuck off and die or I'll end it all." The conversation continued like that for a while. This is the way most suicide interventions go—normally just mouthing off, back and forth for hours—and then the stand-off usually ends peacefully.

*****

I began to reflect on other times we'd been short-staffed and we got SPSU backup. The TOU are responsible for a wide and diverse range of jobs, on average between 250 to 300 a year. An essential requirement of a successful mission is to work closely with other units. Aside from our main roles, the TOU are responsible for conveying high-risk and protected witnesses to and from court, escorting large amounts of drugs to be destroyed and even cash escorts from Sydney Airport to the Reserve Bank of Australia. (These cash runs often involve hundreds of millions, and sometimes billions, of dollars.)

Dignitary protection for high-risk heads of state is another role, with the degree of our involvement dictated by the threat level placed on the foreign VIP or diplomat. A US President or Vice President always requires a large-scale response. The TOU provide armed protection for the motorcade through counter assault teams (CAT), which are heavily armed, rapid-response units operating out of armoured vehicles. Sniper cover is also essential with a substantial number embedded in buildings, rooftops, in choppers and, on occasions, on top of the iconic Sydney Opera House. If dignitaries venture out onto Sydney Harbour, CAT teams in water police RHIBs and sniper support are provided.

A motorcade can comprise 40 to 50 vehicles. This requires an immense amount of organisation and cooperation. The visit is planned down to the second. From the VIP's arrival at the airport, police dignitary protection officers dressed in grey suits can be seen talking into their cuffed sleeves, with highway patrol motorcycles blocking intersections and providing traffic control, and Transport NSW (RTA) traffic light operators ensuring a 'green light corridor' for the entire journey. The riot squad controls the crowds, with bomb and rescue officers, explosives detection dogs and specialist paramedics all playing a role. Then there are the VIP protection squads.

I was assigned to a counter assault team, not sniper duty on this occasion, riding in our V8 Chevy armoured vehicle. An ex-American Special Forces soldier, now a secret service agent, was along for the ride as a liaison officer. Our conversations were jovial and we enjoyed stirring up the good-spirited Yank. He was using chewing tobacco (also known as dip), something all their agents seemed to get into, and spitting into a cup. (They told us it was to help them stay awake.) He filled us in on a seemingly endless catalogue of off-the-record stories about US Presidents past and present.

At the time, Australia's terrorist threat level was 'probable' and, as such, we were on high alert. Our intelligence briefing detailed that 15 rocket launchers had recently been stolen from the army and sold on the black market. The concern was that they might have found their way into the hands of terrorists. As our motorcade was en route to the dignitary's hotel, a report was broadcast over police radio. An unidentified man with a backpack, carrying a long dark item, was pacing back and forth across an overpass directly in the motorcade's path.

"The President's limo may be able to take a direct hit from a fighter jet's missile, boys, but I don't like our chances against a rocket launcher in this old thing," the team leader joked, trying to make light of the situation. 'This could be interesting,' I thought to myself. Our snipers in the chopper reacted, flying ahead to assess the threat while more police were urgently dispatched to the area. All we could do was wait for an update.

"Just some poor silly walking up and down the overpass with an umbrella over his shoulder," came the response from the helo snipers. We all just smiled at each other.

'Buy-busts' are another operation requiring collaboration between units. Firstly, detectives compile evidence on the drug dealers or weapons suppliers, usually over a period of months or years. Our involvement begins when it's known that offenders are armed (and most high-end dealers are). Our role is to protect the life of undercover officers (UCOs) and then arrest the offenders. An embedded sniper unit provides extra insurance. The operation often involves high-risk vehicle stops (sometimes ramming cars off the road), street arrests or our teams being physically embedded in a location. One such buy-bust involving a Chinese Triad gang still sticks out in my memory. After the successful arrest, I observed $2.4 million in cash stacked on the table in $100 and $50 notes.

The location for the 'buy' was a McDonald's car park. It was far from an ideal location, but we had to work with it. I was part of a six-man arrest team secreted in the back of an undercover van. It was a tiny, dark space and we couldn't move or talk. It was summer and there was no air conditioning. Beads of sweat were running down the groove of my back. My overalls and balaclava were soaked with sweat, and I desperately needed a toilet break. The drug dealers had been especially cagey and kept messing the undercover cops around, much to our bladder-strained disapproval.

Finally, it looked as if the deal was about to 'go down'. NSW State Surveillance officers had successfully followed the offenders to the car park, providing a running commentary. The police chopper was overhead. As I quietly prepared myself, I got the usual rush of adrenalin that I loved and lived for. An operator peering through the peephole whispered his observations to us. The armed drug dealers were in a black Holden Commodore ute, driving slowly through the car park and approaching the undercover cop's car. I gripped my Remington 870 pump-action shotgun, loaded with ▮▮▮ ammunition. The ute slowed to a stop, pulling up next to the UCO's vehicle. I took a deep breath and waited. Suddenly, the passenger threw a bag into the UCO's car and accelerated.

"Oh shit, he's bailing out," came the call from the operator on the peephole.

"Go! Go! Go!" called the team leader.

The allocated opener cracked the sliding door before aggressively reefing it open. I was third out. After five hours of being in the same position, as my legs hit the ground, they wobbled slightly under me as my eyes squinted, adjusting to the sunlight. I sprinted after the ute with two operators out front and to my right. One was Browny. I focused on the tiny back window behind the driver's cabin. A small target. I didn't hesitate. I racked the shotgun, chambering a round as I ran. I took a sight picture. It was at least 20 metres in front of me speeding away. I couldn't stop running to fire. It was now or never.

Bang. Chung-chung. Bang. Both rounds hit their mark and pierced the small back window. ▮▮▮ gas instantly filled the cabin and the driver crashed into the brick barricade at the end of the car park. Browny glanced sideways at me with a look of surprise and disbelief. One of our 4WD cut-off teams with the police tactical dog on board blocked any potential escape. Confused and startled onlookers were ducking for cover. (Some cheeseburgers and fries didn't make it that day.) I ran forward and, with the assistance of another operator, ripped open the driver's-side door. A cloud of ▮▮▮ gas instantly hit me, and I felt the immediate effects. I pushed through it, ripping the driver from the car and arresting him.

Special Operations Team paramedics (SOT) quickly assessed the drug dealers for injuries before they were handed over to detectives. All units had played their part. The job hadn't gone exactly to plan but, with quick thinking and ability to adapt and overcome, the mission was a success.

*****

Back at Botany, I made a quick assessment and said to Z, "I reckon that garage door will pop open easily ay."

"With the ▇▇▇? Yeah. Good," he agreed. A ▇▇▇ tool is a bit like a builder's jemmy bar, only more medieval-looking.

"It's just the lock and some metal clothes hangers wedged in," I replied, continuing to position myself. It was going to be my responsibility to get the door open when we got the order. The smell of petrol fumes instantly took me back to so many other jobs, like the time an overseas Chinese student dowsed himself in fuel and then lit himself up in front of us. My quick-thinking partner grabbed a blanket and smothered him in it, but even so, the poor guy sustained serious burns. In an instant, I recalled how his hair had melted and the skin on his arms and chest peeled away in fleshy chunks as he was gently hosed down by the fire brigade. And I momentarily recalled the job we did with the taxi driver who wanted to set himself alight and blow up his car and, with it, the NSW Parliament.

Sash continued to patiently engage the POI in the campervan, but it appeared she wasn't making any progress—although he strangely insisted on making comments about the shape and size of her breasts. She looked over and pointed her finger in my direction and, with a wry smile, non-verbally conveyed the clear message, 'Don't you dare say anything'.

A couple of rescue and bomb disposal staff—one female,

one male, arrived to see if they could help. I knew one of them. "You going to need any of our gear to get that open?" she asked.

"Nah. Looks pretty straightforward. But thanks. We can't use power tools anyway."

"Agreed. Good man," she added.

Z ran over the EA to see what I thought. Like Lindt, our EA at Botany included agreed triggers that were ticked off in advance by the bosses. These were effectively our rules of engagement. "I reckon we're going to get permission to go in soon. You got that door sorted ▮▮▮▮?" Z said in his typically understated way.

"Yeah, I'm all over it."

The Botany EA triggers were to be activated if either the man started to hurt himself or he directly endangered our lives. In both cases, we had authority to use our initiative to save his life—or ours, without the normal complex decision-making considerations from above. I liked the plan—it was how we should operate, and Z appreciated my input.

After hours of negotiations—with no result—we finally got the go-ahead. Permission for a 'breach and hold' was approved—a specific order to breach the garage door but not to move in. Situations like this often provoke a response from the offender; normally they give up and come out. We stacked up in our positions to the left side of the garage, mostly out of view, only about five metres from the POI.

"You good ▮▮▮▮?"

"Yeah mate."

"Pauly?"

"Yeah Bro."

"How about you?" Z continued, tapping the SPSU operator on the shoulder.

"Yep ... I'm ready... copy that," he confirmed enthusiastically.

The new guy didn't say anything. I think it might have been his first operation.

"Righto. Let's do it."

I quickly moved forward to the right with my ▮▮▮▮ tool, while Pauly went to the left. I smashed the locks and levered the door until it popped. Dropping the bar, I grabbed hold of the door and began to reef it up. Pauly immediately came to my assistance. Unfortunately, this triggered the worst possible reaction from the POI who jumped back into the van and slammed the door. Then I heard a horrifying sploshing sound and saw a jerrycan suddenly appear through the curtains dividing the front cabin from the back. The man was splashing fuel over the dashboard. This wasn't expected. There had been no indication that he had any more petrol.

"He's dousing the van," I yelled at Z.

"That's not good."

"No, not good at all."

"Shit!"

The SPSU guy was out front on the riot shield. Pauly was next, with me third in the stack, holding the ▮▮▮▮ tactical bar. An SPSU operator was standing in the parallel garage at the ready with a hose connected to a fire brigade truck. Another SPSU operator was behind me with his knife gloves on. The plan was a good one but discovering that the POI had a full 20-litre jerrycan of fuel was a critical development. If we'd known, we would've had our breathing apparatus on, the same as the fire brigade use, but now there was no time.

"Get ready boys. We're about to do this," Z said calmly.

My thinking had completely changed with the situational update. I'd been relaxed—but now I faced the very real possibility of being seriously injured, or worse, incinerated to death. I momentarily thought about Lisa and my girls at home as I did at Lindt. I readied, putting the other out of my mind, rehearsing what steps I'd need to take next. I tightened my grip on the ▇▇▇▇ tactical bar.

"Righto boys, everyone set?"

"Ready!" we answered Z in unison.

"Cobra! Cobra! Cobra!"

The SPSU bloke ran forward with the Perspex riot shield, turning to face the door providing Pauly with cover. Pauly reefed on the van door handle a couple of times without success, before pushing forward. I lined up the window from my position. *Smash.* I got through. It was laminated safety glass, so it needed a couple more hard swings. I paused momentarily, anticipating a burst of water from the fire hose to my right.

Suddenly, there was a blinding flash of light and a massive explosion. *Bwooofff.* I found myself flying through the air, hitting someone or something behind me. I landed on my back a long way from the blast zone—the entire length of the underground garage. I got to my knees, shaking my head, stunned.

Then I saw it. A huge wall of fire—floor to ceiling—everything else was black with thick choking smoke. I could no longer make out where the van was, or where any of my team were. Z was the first to react, appearing from my left carrying an industrial fire extinguisher. I jumped to my feet, and we pushed forward together. The fire was so intense, so hot; it was burning the exposed parts of my face. I grabbed hold of Z's belt with both hands as he sprayed the fire extinguisher ahead of our position in sweeping protective arcs. We were both being rag-dolled by the intensity of the fire hitting us in powerful pulsing waves. Momentarily, I was again able to make out the vague shape of the campervan. Z started yelling, "Get that fucking fire hose going." The SPSU guy moved back into position. I needed the hose to activate to save our lives. He pulled on the lever but hardly a trickle came out, not even as much as a garden hose, just a dribble.

"Bugger!" Z yelled. I looked up again at the wall of fire. There was no way we were going to get through it. I pulled my balaclava up as high as I could but it did nothing to stop the skin on my face from scorching. I could smell my own hair burning. The man in the back of the van was being burnt alive and soon I would be too. "Oh shit!" I yelled, "Pauly's in there." Z started again with the fire extinguisher, but our situation was deteriorating—rapidly. I again plunged into the wall of flames, desperate to get to my mate. The pain was excruciating. There was no oxygen in the air and my body was on fire. I just couldn't push through. The man in the back of the van shrieked in terror. I could hear his blood-curdling scream over and over in what must have been a hellfire nightmare. It was horrendous but, at that moment, there was no way I could get to him and my priority was to find Pauly and the SPSU bloke.

As I collected my thoughts and mustered for a final push, there was another massive explosion. *Bwooofff* then *Boom*. A powerful blast erupted from the van, blowing me back again. The POI had managed to open the sliding door and the rush of air instantly ignited the remaining fuel. Then I saw it. A huge rolling fireball appeared from within the van before rushing straight for us. The immense fireball clipped my right arm on its way past, swinging me around on impact. Z was knocked to the ground as well but quickly recovered. I watched in shock as the figure of the man from the campervan emerged, lying face down, screaming and writhing in agony as Z covered him in white powder from the extinguisher.

Then the whole world turned black. It was overwhelming me. I pictured Pauly being burnt alive as I desperately pushed forward into the flames. With each step, I fought against every instinct of self-preservation. I put my right arm in front of my face and pushed on into the searing blizzard. A figure appeared. It was Pauly, staggering towards me with his hands held out, ablaze. We locked eyes. Flames were lapping up his body and on to his face, burning his helmet. He reached out his hand in desperation. "I'm on fire. Ben, help me!" I grabbed hold of Pauly and pulled him backwards out of the inferno. Then, horror struck. I saw the life go out of him as he collapsed to the ground. At that moment, the past came crashing back. Those critical seconds between life and death at the Lindt Café, where time stood still and the world turned into a slow sepia shadow: it was just Pauly—my shield man and me—facing death, all over again.

I looked for help, desperation crashing over me like a tsunami. Z must have dragged the man to safety and who knows where the others were. I looked down again at Pauly. There were no signs of life. I slapped the flames out on his head and body with my gloved hands and grabbed hold of his vest. With all my strength, I dragged him in the direction of where I hoped the exit was. The only light was from the fire. Everything else was black. Pauly was a big lump of a man and now a dead weight. Adrenalin was still surging through my body; I couldn't get him out quickly enough. I needed help—now. I bellowed as loudly as I could while continuing to drag him.

"Man Down! Man Down! Man Down!"

Then, out of the toxic smoke Z appeared. He stopped beside me and looked at Pauly before glancing back. He was shocked too. Z took hold of the other shoulder strap and we dragged Pauly together. As we did, I saw my mate's head bouncing face down along the concrete. I shouted to Z, "Pauly's gone." Rays of sunlight started to appear from the exit. I pulled harder.

Suddenly we were free of the smoke and into a scene of utter chaos—as Lindt had been. I looked around, my singed eyes adjusting. I saw a group of ambulance officers working on the POI. I walked over and let rip. "Hey! Come over here and help my mate—not that gronk. I mean RIGHT NOW!" Two of them immediately attended to Pauly. I didn't want my worst fear realised so I turned away and tried to take in some fresh air. That was when I felt my lungs. They were burning with every breath in and out, but that was of little concern to me now.

I blinked in total disbelief—like waking from a nightmare. Pauly was up, well, sort of. He was on his hands and knees with a fire brigade officer gently hosing his face. How could this be? I walked back and knelt, placing my arm around him. Chunks of skin were falling from his face. Our inspector looked down too. The TOU are a tight-knit group who care for each other— as good mates should. I'm not a man who often shows emotion, but I was nearly overwhelmed with relief. Pauly looked up at me, "Fuck me Benny, that was hectic."

"Tell me about it bud, that was totally fucked up."

He turned to look at me. "Be honest with me mate, is my dial gunna be alright?" Parts of his face still had skin attached; other parts were flapping loosely.

"Yeah man, she'll be right," I said in my most unconvincing but reassuring voice. It was an emotional rollercoaster. At first, I was sure Pauly was dead, then he was alive but with his face badly damaged. Pauly was rushed to hospital. I waited with Z as the ambulance sped off. We just stood there, silently, until fire brigade officers broke the spell, running their hoses into the garage in full breathing apparatus. "That would've been nice to have on," I said as they ran by, adding, "It looks like you've got your fire hose working now ay fellas."

"Shit happens," Z added philosophically.

I started to repeat something Pauly had said at Lindt, but then stopped myself. 'But not when you want it to …'.

Then, out of the darkness came the new bloke. The fire

hadn't even been extinguished and toxic black smoke was still billowing out of the entrance driveway. He was attempting to carry all the equipment by himself. Z and I just looked at each other and laughed out loud. God knows where the new bloke had been. Pauly and the SPSU operator had been at the front of the van, trapped on the other side of the wall of flame. Pauly bravely rallied the two of them to run through the towering furnace. As they did, he was smashed by the second blast. Thankfully, the SPSU guy was safe, sheltering behind the shield. Sash was okay. Matt too. Matt had helped Z drag the POI to safety.

"Your lungs sore?" I asked Z who was coughing violently. "Mine are killing me."

"Yeah, mine too. We'd better get checked out," he replied. We finished loading up and got a lift to hospital with the inspector.

"Boys, when that explosion happened, I thought that was the last time I'd see any of you, for sure. It nearly knocked us over and we were more than 50 metres away."

"Yeah. I thought we were all fucked," I said agreeing with the boss, but being a bit more technical.

"After the explosion, there was nothing but smoke. I couldn't see anything. There was no way any of us could get to you," the inspector added apologetically. "Then there was that second explosion, what was that?"

"That was when old mate got his van door open. That's the one that got Pauly I reckon," Z replied.

The inspector continued, "Big day at the office ay boys. You all good?"

I looked at Z. "We'll be right, better than Pauly anyway."

The acting inspector was one of the boys. He'd been working in teams with us for years. I could tell that he was rattled as well. I've never been in his position, seeing something happen to your mates at a distance and not being able to do anything about it—and I never wanted to be. The snipers must have felt the same way at Lindt as we made entry.

We arrived at Saint George Hospital Emergency Department. The triage nurse was expecting us and ushered Z and me into separate treatment rooms. I was frustrated because I thought I was fine and just wanted to check on my mate's welfare. As I sat on the trolley waiting for the doctor, I couldn't stop seeing flashbacks. The explosion, the wall of fire, Pauly suddenly appearing, with desperation in his eyes, and then the flashbacks to Lindt—again and again and again, with the seemingly perpetual memory loop of Katrina Dawson dying in my arms. I tried to block it out but it just wouldn't leave me. The doctor walked into the room, momentarily snapping me out of my dark daydream.

He began by asking me details about the incident. I answered his questions but insisted I was okay and just wanted to go and see how Pauly was.

"We need to check you out first."

"My lungs hurt when I breathe in. It might be smoke inhalation or something, but I'll be fine," I said.

"Were you close to the flames?"

"Yeah. I was in the fire numerous times."

"You need to be very careful. If you breathed in the flames, blisters can form on your lungs and burst during the night and then you'll choke to death on your own blood." (He now had my complete attention.) The doctor wouldn't let me go until he knew that I'd have someone closely monitoring me during the night. When I told him that my wife was an emergency nurse, he was reassured. I could leave to see Pauly. Conveniently, Z left his medical assessment at the same time, and we were escorted to where my mate was.

I heard him before I could see him. Pauly was always

loud. Two of the boys from work, Robbo and Immo were there with him. His face was wrapped up like an Egyptian mummy, but it didn't stop him from yelling and being inappropriate—perhaps it was the morphine—then again, perhaps not.

"That you Benny?"

"Yeah mate, I'm here."

"What the hell was that, ay? Never experienced anything like it. You know they put that dickhead two beds up from me."

"Seriously?"

"I tried telling them that if they didn't fucking move him, I was going to kill him."

"You know you're yelling don't you mate? It's a wonder you can talk at all, bandaged up like that." Some people might call my mate a bit rough, but Pauly was a loyal friend, a skilled tactical operator, and a brave man—and that was what mattered to me. We stayed by Pauly's hospital bed. He was the centre of attention, just the way he liked it. We subconsciously formed a protective perimeter around his bed. Then Pauly's wife arrived. I felt for her immediately. She'd been through a lot as the partner of a TOU operator, just as Lisa had. I said my farewells.

"Cheers Benny, you've always got my back. Love ya bro."

"I'll always be there for you, you know that Pauly. See ya big fella. Look after yourself." I knew he was getting the best care and there was nothing further I could do, but it was hard leaving him after what we'd just been through.

I finally found Lisa. "Ben. Are you OK?"

"Yep."

"Is Pauly OK?"

"He'll live. His face is burned up pretty bad. We'll just have to see," I said in a low voice. Poor Lisa kept trying to get me to talk but I just couldn't. I looked out the car window for the entire way home. I was trying to bottle it up, as I'd done with everything in the past, but I knew my emotional cup was about to overflow.

That night, I lay on the couch at home in my own disturbed shadow world. Lisa and the two girls were asleep. I was watching something on television in the dark trying to distract myself from my racing thoughts, but it just wasn't working. My phone buzzed. It was a long text message from Pauly's wife. "Ben, I appreciate you always being there and looking out for my Pauly, but I'd really like it if you two didn't work with each other ever again. You and Pauly are always in such massive shit fights, and I don't think I can take it anymore."

I was a shit magnet. I knew that. And the truth was—I loved it. I'd been on most big jobs the TOU were involved in. I was always the operator who pushed forward to be right amongst the action. (Pauly and Gus were the same.) I had a reputation as the bloke you wanted around when 'the shit hit the fan'. I could handle myself well under pressure and then do whatever was needed to be done. I was the man who could be depended on to pull the trigger. But suddenly, I was aware of the cost of this to everyone around me. I understood. I read the text again. She was deadly serious—Pauly and I really had been involved in too much together. There had been hundreds of situations where we put our lives on the line, Lindt, of course, and now this. I replied, "I know where you're coming from. You're right. Unfortunately, I can't say there won't be more but I promise to always be there for him."

"Ben. I suppose that's the best that I can ask for. Thank you," she texted back. She then innocently signed off with a smiley face emoji. I just stared at the screen. The job had hit home. Even with all my training, experience, and confidence, I was now painfully aware that eventually there was always a price to be paid—and not just by me.

Pauly was wrapped up for weeks but, amazingly, it barely seemed to affect him. (Admittedly, my mate had a rough head to begin with.) The man in the van somehow survived and my lungs eventually got better. But I'd just been exposed to too much trauma. Like my childhood pony Tarago, the sturdy creature with a good temperament, I had my limits too.

I never let anyone know about the flashbacks, the nightmares, my racing heart, and the constant pains in my chest that started after Lindt. I was a highly trained state asset and an experienced and reliable professional. I denied it to myself as best I could. Physical injuries were one thing—like when I was a kid, but this was very different.

One day at work, one of the junior guys asked me about 'Botany', and I nearly broke down. I had to get up and walk away. The only time this had happened to me before was at Lindt. I was tough, too tough for emotions. Or so I thought. I went on like this for another four years—more Thornleighs, more Botanys, more danger, more trauma, more human suffering—with Lindt always hanging over me.

The Nuthouse

We'd just moved to our little piece of paradise south of Sydney. It was my youngest daughter's Peppa Pig-themed pool party. Many of my TOU mates and their families came too. (We might've been tough SWAT cops but, we were also skilled in changing nappies and tying ponytails.) A lady in a pink and red velour costume had my two-year-old convinced that she was in fact 'the real Peppa Pig' but, not my eldest daughter who whispered in my ear, "Daddy I think there's a person inside."

I got talking to my father. He'd been in excavation most of his working life and I asked for his advice. Near the back boundary of our new property there was a full-length retaining wall made of treated pine sleepers. It was head high at one end. The wall was collapsing, and the area was completely wasted with a Death Valley-like scorched garden bed and an ugly, spikey Date palm. "I want to pull this wall down and dig all the dirt out so I can make an entertaining area next to the pool," I said to my dad.

"Hmmm, okay," he replied, looking the area up and down.

I continued, "But, I've got a little problem. I can't figure out how to get all the dirt out to the street so it can be taken away."

"Hmmm," he said again, as he walked around evaluating the project. "To be honest young fella, there's really no way to do it. Unless you want to crane it out," he reflected, shaking his head.

Early the next morning, I started to dig. Over the next six months, every day off work, I was back out there from first light until after dark. I even took a month's annual leave to get it done (and went through three shovels). A man came to the front with an excavator and dump truck, hauling away 67 tonnes of dirt and clay. He shook his head when he found out how I got it all out—by wheelbarrow.

"What do you think of my progress?" I asked Lisa one day.

"To be honest Ben, I feel like a single mother with you out there digging all the time. Do you think you might have a problem?" Lisa said to me, annoyed but genuinely concerned at the same time. She was of course right. I did but, I was nowhere near admitting that to myself. (The digging was only the start of the project, which took over two years to complete, beginning with facing the challenge of excavation, to laying foundations, to reconstruction using the best materials and methods available.)

I mostly worked on my own, although I did have occasional 'moral support' from my old pensioner mate Bill. Bill had a sad story. He was an ex-heroin user who had spent most of his life in gaol. We were the odd couple—friends— the cop and the ex-crim, a genuine 'school of hard knocks' character who was trying to make up for bad decisions and lost time through good deeds. The truth was that I had to stay busy to distract myself from constant flash backs—and not just the usual 'head noises' from Lindt.

The constant exposure to violence and suffering had taken its toll on me. Seeing a dead body is one thing but, experiencing the brutality of someone inflicting extreme violence on themselves or others, or dying in front of you, is many times more traumatic. The theatre of my imagination now featured hundreds of horror scenes that played over and over the moment my focus on physical activity waned.

It was around this time that Lisa and I got married on the sand at our local beach under a huge arch decorated with wildflowers. Our two girls were dressed like little angels in frilly white dresses. Our family and close friends gathered to celebrate. My best man Gus had his fractured leg in a plaster cast. Pauly was more than happy to throw him over his shoulder and carry him, much to the amusement of my other TOU mates. Festivities kicked off straight afterwards in the surf club. Lisa, with her love of music, had hired three separate live bands that played into the night. It was so much fun and a reminder of the way I used to be.

*****

It took another work-related injury, to my left knee, requiring a third round of reconstructive surgery, to force me into facing some hard truths. "As difficult as this may be for you to hear Ben, you're going to have to find a new career. I break the same bad news to professional rugby league players all the time," the orthopaedic surgeon told me with a hint of genuine concern in his voice.

"A career like what, exactly?" I questioned him.

"One like mine, where you mostly have to sit behind a desk."

"No disrespect doc, but you obviously don't know me very well. That just wouldn't work," I said shaking my head.

"If you weren't so young Ben, I'd be putting a knee replacement into you right now!" the doctor continued, now speaking in a more serious tone. I wasn't even 40 years old. I took this advice in my usual way—as a challenge. I'd prove him wrong and get back to operational duty in no time. I'd done it before.

After the surgery, there was a long period where I couldn't distract myself with physical activity. The knee just wasn't getting better, and I had too much time to think. An ex-police rescue mate of mine who had struggled with PTSD believed I had it too. I denied it immediately, telling him he was dreaming. He didn't give up. I casually mentioned our conversation to Lisa. "We can't go on like this any longer Ben. You need to do something!" she said with an urgency in her voice I'd never heard before.

"You're serious, aren't you?" I said, knitting my eyebrows in a concerned frown.

"Very!" she said, staring intensely at me. Lisa had had enough. And I knew she was right. I'd shut her out. I was emotionally numb. Nothing made me happy. I was always on edge, ready to explode. I'd just thought, or at least hoped, that I might've managed to hide it better.

I really didn't have any time for 'shrinks'. This was a result of the off-target predictions about Malcolm Naden and the Lindt terrorist and of course the box ticking 'well checks'. I struggled to see how they could relate to me and my operational experiences. How could they offer me any real advice especially from something they'd only ever read about in books? After Lindt I'd agreed to see someone under the employee assistance program, but it wasn't a good experience. At the time, I outlined to the blonde, fair, 30s-something psychologist how much the Lindt operation had disturbed me and described my worsening symptoms: chest pains, extreme hypervigilance, flashbacks, and nightmares.

I also confided in her that every time I saw a blonde, fair, 30s-something woman on the street, or anywhere, I was instantly convinced it was Katrina Dawson and then, my heart felt like it was going to explode out of my chest. (There was a woman fitting this description working downstairs in the ███████████████ that I saw daily for years; and every time I did, I had a well-concealed panic attack.) I'd also constantly picture random strangers being shot and bleeding out in front of me. As a result, I'd always have my hand resting on the grip of my Glock, ready for the next firefight.

After a few sessions—which was all the police normally provided funding for—the psychologist said, "Okay, so I think we're pretty much done here. I'll give you a call in a week to see how you're going." The police would've approved more sessions, I'm sure of that, but nothing happened. It seemed the psychologist just couldn't be bothered filling out the paperwork—so I didn't return her call; and that was that. This time, however, I decided to consider the option. The reasons I gave myself were to please Lisa and get my mate off my back. I took a phone call from the new psychologist who explained that there was no pressure and that I could come in and see her anytime. I put it off for another two weeks before I booked an appointment.

I was greeted in the waiting room by a kindly-looking, chestnut-haired, middle-aged, Italian-Australian woman. Her name was 'Angela'. She was tall and lean and was wearing a modest ankle length dark dress complimented with makeup and jewellery. I was surprised by the contrast with her consulting room. The carpet was a weird blue colour clashing with two dark green single leather couches. There were no pictures on the plain white walls—just hangers—and no natural lighting. Instead, the room was overly lit by naked fluorescent ceiling tubes that reflected off a harsh glass-top computer desk. Next to one of the chairs was another glass side table with an extra bright crane light that would've looked more at home in a dental surgery—or a torture chamber. There was a black steel-framed fake timber bookshelf on the back wall with some mindfulness books randomly strewn across it, a stack of mismatching pillows and blankets and two artificial plants, jammed side by side, one in a Fanta-coloured plastic pot, the other in a ceramic jar. I felt like running away.

"So … Ben. Can I call you Ben?" Angela began.

"Sure, why not?" I replied adjusting my position in the green chair, searching for a window in the windowless room to look out of.

"I've been speaking to your friend, the one who recommended that we meet," she continued in a caring, quiet voice.

"Oh yeah, did he?"

"So, you think that everything is fine, do you?" she persisted.

"Yeah, all good. I've got some issues, sure but who doesn't in my line of work; just man up and get on with it—that's the way I was raised."

"Could you tell me about your line of work and some of the things that you're talking about," she masterfully engaged me. I pulled up abruptly when I realised what she was doing.

"Look, to be honest, I haven't had a good experience with shrinks … sorry psychologists," I added, correcting myself mid-sentence.

She laughed and smiled, "That's okay Ben. I honestly don't mind."

Somewhat surprised I continued, "So … Angela, can I call you that? Before I go telling you everything about myself, I need you to tell me a little bit about you."

"Yeah, sure. No problem," she replied. I didn't expect that. It was all very personable. I agreed to see her again. As the first few sessions came and went, we developed a rapport that involved a lot of banter. The state of her office was always the icebreaker. We both knew what I was doing but she went along with it anyway.

After some weeks, my level of trust increased, and I began to open-up. I'd managed to bottle it all up—especially Lindt; most people wouldn't have noticed. I could see the concern on the psychologist's face grow as I gained the confidence to rattle off descriptions of operational traumas; it was as if my emotional flood gates had opened—at first a trickle—and then a torrent. At times I felt overwhelmed. There was still no way I could go anywhere near Lindt.

"Ben, this is going to be hard for you to hear, but I want you to consider going into the psychiatric hospital to do a PTSD-awareness program," Angela said in a serious tone.

"The nuthouse? Seriously? I honestly can't think of anything worse. So, you think I'm insane, do you?" I responded in a patronising tone.

"Definitely not, but my professional diagnosis from our very first session is that you have PTSD. Ben, you understand that PTSD is a mental illness, and the result of your long-term exposure to extreme violence?"

"Ha ha, seriously? Nah, I reckon I'm all good. I've just seen some bad shit," I shot back.

"Yes, you've experienced a lot of terrible things Ben," she continued before letting me fill the awkward silence with my next reply.

"Not that I've got any interest in doing it … but what exactly is involved in the program?"

"You'll have to stay in hospital for three weeks and be placed in a small group with five other people who have similar issues. I really think it'll benefit you and your family."

"Look Angela, to put it bluntly, I can't think of anything I'd prefer to do less—sitting around listening to a bunch of people talking about their feelings—uggh. I don't do sympathy well and I don't do victim. It's just not going to happen," I insisted.

"Ben, I'm asking you to trust me. It's not like that at all," she butted in, talking over the top of me. From then on, every session, she brought it up and I gave her the same response.

One day, some months later, I was chatting to Lisa who was now on maternity leave with our new baby. "My psychologist keeps harassing me. She's telling me I need to go into the psych hospital to do some sort of PTSD program. I'd rather torture myself with a *Gilmore Girls* re-run," I said, trying to make light of it.

"Ben, you need to do this. If you don't, you're going to lose your family," she replied unexpectedly. This shocked me. My first thought was that I must be worse than I realised for her to say something like that because, for her, family was everything.

"But, we've just had our third baby. We couldn't possibly do it."

"Ben, it's going to be really hard, for both of us but it needs to happen," she said bluntly. "I never told you this before. Remember when I was in labour, and the anaesthetist tried to get the second epidural in after messing the first one up? I knew something was wrong because I had flushes through my entire body," she explained with a strained look in her eyes.

"Of course, how could I forget?" I replied, shaking my head.

"When the doctors came running into the room, you were pacing up and down. In that moment, I thought I might die but I was more concerned that you were about to go off. I had to call my friend the midwife to calm you down. I know you can't handle incompetence and, since Lindt, you've got a very short fuse."

What Lisa said was true. I was happy and easy going when we first met. Never stressed about anything. Now almost everything irritated me. And so, I was better off staying at home just avoiding people. And Lisa—the life of the party, was going down the rabbit hole with me. I could see the look of trapped desperation in her eyes.

After a sleepless night and a restless drive in, we arrived. I glanced up at the sign, 'Psychiatric Hospital'. As a police officer, I'd only ever put people in the looney bin but now I was about to be a patient there myself. I looked at my three girls. They all adored me, and I did them. After giving my six-week-old a final cuddle, I took a deep breath, much like I would have done in a dangerous operation; I got out of the car and paced towards the entrance. There had only ever been one door harder for me to walk through—to a certain café in Martin Place, six years earlier.

    I was only one step inside the psych hospital before being subjected to a temperature check, mandatory Covid-19 testing and paperwork. I didn't have my Medicare card. Apparently, this was a big issue, and I was made to wait for what seemed like hours. "Stuff this for a joke. I shouldn't even be here," I reacted out loud. My patience was finally at an end. I was about to walk out before realising that this was something I would never consider in a TOU operation. I was trained to move deliberately towards danger, not away from it but, before I had time to spit the dummy again, a clerk miraculously resolved the issue. A patient identification band was clipped onto my left wrist. I was now officially crazy.

    A nurse escorted me up to the level reserved for emergency service and military personnel. After exiting the lift, I followed her past the nurse's station and through the common room. I just looked at the ground, although I did notice exercise bikes strategically placed in each hallway. At the end of a long corridor was my room. The nurse sat at a small desk, and I took a seat on the end of the bed. She handed me the standard care package in a white plastic bag which included a stack of forms and pamphlets, a coffee cup, and a water bottle with the name of the hospital displayed all over it. (It wasn't something I planned on using after my discharge.)

The nurse was in her 40s, heavy set, with serious glasses, dressed in no-nonsense dark blue hospital scrubs. She asked me to give her a brief outline of traumas I'd been exposed to and to describe any physical symptoms I was experiencing. She paused in response, looking up at me over the top of her glasses. "Oh dear, you have seen quite a lot," she said with genuine concern. I just nodded, pursing my lips. "You'll need to hand over any sharp objects such as razors, scissors and nail clippers," she continued.

"Sorry, what?" I replied, puzzled.

"Your razors and anything sharp," she repeated.

"Seriously? And what do you think I might … ." I stopped myself mid-sentence, as the reality of being in a psychiatric hospital hit me.

"And you'll need to give us any chords or leads or belts you have too."

Putting on the inpatient identification band after checking in was one thing but preventative self-harm measures were entirely another. "I think we should finish this later," the nurse said placing the folder down.

"What? This questionnaire?" I said confused.

"Yes, you appear to be getting agitated. I can see that you can't stop fidgeting." I looked down. My right knee was jiggling, and I was clasping my sweaty hands together in a tight ball.

"Nah, seriously, let's get this done, I'm fine," I said unconvincingly.

"Are you sure?" she replied, looking doubtful.

"Bloody oath."

Finally, I was left alone in my room. I glanced around at what would be my home for the next three weeks. It was a tidy space with a double bed and a television. There was also a small balcony. I pushed the glass slider open before trying the security door, but it was welded shut. At least I had some fresh air because, without that, I wouldn't have lasted 10 minutes. The ensuite bathroom had a shower, a sink, and a toilet, with all the handles replaced with rounded knobs eliminating 'hanging points'. I laid back on the bed and closed my eyes, hoping that when I reopened them again, I'd be somewhere else.

I had my first appointment with the hospital psychiatrist. She was a middle-aged Korean-Australian woman with a kind face and a gentle disposition. After an extensive interview, she appeared concerned. "I need to issue you with medication," she advised me.

"Nah. I hate the stuff. I don't even like to take Panadol," I said refusing.

Her tone completely changed, and her expression hardened. "Listen here Ben, you said that you were willing to commit yourself to trying everything in this program; medication is necessary."

I realised that although caring in nature, she was to be obeyed. "Okay then," I said making a necessary tactical retreat.

Back in my room, as I was sitting with my head in my hands, trying to gather my thoughts, there was a knock at the door and a male nurse entered and greeted me with a cheeky grin. "Would you like a tour mate?" He was a short, round, eccentric Maltese-Australian but much more than your average scruffy 'harry high pants'. Rather, he turned out to be a surprisingly free spirit. I liked him immediately and just seeing him around made me feel more at ease.

The hospital wasn't that large, with only four levels but he kept getting lost. The male nurse, or is that 'murse', did however manage to show me the tiny gym, which I was grateful for, as well as 'the art and creative space', which looked as if no one had ever used it. It was at that point that I became distracted by some of the other patients, many of whom appeared heavily sedated; some were visibly shaking. 'Zombie apocalypse' might be unkind, but for me this was a confronting experience. I didn't need to be shown the outdoor smoking section because the penetrating, toxic stink was oozing through an open double door. I was after all, a reformed smoker.

In the only other outdoor section, a full-size mural of a clichéd tropical beach scene was painted across one of the claustrophobic prison-like walls. A jumble of mismatched white plastic chairs made the space feel chaotic. The suffering outdoor plants were clearly neglected. If the area was designed to make you feel more relaxed, then it failed. It made me think, 'How far gone would you have to be for this to make you feel better?'

Laying on my bed, going over the timetable of treatment, I realised it was dinner time. As I walked into the dining room, I searched for a chair at the back but, apparently, I wasn't the only one who suffered from hypervigilance. Settling for a position down the front, on a single table, as far away from other patients as possible, I was quickly losing my appetite. A kindly Pacific Islander kitchen lady appeared beside me.

"You want some soup dear?" she said.

"Yes please," I nodded, looking down, keeping completely to myself. Still, I couldn't help but notice a heavily medicated, heavy-set woman, dressed entirely in black, except for a small Aboriginal flag on her hoodie. She had short-cropped hair and wore a rainbow lanyard and was being led by two nurses to the next table. As I sat awkwardly sipping on my soup, I glanced sideways at her out of the corner of my eye, just as she collapsed forward into her mashed potato and gravy, falling asleep, snorting and spluttering. "I'm done. I'm out," I said out loud, as I pushed my plate away, jumping to my feet and heading for the lift. As the doors closed, I was confronted by the overbearing stench of beer and cigarettes. Clearly, the drug and alcohol detoxification courses weren't going too well. "Are you okay?" a nurse enquired, as I exited on level four.

"Can't complain," I lied, still holding my breath, as I quickly walked to the sanctuary of my room. I'd just started to calm down again when an early 20s-something, pretty-bleached-blonde unexpectedly appeared in my doorway.

"Just doing the rounds," the nurse announced, forcing a smile through her heavily collegian-filled pillow-face lips.

"Oh okay," I said, trying to work out what was going on and also why someone would willingly do something like *that* to themselves.

"Have you had your meds yet?" she continued in a matter-of-fact way.

"No, no, but I'll be there soon, for sure, hundred per cent," I said hoping she'd forget about it—but it couldn't be put off any longer—and as cliché as it sounds—it was 'medication time'.

I was shown to the waiting area and directed to sit in one of four single couches set out facing each other over a coffee table. It was very strange. I just couldn't see the sense of it. A flush of embarrassment washed over me, although the two other patients waiting for their sedation seemed to be enjoying the experience—even excited about it, which totally confused me. In fact, some patients appeared to be in competition, like it was a badge of honour, for how many pills they were taking. It was like saying, 'I'm more damaged than you are because I'm on more medication'. With only three pills in my cup, the others must have thought that I was in the place under false pretences.

The staff were locked in a heavily fortified room with steel bars. A tiny, toughened glass window slid open, my file was checked and a nurse looked up at me. "Oh, you're an easy one—you don't have much at all," she smiled, signing off a medication chart.

"Umm … I suppose I should say … thank you," I said *sort of* sarcastically, forcing back a smile in return. I'd noticed that the two in line before me were served a plastic cup, full to the brim, with caplets, capsules, tablets and wafers of every colour and shape. They looked happy.

I was sitting on my bed in silence, sipping tea from a white polystyrene cup, when I noticed how drowsy I was feeling—it was the medication. Since Lindt, I'd struggled with sleep, but this was an entirely new experience. Even the constant high pitch buzzing from my tinnitus wasn't bothering me so much. I lay back on the bed and looked up, immediately noticing that the smoke detector appeared to be moving around on the ceiling. A gentle breeze blew through the security screen as my eyes closed and I drifted off. Suddenly, a nurse burst in shining a torch directly onto my face. I jumped up out of bed, my heart pounding, my eyes struggling to focus. "You all good?" the nurse enquired, again in a strangely matter-of-fact tone.

"Yeah of course, *why?*" I said confused and startled.

"Okay, thank you," she responded. And with that, she was gone.

I lay still, again staring at the ceiling as my heart rate slowly returned to normal. I desperately wanted to go home but I knew I needed to see it through. 'It's an alternate universe—like TOU selection,' I told myself, but this time it was for my family. As I slowly began to doze off again, I discovered, the hard way, that the nerve shedding 'tick and flick patient checks' were going to happen every two hours. Then, at around 4.00 a.m., I was awoken by a man down the hall shrieking in terror. The nurses were checking on him more frequently.

After the fourth and final check of the night, I didn't jump out of bed. Instead, I felt groggy from the medication and the restless night. The sun was up, and I forced myself into the shower, twisting the weird little knob, only to find that the water was lukewarm—yet another measure to prevent me from hurting myself.

"How'd you sleep?" a nurse asked me, and then the same question every morning after that, at the exact same time; it was like *Groundhog Day*. Then I remembered, something was different—it was my birthday.

The lifts were slow and small and stopped on every level. An old, pastey-skinned, alien-like, completely bald man with blackened teeth and yellow tobacco-stained fingers, wearing a worn-out purple suit walked in. "G'day, how's it going?" he said in a chirpy high-pitched voice.

"Not bad," I deflected, trying to shut the conversation down before it even began. He just stared at me, his entire body shaking. I looked away. There were large 'Where's Wally' posters plastered on all the walls in every lift, obviously for awkward interactions in a confined space such as this and to distract you from your own thoughts. I got right into it.

I walked into the room for my first group session. Several people were already seated in an 'L' shape along the walls with the psychologist and her assistant at the front. There was a small, struggling plant in the corner, a poster-sized photograph of yet another beachscape and a portable whiteboard on wheels. Making their introductions, the psychologist and her assistant both seemed pleasant. The other patients just sat quietly not saying a word.

Although small in stature, the psychologist clearly commanded respect. (At our first session she raved on and on about being into Cross-fit and Muay-Thai.) Her dark, wild frizzy-haired, tanned, and early 40s-something stocky looks, contrasted with the appearance of her assistant who was fair, blond, thin and in her early 30s. She had just finished her degree and was there to observe group sessions. We were told, that as everyone was there to get better, everybody must participate. No one was to go into their personal traumas but rather only talk about their 'feelings' and associated physical effects. (Angela had reassured me that this wouldn't happen; she was going to hear about it when I got out.)

The psychologist then proceeded to lay out the rules. This included writing a list of 'banned words and expressions' on the whiteboard such as, 'all good, can't complain, fine, I'm okay, no dramas and sweet as bro' (for any New Zealanders). We then went around the room and introduced ourselves. There was a dog squad operator, a veteran GDs cop (who had worked across almost the entire spectrum of policing), an army warrant officer, a navy leading seaman, and a random civilian who continuously played with a string of stress beads. This constant fidgeting seemed to consume her. (I never did find out why she was in our group.)

I was the only patient who hadn't attended a similar course before. The others were all overweight. Most had had a marriage breakdown—I was still clinging to mine. There were no smiles and the vibe was flat and sad with the others seemingly caught up in their own private ordeals. I noticed how rugged up the psychologist and her assistant were. They explained that PTSD sufferers felt hot most of the time and, for that reason, she always turned the air-conditioning down for courses. (And I'd always thought that Lisa was the one with the problem.)

*****

Late that same afternoon, I was allowed out to see Lisa and the girls—for my birthday. They had parked around the corner from the hospital so that my seven-year-old didn't see me walk out and start asking questions. I was nearly overwhelmed when I saw the four of them. The weather was cold and windy. We drove to a nearby wharf in the harbour and sat in the car looking at the view. Lisa had baked a cake (with the girl's help). It was sitting on the middle console between the front seats. My oldest girls had made me a card each. I sat awkwardly as everyone sang *Happy birthday*.

We couldn't stay in the car any longer, so we braved the howling gale and walked along the pier to watch the sunset over the ocean. I held our rugged up six-week-old baby girl close to my chest. Our two older daughters ran around chasing seagulls. Lisa and I watched as a large wave crashed, nearly washing a fisherman off the rocks. A pelican stalked its way over to the man's bait bucket as he floundered in the whitewash, helping itself to a fish, before the fisherman finally regained his composure and chased the bird off.

That night, after another awkward elevator and dinner experience, I gave Lisa a call.

"Ben, I think I may have done something silly," she told me straight up.

"Oh really?" I said intrigued.

"I need you to check the bag with your presents in it," she continued.

"Lisa, why? What for?"

"Well, you know that knife we used to cut your birthday cake with—I can't find it."

"You're kidding me?" I said.

"I wish I was," she continued. I looked and there it was, hidden in the bottom of the bag.

"They'd absolutely lose their minds if they knew I had a

large-bladed knife in here—I reckon the whole floor would go into lockdown," I replied, imagining the scene.

"They might call the TOU," Lisa teased me.

"Imagine Gus and Pauly turning up," I answered, seriously thinking that this might be on the cards.

"Oh God, what are you going to do?" Lisa continued, now in a more serious tone.

"I might try and smuggle it out, although if they find it on me, then all hell will break loose."

"I'm sorry—the baby—I'm not sleeping—that must be it."

"I wouldn't worry about it. I'll sort it."

I'd just smuggled a kitchen knife into a psychiatric hospital where the staff panic if they find a pair of nail clippers. I considered admitting the mistake, but I knew it wouldn't go down well. They'd either freak out and blame themselves or think that I'd done it intentionally. I decided to hide it. I really didn't want to have room checks increased to every five minutes.

*****

With each session, I was becoming increasingly frustrated by two patients in the group, although I did become friends with the ex-dog squad officer. He was a good-hearted, knock-about bloke from the country, and we clicked straight away. On the other hand, the GDs guy was just a sad sack revelling in his own misery and the warrant officer obviously loved attention. He was doing his best to make the sessions all about him, constantly reflecting on what he'd learnt in the army's PTSD course, one upping the psychologist about what we were about to learn ourselves. I was at least aware that my symptoms included angry outbursts—and this group was about to provoke one in me.

But despite myself, I was learning about PTSD. I found that I suffered from just about every one of the symptoms, which, in addition to everything else, included feeling emotionally numb, self-blame, lack of interest in life, struggling to ever have a happy thought, negative beliefs about myself, avoiding social interaction, feeling cut off from others, hypervigilance, insomnia, and increasing alcohol consumption; the list went on and on. However, it was my cognitive decline that was really concerning me—feeling exhausted all the time, memory loss and not being able to focus on the most basic tasks.

The senior psychologist could obviously sense my denial, so I was targeted in group sessions and specifically asked to talk about how I felt. She was clever and determined but I just couldn't let an opportunity slide to get one back at her. In one session, she earnestly asked me, "So, Ben, tell me, what would it be like if we made all of our decisions in life based entirely on our emotions?"

I paused for dramatic effect and with a cheeky grin answered, "Then, I suppose, we'd all be female." She gasped, speechless. It was the first time I'd heard the other group members laugh. They all obviously appreciated that silencing her was a major accomplishment.

She gathered herself and with pursed lips replied, "I have to say Ben, I'm using absolutely all of my professionalism not to respond to that comment." As the session ended, the psychologist asked each of us to share one thing that we'd learned.

"Well, I've learned how to trigger you," I said to the high-spirited, universal approval of the entire group. It was gold.

The psychologist paused herself before responding. "Oh really?" raising her dark eyebrows with what I hoped was a hint of a smile.

As we got to the lifts, I said to some of the others, "Bloody hell, she's really going to come after me tomorrow."

The dog squad guy just smiled and said, "You're a braver man than me mate."

Each of us were appointed our own psychologist for individual sessions. This was partially to determine our eligibility to be placed in the 10-week PTSD prolonged exposure therapy course, although I wasn't aware of that at the time. I was assigned the assistant who always wore a black well-fitting business suit and fashionable knee-high leather boots. Her blonde hair was pulled back in a tight, neat ponytail. She asked me to compile a list of traumas and speak about them. As I'd done when I first met Angela I struck first. "So, before we start, could I ask you a little bit about yourself … before I reveal *everything* about me?"

"I'm sure that's not how it works Ben," she politely smiled back.

"Okay then, cool. I'm pretty sure I know enough about you anyway."

"Yeah, like what?" she replied inquisitively.

"I'd say that you're from the inner west of Sydney, you like Indy rock bands and I reckon you only go to hipster cafés," I grinned.

"You are observant, aren't you?" she smiled back. I was right on the money and we both knew it.

"I really can't talk about Lindt. I'm just not ready for that," I said returning to her question.

"That's okay, what about other traumas that you've been exposed to? I'm sure there have been some," she replied in a caring but naive way.

"Yeah, a few," I said nodding. "I jotted some down as you asked. So, I'll start then?" I enquired.

"Yes please," she said innocently, completely unaware of

what I was about to deliberately inflict on her.

"Where to start? A man stabbing himself over and over in the stomach before we ran forward to stop him, his intestines now protruding through deep gashes; another man shoving a knife into his neck, before repeatedly smashing his head and the handle against a table to get it in deeper; a young woman with schizophrenia forcing a butchers knife into her mouth and down her throat; a methamphetamine-crazed man in his early 20s holding his girlfriend and baby hostage, barricading the doors and refusing to let anyone in or out."

And then something very strange happened. I found myself in a daydream, not in the room with the psychologist at all but back in time, as my grandfather had done all those years ago when he was telling the story about his mate in the bomber. In my waking nightmare play list, the young man shields behind his terrified partner, pressing the point of a carving knife into her upper chest while she desperately tries to hold onto their screaming baby. As our stack advances, he drags his partner backwards onto an old couch and holds the stainless-steel blade up against the baby's throat. "Youse pigs come one step further and I'll cut the fuck'en baby's head off!"

We've been called to a job in the Inner-Western Sydney suburb of Enmore. Police have cornered a Russian national who shot his wife in the leg as she tried to get away from him. As we arrive, the man walks towards us holding a loaded revolver. He looks to be in his early 50s, with salt and pepper dark hair and a hard face. I have my UMP40 sub-machine gun trained on him ready to engage. The man is convinced he's going to gaol for the rest of his life. (He obviously doesn't know the Australian legal system as well as I do.) Police negotiators were trying to speak with him from their position behind us. The POI is now only five metres away, waving the gun around wildly. "I'm never going to prison," he yells, and with that, he puts the gun to his right temple and pulls the trigger. *Bang*. He drops to the ground, hard and fast, like a puppet with its strings cut.

Our team rushes forward before I kick the gun away. There is blood pulsing and squirting out of a still smoking hole in the side of his head. Armies places a trauma bandage over the wound attempting to stem the flow of blood, with Gus commencing chest compressions. Bright, frothy blood streams from the man's mouth and nose. I look down at the dead man's face and wonder how much longer the resuscitation attempt will continue. The boys were really hooking in.

"He's brown bread," (slang for 'dead') I say to Gus.

"Not good," my mate confirms, wincing, as he continues CPR.

Then, suddenly, the man's eyes blink, his head lifts off the ground, his mouth gapes open and out comes a mummy-like silent scream as he gulps down a final squelch of air and blood. In Bankstown, I'd seen scores of bullet-riddled bodies, a result of the 'Romeo and Juliet war' between two local Lebanese crime families, although this was different. The horror movie-like resurrection really was next level gruesome.

At a printing warehouse, in South-Western Sydney. There's a 'bikie' dispute over money. Three men return with handguns although they weren't expecting the owner to greet them with an SKS assault rifle, which is very similar to the better known AK47. On arrival, I observe a man lying dead on the ground in a pool of blood. GDs police report that the POI with the SKS is holed up in an office on a mezzanine level with employees still on the factory floor, hiding behind pallets, too terrified to move. After hours of unsuccessfully trying to raise the shooter, we push forward.

Our team take cover behind the armoured vehicle which is driven forward as far as possible. I'm on the ballistic shield with Gus as my cover man. (The small shield appeared even smaller that day.) The only access to the second story is up an internal flight of steel stairs. We request the use of tear gas, deployed by a 40-millimetre ▮▮▮▮▮ launcher but this is declined by the bosses. The risk of the office catching fire and the cost of the clean-up apparently must take priority. The bosses did, however, allow the use of manually deployed CS gas grenades and, for that reason, we had our respirators on. As Gus and I cautiously step up each serrated steel tread, with the stack right behind us, our masks inevitably begin to fog up. I brace for a volley of heavy calibre shots. If SKS 7.62-millimetre rounds were fired on us, the shield would've done little to protect me, let alone our entire team, and many operators would fall.

Noticing that the office door was open, I peer through the rectangular bullet-resistant glass viewing port, draw a deep breath, and take another step. As I round the crest of the stairs, I can see a heavily tattooed man, dead on the ground, in a pool of his own congealed blood, with the weapon lying in front of him. "He's down, he's down," I yell. Part of his head is missing. He's shot himself under the chin and there's brain splashed across the ceiling and walls.

Gus and I do our own on the spot CSI investigation working out that he'd been wearing a baseball cap at the time he shot himself. It's been blown off his head, flipping over and over through the air before coming to rest, right side up, on a nearby table, with a perfectly round finger-sized bullet hole in the top. I'm still reminded of this each time I put on my cap.

The job is a two-day siege in The Blue Mountains west of Sydney. All we're given to eat is one soggy 'three-inch' Subway each. I didn't know you could get one that small—half the size of the miserable six-inch subs we were given at Lindt. (The government and police hierarchy threw money at the TOU after Lindt, rather it was our Kim Jong Un-style dictator boss who is behind the cost cutting catering outrage.) A man has taken his elderly mother hostage, menacing her with a high-powered hunting rifle but, his intention is clearly to provoke us into shooting him—a 'suicide by cop' scenario. He's an intravenous drug user with hepatitis C and terminal liver cancer. The POI is pointing his weapon at our armoured vehicle and screaming out threats.

All the windows have heavy curtains drawn. Darkness falls and we need to know his exact location. Approval is finally given to move forward in the armoured vehicle and use the hydraulic ramming pole to smash out a bedroom window. However, this doesn't reveal his location, so we work our way across the front of the building smashing out every window one by one. The only thing left is the ornate wooden front door. We smash that down too. A large portion of the house is now visible, but we still can't locate him. I'm wary of a similar job I was on in Kurnell, in Sydney's south. Also armed with a rifle, another man intentionally fires numerous times over the top of our armoured vehicle attempting to provoke a suicide by cop response. He then shoots at a TOU operator who carelessly steps out from behind cover. Two operators return fire hitting the man in both hands and in the shoulder.

Back in The Blue Mountains, police negotiators receive a phone call from the POI informing them that he's shot himself in the head. Is his strategy to draw us in? I grab the ballistic shield, hold it close to my chest, and draw my Glock. I activate the light source, now with its unique green laser pointer. The different colour laser distinguishes a pistol in a firefight from a rifle, which uses a red laser pointer. All operators had been issued with new rifles, a Sig Sauer MCX with a suppressor (a silencer). The rifle uses a larger non-fragmenting 7.62mm Blackout round that helps bring a target down sooner without the danger of uncontrolled shrapnel. (These were some of the many NSW Coroner's recommendations the TOU adopted after Lindt.)

I have two cover men, on either side of me. One was 'Translucent', or 'Rice Bubble', so named by Gus because of his unnaturally pale, paper thin, vampire-like skin. The other operator, was 'Hightower', so named due to his height (taken from *Police Academy* movies.) Our team ease out and slowly move towards the ruined front door. The plan is to deploy a remote control 'throwbot' (one of many specialised devices the TOU use). At any moment I expect the man to fire on us. Pulling up on the front balcony, I peer through the large hole where the front door used to be, into a dimly lit room. Unexpectedly, a man's blood-soaked arm emerges out of the darkness, clawing itself along the ground towards us like a damaged terminator. We push in quickly and secure the rifle. The man is bleeding heavily from a wound to the middle of his forehead, but, incredibly, he's still alive and still conscious—and still talking. "I have a fuck'en bastard of a headache," the man groans in pain.

"Of course you do old mate, you've shot yourself in the fucking head—and look what you've made us do to your mum's house," says Translucent. The bullet penetrated the man's forehead and travelled anticlockwise around the inside of his skull before coming to rest at the top of his spinal cord. And it was at that point that I shook myself out of my daydream, much like I do every night around 4.00 a.m. from whatever savage nightmare is tormenting me, drenched in sweat, my heart pounding.

The figure of the psychologist again filled the room. But now I was suddenly and painfully aware of her youth and lack of experience. She looked pale. All her professional confidence had evaporated as she took refuge in the safe harbour of stock standard cliche questions. She readjusted herself in the chair a couple of times, trying to compose herself. "So, Ben, why do you feel this way?" and "Do you think it's okay to think like that?"

At that very moment, I began to question myself. What the hell was I doing? Was I being like the guy in my PTSD group who irritated me so much, always trying to one-up everyone like it was a badge of honour to prove how damaged he was? Surely my situation was different? I hated the idea of being a victim. I just wanted to show her the trauma I'd been exposed to and explain why I was here. Is there anything wrong with that? And then it hit me. I was doing exactly the same thing.

*****

Gus and Pauly had arranged to visit me. They meant well and were just being concerned friends, but I was still anxious about it. The three of us met in a café around the corner because I couldn't bare for them to see me in the funny farm. They were already waiting. We sat down together before looking awkwardly at each other across the table. "So, who's the mad dog now, ay Benny boy?" Pauly said, breaking the ice with his usual lack of a social filter.

"I reckon you've still got me covered mate," I said smiling, glad that he was being himself with me. "But I'll tell ya boys," I continued, "Some people in there even make you look normal."

"Yeh, like what?" Pauly said intrigued.

"Well, there was this one joint group session where a young bird at another table stood up, started looking around, and then the next thing you know her eyes are rolling back in her head. Then, she hit the ground hard and had this mad fit—the poor thing. The weirdo shrink just kept talking and my fellow looney tunes barely seemed to notice."

"Bloody hell, was she okay?" Gus asked in a concerned tone.

"Yes mate. An ex-Ambo lady in the group helped her," I reassured him.

"So, are the shrinks just as mad as the patients?" Gus added, fishing for another story. I told them about one psychiatrist who wore a brown velvet suit jacket with brown leather patches on the elbows, a matching brown vest and what looked like urine-stained brown suede loafers, topped off with Albert Einstein-mad-scientist curly brown hair. I explained that he even wore tortoise shell framed reading glasses. (I was unsure of his eye colour but, I imagined they were brown too.)

"That's one brown bastard," Pauly exclaimed.

"Mad as a meat axe," I smiled.

"Looks like they're feeding you well in there ay ▮▮▮▮," Gus said, looking me up and down changing the subject

"Says Chris Hemsworth," I shot back. For a moment it was like the old days. The boys filled me in on the latest office gossip and I told them stories about some of the other things I'd seen in the looney bin. "So, any decent jobs?" I enquired as the coffees were delivered to the table.

"Nah, not really, not since the official TOU shit magnet flew the coop," Gus said with a cheeky grin.

We spoke together about past jobs, even touching on Lindt, before Gus, looking concerned, unexpectedly turned, and asked me, "▮▮▮▮, who's going to be protecting us the next time there's a shit fight?" I was speechless. It was another issue that I hadn't allowed myself to consider. Pauly was obviously thinking the same thing.

"I guess you wouldn't be any good to anyone anyway with that Rosanne Barr knee of yours," Gus continued, attempting to rectify the awkward silence he'd inadvertently created with one of his off-beat descriptions.

"I still prefer it over your knock knees," I replied. We all laughed together. As I walked up the busy street back towards the hospital, I heard a car horn beeping repeatedly.

I turned to see Pauly hanging out of the window yelling, "See ya Benny, ya mad unit. Love ya Bro."

That night, I lay on my bed with the lights on staring at the ceiling. Despite medication, Gus's words ran over and over in my head. The realisation had hit me—I wasn't going to be there for the boys ever again. And I'd even made a promise to Pauly's wife after Botany that I couldn't keep. The chest pains that I had since Lindt got increasingly worse before turning into a deep throbbing ache. I felt a rush of adrenalin surge through my entire body as I began to hyperventilate and then sweat. My heart was pounding like a sledgehammer to the point where I was sure it would beat out of my chest. I was stricken with panic.

I tried changing television channels to distract myself, but it just got worse. I jumped to my feet and thought to ring Lisa but, I wasn't sure I could dial the number let alone talk. My face was so hot it felt like it would catch fire. After previous panic attacks, I was told, 'I should try vigorous exercise to snap myself out of it', so I dropped to the floor and did push-up after push-up—nothing. I became irrational, no longer in control. Suicidal thoughts washed over me. I couldn't take another second of it. It was as if killing myself was the only solution. I needed to get out of my room before I acted.

I dragged myself down the dimly lit hallway towards the nurse's station, convinced that the walls were collapsing in on top of me. No one was there, they must have been doing their rounds. With nowhere to go I returned to my room. I grabbed two pillows and pulled them into my chest as hard as I could to try and stop the pain. I forced my face into them, screaming and rocking back and forth. Thoughts of killing myself almost overwhelmed me. (Two of my former colleagues had committed suicide.) I must have been like that for at least an hour. If I had a rope, I would have made a noose. Thankfully, I didn't think of the birthday cake knife.

I fell to the floor and started doing burpees. I'd never had so much energy. Yelling out loud, I completed repetition after repetition, raging against the idea of taking my own life. Then I began to feel my heart rate slow, even as I frantically continued to push myself beyond my physical limits. It was my lowest point. There was only one time that compared. It was the day after the Lindt Café siege.

*****

I was at work. An assistant commissioner and the homicide squad inspector running the coroner's investigation summoned the Alpha team into the situation room. The assistant commissioner stood up. "So, gents, I won't beat around the bush. I want to brief you before this hits the media. An autopsy of Katrina Dawson's body has been conducted. It has been identified that the cause of death was the result of wounds sustained from a police bullet." In that second, my entire body flushed with horror, panic, and revulsion. I wanted to vomit. Some of the boys came over and put their arms around me. I knew my mates were talking to me, but I couldn't make out what they were saying. My worst nightmare had been realised. I had killed Katrina Dawson.

An inspector and Pauly walked me to a nearby café

in an effort to console me. I felt just as I did on the night of Lindt when Gus had to physically assist me up the street. I later went to the outside smoking area at the ███████ ██████, withdrew from the world and chain smoked, cigarette after cigarette. The image of Katrina Dawson dying in my arms played over and over.

Some hours later, Pauly interrupted me, "We've got to get back to the office man, the big boss and the inspector from homicide are back again."

The assistant commissioner again addressed our group. "I have an update for you gentleman. Further testing has now revealed that Katrina Dawson wasn't killed by a complete police round but, bullet fragments." Pauly and the boys swarmed around me again.

"Those fragments could've come from anywhere," Pauly said with conviction. "You saved heaps of us bro. And after executing the manager, that bastard was just going to keep shooting hostages." I knew that I should have been somewhat relieved by this, but I couldn't stop blaming myself; and the assistant commissioner's words were obviously no consolation to the Dawson family. It was at that precise moment that the idea I deserved to suffer for what I did started to grow deep roots within me.

Back in my room, there was a knock on my door. "Are you okay in here?" asked the nurse.

"Yeah, I am now."

Every night during the PTSD course, I fought through panic attacks but, I was determined to throw myself into everything with an open mind, and that even included Yoga. As I waited nervously for the class to start, I overheard two female patients speaking to each other. "The hippie lady instructor, from the last class, was telling all the girls to breathe through their vaginas." (This was obviously beyond my biological capacity and mental comprehension) but, one day on the beach, I did try a mindfulness exercise, although I was constantly distracted by the thought, 'What would Gus and Pauly think of me?'

I made a concerted effort to apply myself to the group sessions. When I became 'emotionally triggered', the blonde assistant psychologist appeared to me as Katrina Dawson. The head psychologist noticed that, when I looked at her assistant, I squinted my eyes for a few seconds before reopening them. I was given the challenge to stare at the assistant in class and, over time, I stopped wincing. We developed a good rapport, the head psychologist and me, and eventually I even got used to the constant checks throughout the night as well as waking to other peoples' screaming night terrors. I never did get used to the elevator.

Walking towards the front door on my way out of three weeks in treatment, I reflected on what I'd achieved. Exiting, I looked up and noticed blue sky for the first time in a very long time. Then I thought to myself, 'I definitely have PTSD,' closely followed by, 'I miss my family'.

Katrina, I'm Sorry

"First things first Angela," I said with a smile. "You promised me that I wouldn't have to sit around and listen to a bunch of people talking about their emotions and feeling sorry for themselves."

"Oh my gosh. I know Ben. Sorry about that. I wish I could've been a fly on the wall in the first session," she smiled and then chuckled, barely able to contain herself.

"I nearly rang you, you know. I got in trouble for rolling my eyes at one of the guys in the group who just kept talking about himself. They made me watch and listen to him intently for a whole session after that."

"Was that a good thing or a bad thing?" Angela questioned me.

"Shit no. It was a full on punish," I added smiling.

"You're a classic Ben but admit it, you got something out of it didn't you?" she said, hopefully.

"Well yes, I suppose I did. I never want to go back in there again, and I admit ... I do have PTSD!"

"Finally!" she replied with a huge grin.

"Glad that I can make you happy Angela," I said with an exaggerated eye roll. "But seriously, they want me to go back in for another 10-week program called prolonged exposure therapy—and that just ain't *gunna* happen," I added, shaking my head. Angela explained that, as my traumas were so deeply buried this was necessary if I wanted to learn how to live with PTSD. Thankfully, she came up with a compromise in consultation with my psychiatrist. This involved two-hour long appointments with Angela, twice a week. Every other day, I had to listen to audio recordings of these sessions—and that was essentially exposure therapy. The idea was to repeatedly relive the experience until I could process it as a memory and not just as a locked away emotion. This, however, came with a caution from Angela.

"Prolonged exposure therapy makes you constantly revisit your traumatic experiences. Symptoms are likely to increase at first but, with time and repetition, hopefully you'll be able to recall the memory without the same distress you feel now. But in your case, there're also the added stresses of day-to-day life that can compound feelings of being overwhelmed. I know that you and your wife have a new baby. For this reason, it isn't advised," she said. But I was determined, so that was that.

To begin, Angela and I started talking about the Botany job. As I closed my eyes and recalled every harrowing detail, I was instantly taken back to the human fireball. It was as if I was literally there, reliving every part of the experience: the petrol fumes, the explosion, the wall of flame, the pain from my burning flesh and all the emotions that went with it. After weeks of what felt like torture, in one session, I made an important connection. At Lindt, I was certain that Pauly and I were running into certain death from a huge explosion. Then a year and a half later at Botany, both of us were enveloped by an enormous blast where I was convinced my mate had died, just like Katrina Dawson had, in my arms. The explosion themed nightmares didn't stop—but from that day onwards, they didn't seem as horrific either.

I fought on with exposure therapy—my new challenge. Between sessions with Angela, I also had regular appointments with the psychiatrist. Angela and I even managed to start talking about Lindt. Lisa had hoped that I might've shown some improvement by this stage, but it appeared the opposite. As Angela predicted, my symptoms immediately got worse, especially the constant threat of a panic attack. As a result, I became very anxious about social interaction. One day, Lisa pushed me into meeting up with some non-TOU friends at a local burger bar and I felt one coming on. It was going to hit me like a freight train, so I escaped to the toilets—just in time. When I re-joined the group, a long time later, I offered the feeble excuse of having an upset stomach. Lisa put on a brave face—but it really did ruin what was now a rare outing for both of us.

Through constant and repetitive exposure, I began to recall long-forgotten details from Lindt. Still, some memories were just too traumatic, and my body shut me down through a panic attack. After these rigorous sessions I needed to chase away some demons before getting home to my family. I decided to start riding my mountain bike to and from appointments at full tilt to the point of physical exhaustion. I found vigorous exercise really helped, although Gus did warn me, 'If he ever saw me in Lycra, then we just couldn't be friends anymore'.

After one especially torturous session, I was traveling along the cycle path at what I thought was a great speed. Then, to my right, I saw a shirtless, skinny, millennial hipster with a man bun and a ridiculous Captain Hook-style moustache, twirled at the ends, speeding past on an electric skateboard. This just couldn't be allowed. I attacked the bike and began to catch him. Although sure my lungs were going to burst out of my chest, I finally eased past, glancing sideways at the young bloke with a look of exhausted satisfaction. He had no idea of what I was doing, humming along to some music playing on his single ear pod, looking up at the clouds, without a care in the world.

Another thing that helped with exposure therapy was when Angela suggested that I write things down. Then I read what I had written over and over and over, hundreds of times. However, to complicate matters, I was now in the final process of a medical discharge from the police force. This was a huge issue for me. My identity crisis was as challenging a struggle as PTSD. Being a cop is who I am.

From the very first day, when I threw my hat in the air at the police academy, I never imagined my career would end in a medical discharge. Now, aside from the pains in my chest, extreme hypervigilance, and panic attacks—I was deeply depressed. I started to question my decision to see a shrink in the first place because now my emotional flood gates were fully open. I was mentally and physically exhausted—all of the time.

*****

The truth was that the night of Lindt, with all its atrocities, was far from where the trauma ended for me. The terrorist siege had rocked Australia. Afterwards, there was a public outpouring of grief demonstrated by the thousands of floral bouquets laid out in Martin Place. It was the first large scale terrorist hostage rescue in Australia's history. The Prime Minister, Tony Abbott, NSW Premier Mike Baird, and Police Commissioner, Andrew Scipione, all wanted to thank the 'boys in black' who had run into the Lindt Café and shake our hands. But, after the formalities, everything would be scrutinised during the most expensive and extensive inquest ever conducted in Australia—and of course, there was to be another trial—by media. Innocent people had died, and the press was looking for someone to blame—as they do.

Killing in the line of duty is a life changing experience for a police officer. It has very personal consequences and this is compounded by the pressure of inquiries and investigations. In my childhood fantasy world of cowboy gunslinger shootouts, I was the local sheriff, the quickest draw in the West, facing a band of desperadoes. It always ended in a duel against the leader of the outlaw gang, man to man, good versus evil, facing off and staring each other down, just waiting for one or the other to make the first move. *Bang.* The bad guy got blown backwards, off his feet, before landing on his back on the dusty ground, instantly stone-cold dead, with me blowing pretend smoke from my toy colt revolver, spinning it around my finger and re-holstering. The reality of taking someone's life is, however, very different. After Lindt, I struggled with television dramas or war movies that were essentially dishonest in the way they presented death by gunshot as something clean and neat and emotionally uncomplicated.

I often reflect on the moment I stood over the terrorist's bullet-riddled body. I'd taken his life. He'd forced my hand. I understood that. And after he mercilessly executed Tori Johnson, it was him or the other hostages, or all of us. The truth was that the terrorist took something from me that day. I felt like a different person after intentionally and violently killing another human being—removed from people—even loved ones—often isolated and lonely. I'd spoken to diggers who told me that up close killing was something they'd only talk to other soldiers about. Now I understood that too.

As the 18-month long inquest played out, I tried my best to avoid the frenzied media coverage, but even in our meal room at work, there was always a newspaper laying around and a television on the wall with photos of Katrina Dawson and Tori Johnson constantly aired on news bulletins. The bosses were getting dragged over the coals for the decisions they made on the day although, there was one report of a forward commander, who admitted taking into consideration the lives of 18 TOU operators as well as the remaining hostages. He argued that everyone would have died in a blast the moment we made entry into the café. (The commander was clearly also convinced that the terrorist had a bomb.) He was ridiculed in the inquest and then crucified by the media for his point of view.

Social media was saturated with it. Everyone had an opinion. A lot of advice came from armchair warriors whose expertise was limited to video games like *Call of Duty* and Vin Diesel or The Rock action movies. Then there were even allegations of cowardice or claims that we were either incompetent or not trained to deal with the situation. Inevitably, the conspiracy theorists also came out of the woodwork: 'A government cover-up' or, that Lindt was a 'false flag operation'—made up—fake.

No one, except senior legal counsel, was allowed into the closed court sessions, with ASIO (the Australian spy agency—the equivalent of the American FBI) protecting their knowledge of what happened and their probable involvement. And then there was the question of how and why the terrorist had been allowed out on bail in the first place. The solicitor who mismanaged this even had their identity suppressed or was it the whole NSW Director of Public Prosecution's (DPP) fault and they just found a convenient fall guy? My mates at the TOU thought the same thing: 'Why the hell did the lawyers get a closed court session? Protecting their own kind's incompetent fuck up?' On the other hand, my actions in the three to four seconds that I was shooting the terrorist were broken down into milliseconds and methodically scrutinised—over many months. Ballistic experts, crime scene officers, homicide detectives and a legion of highly paid barristers and solicitors all joined the circus. (I was only allowed in to provide my evidence. I wasn't permitted to see others provide theirs.)

Fortunately, there were just enough people with good things to say, including many letters of support from the public.

One was handwritten by a kindergarten boy who told us that we were 'his heroes' and that, "When he grew up, he wanted to be a SWAT cop too." He even drew a picture with a texta of a TOU operator shooting a terrorist. It reminded me of myself at that age. And, in recalling the innocence of children, I imagined how many so-called 'grown ups' would be offended by such an unselfconscious drawing. A lady's embroidery club even hand stitched a full-size quilt for us. (This is still on display in the TOU office.) And then there were three boxes of 'top shelf' alcohol, addressed to 'the brave boys in black', donated by Australian businessman Lindsay Fox.

I participated in a videotaped walk-through interview of the café conducted by senior homicide squad detectives one week after the siege. I was reduced to tears when I recalled where and how I found Katrina Dawson. And seeing the actual holes from the terrorist's shotgun blasts just above our entry point was a visual reminder of how lucky we'd been. (One of the 12-guage rounds was comprised of larger calibre SG ammunition, which would've taken my head off.)

The autopsy revealed that the terrorist sustained 13 gunshot wounds to his body and had at least two, if not up to four, bullets in his head. Crime scene investigators revealed that Katrina Dawson was struck by fragments from a police round after passing through the leg of a wooden chair. Investigators were never able to determine which round had been fired from whose rifle as every bullet fragmented on impact, making them completely untraceable. Investigations also revealed that the terrorist had somehow managed to partially rack yet another round into the chamber of his pump action, despite being shot so many times.

The number of bullets I'd fired in the operation became a media obsession and it was seriously getting to me. One day, the inspector who ran the Lindt operation told me he had something to show me.

"Ben, I have a mate in the SAS who wanted me to give you this letter," he said passing me an envelope.

"Cheers boss, thanks," I said intrigued.

Dear 'Officer A' (Ben),

I would like to take this opportunity to offer a letter of support to the members of the TOU involved in resolving the Lindt Café siege and to the officers who directly engaged the gunman. I have no doubt that members of your team and your immediate families are the cornerstone of your support network, however, allow me to offer my own words of encouragement.

I recently had it explained to me the anguish and stress that most police officers go through as they await the outcome of a lengthy investigation or trial. I now better understand the self-doubt and over analysis that can lead officers to question their actions to the point of madness. It is for this reason that I am writing to you.

What I can offer, from soldier to police officer, reflects my own experience. In 2011, I shot and killed my first enemy combatant in an obscure and remote corner of Oruzgan Province, Afghanistan. In that instance, the distance between 'the threat' and the initial engagement was less than 10 metres, not dissimilar to what you faced at Lindt. I fired 13 shots, six on initiation, six as I closed the distance and one as I arrived at the threat's position. However, it was the last shot that was most important because it was the one where my brain was able to process that the combatant had been neutralised.

Ben, this illustrates that your actions, and the number of shots you fired in the Lindt Café, are in keeping with what I know to be a completely normal human fight or flight reaction. I can only imagine how frustrating it must be for you to have this called into question by people who wouldn't know one end of a rifle from the other, let alone appreciate how it feels to have rounds cracking past their heads.

I have no doubt that your Emergency Action and Direct Action Plans (which you call a Deliberate Action Plan) would have been similar to ours. As members of the profession of arms, we both know that a Direct Action Plan has the best chance of success because we choose the circumstances and timing of the encounter; but we also know that if our hand is forced and there must be an Emergency Action Plan, then there will be casualties.

It is right for us to mourn the tragic loss of Tori Johnson and Katrina Dawson, however, make no mistake, everyone's life in that café was already forfeit the moment the gunman revealed his hand and made clear his intentions. For all intent and purposes, every hostage was already dead.

The actions of the wider organisation are not my concern here and should not be yours either. As a tactical officer, you are but one piece in a larger puzzle. All you can do is understand your thoughts and decision-making processes.

We walk an ever increasingly difficult line, people like you and I, where we must be able to take lives and yet still somehow function in society and be able to shift the subtle shades of grey and make black and white decisions in an instant. Reconciling these decisions can be difficult when our actions are subject to scrutiny by the very people we serve to protect.

In my current role, I am working at building resilience in our young soldiers and in the next few months we will look to expand into helping our returned veterans with PTSD as part of our ongoing performance initiatives. I would like to take this first step in reaching out and offer you the same additional support.

Stay safe.
Your SAS mate.

The letter couldn't have come at a better time. Everything he said supported my actions in shooting the terrorist 15 times. My unique operational challenge, however, was the backpack bomb and not allowing the gunman to blow everyone up. I later had the honour of meeting the Victoria Cross recipient Mark Donaldson. He was instructing me and other TOU boys together with SAS troopers on a weapons course. I asked him about the author of the letter. "A truly impressive individual" was his response.

*****

The coroner's inquest received extensive and sustained media coverage. Firstly, there was broad denial that the siege was even a terrorism incident. This was despite the terrorist proclaiming that he was a representative of Islamic State undertaking a 'textbook' lone wolf terrorist attack. (ISIS acknowledged this in their online magazine *Dabiq* and also claimed responsibility.)

Then sections of the media began to portray the attack as merely the work of a nutjob with a shotgun and fake bomb. Was this to reduce the risk of offending the Islamic community or possible reprisal? Or was it just another way of attacking the police? Then the ideologues used the siege as an opportunity to push an agenda through the online campaign #illridewithyou. This was later proven to be fabricated.

Some in the media, with the benefit of hindsight, just simply removed references to our best intelligence and operational experience that supported the informed view that the terrorist's backpack contained a bomb. (At the inquest it was revealed to be a besser blocked-sized and shaped radio speaker.) Some sections of the press called this 'a mistaken belief'. I thought, 'What if the bosses assumed there wasn't a bomb and there was? Would this be a 'mistaken belief' too?' In my mind, this was a deliberately tricky, mean-spirited, bullshit strategy to frame the TOU and the NSW Police Force as incompetent—and then to create convenient scapegoats—us and them—black and white. For the very worst of them, it was as simple as—a, b, c.

My old school solicitor was an ex-cop turned lawyer with a sharp wit and no time for bullshit himself. He had the look of a man who had seen it all. (My barrister, a younger man, had worked in the Australian Army Legal Corps and the three of us made a great team.) "Ben," my solicitor briefed me, "When you give evidence, those bastards ... sorry *barristers* in there, are going to have a good crack at you. I want you to realise that the most dangerous situation they've ever faced is a paper cut."

One such barrister was short and slight and dressed in black, with black parted hair and matching black rimmed glasses. He kept pronouncing 'the Alpha team' as 'the *elpha* team', in a voice that sounded deliberately pretentious. "So, Officer A, you shot a total of 15 or was that... 17 rounds? Is this correct?" he said as he strutted around the landlocked space behind his legal team's table.

"Fifteen I believe, yes," I replied. (I then explained how a round found its way into my top pocket but, he wasn't remotely interested in that.)

He continued with his line of well pre-prepared questions, feigning a look of genuine enquiry. "And you state that you shot all of those rounds in ... what was it... three to four seconds?"

"That is my recollection, yes," I replied.

The barrister then strategically raised his voice. "You can't *possibly* be sitting here today giving evidence in front of all of these people, including the honourable Coroner [looking towards the bench, pausing for dramatic effect—as he prepared himself to question my integrity], and seriously tell me that you were able to achieve this and still abide by the NSW Police Force's policy for the discharge of a firearm, of—'shoot, assess, shoot'—are you Officer A?" It was all very theatrical but, it was also wrong.

"Yes, I am saying that," I replied confidently. "I'm well-trained. But you've forgotten something important," I continued.

"Oh yes, and what is that?" he replied, turning on the spot, lifting his eyebrow in an exaggerated show of faux indignation, tilting his head like a goose, looking at me with one cocked eye.

"It is actually assess, shoot, assess," I said pausing for effect myself. "That first step is extremely important," I added just to rub it in. From the constipated look on his face, I could tell that he wasn't accustomed to being corrected by anyone—let alone a mere grunt policeman. From the far side of the room, my ex-cop solicitor gave me the double thumbs up signal.

And then it was Pauly's turn. "In 30 years of policing, with all the crooks I've charged and put before the court, I've never heard anyone swear in the box as much as that fella," The old school boss from homicide said to our inspector.

"Seriously, you mean our Pauly?" he replied.

"Definitely! What a character and they absolutely loved

him," he said with a big smile.

"You should have heard it," he continued, recalling from memory some of what my mate had said under oath.

"And then we got the code word and I fuck'en took off, like Captain America with his shield, to the fuck'en front door as fast as fuck'en Usain Bolt!" It was raw, and it was certainly unfiltered but, they couldn't say that Pauly wasn't being himself—a knock-about Aussie bloke from the Alice.

*****

For TOU operatives lucky enough to be selected, the sniper course is the ultimate. (Although the breachers mightn't agree with that.) At this stage I had been a TOU operator for eight years. On completion of the course, I would still be an assaulter, but also a sniper. Some of my favourite times in the TOU were in the sniper unit. Shooting from boats at sea (Captain Phillip's style) to firing from choppers, engaging moving targets, using glass cutting and armour piercing rounds, to a later course conducted by an ex-SAS sniper, effectively shooting small targets out to 1.2 kilometres with confidence.

This elite course is conducted at the Australian Army's School of Infantry, in ▮▮▮▮▮. Approaching the range master's office, together with other recruits, we were greeted by a decommissioned Leopard tank, just off the driveway in between some trees, with its main-gun pointed straight toward us. (Although later, someone in the military felt so confronted and frightened by this that they were forced to turn the whole thing around and face it harmlessly into the bush.)

"We're back at Jurassic Park again, ay guys. Watch out for dinosaurs," said a spirited Perro, who was one of the course instructors. (He just loved being out there with the boys.) ▮▮▮▮▮ army base has an abundance of wildlife. There are feral pigs, brumbies (wild horses), emus, foxes, goats, and kangaroos in their thousands. "You gotta be really bloody careful fellas not to shoot any of the animals running onto the range during sequences because, I'll tell ya straight up, the animal liberation fruitcakes will go nuts and it'll end up on the front page of the newspaper." (Or worse, I thought, the inevitable ABC *4-Corners* 'special report' into the NSW Police Force's indiscriminate massacre of innocent feral animals'.)

The sniper course is both demanding and rigorous. In one of my many assessments, a time limit was set to stalk into an effective 'hide'. As well as being completely concealed, the perfect position needed to provide a clear 'firing lane'. I set myself, peering through my high-powered scope at the target before glancing at my watch. Time was up. It was now over to the instructors to spot me. I lay in the blazing sun, in 40-degree heat, for five hours, not able to have a drink. I observed the instructors 500 metres away standing beside the target, combing the bush with their binoculars, trying to discover my position. Unexpectedly, there was a rustling in the scrub just in front of me and then the sound of dry leaves crunching. It was getting closer. If I moved, I'd be spotted, and that would mean an instant fail. The noise was now right on me. My right eye remained focused on the scope, with my left eye looking directly ahead. All I could do was wait for whatever it was to appear.

Then, the prehistoric-looking head of a massive goanna suddenly emerged through a clump of tussock grass. Face-to-face, the goanna's long, red, forked tongue flicked out, nearly whipping my cheek, the creature's huge talons protruding from its leathery feet. We both froze, staring at each other—eye-to-eye. (Goanna attacks on humans are known to produce horrific injuries. Its toxic bite not only induces excessive bleeding but also causes blood poisoning, requiring urgent medical attention.) It was a stalemate. I breathed in slowly, paused and then quickly blew out all the air in my lungs in a silent attempt to make the creature retreat. Affronted, its head jolted backwards; it arched up onto its hind legs and hissed at me before running up an old gum tree directly to my left. My racing heart slowly began to return to normal.

The instructors were still searching, now only 80-metres from my position. Then a scurrying noise as pieces of bark began falling onto my arm. The goanna was making its way back down. I thought to myself, 'Here we go. What now goanna?' The instructors were a mere 50 metres away and the goanna was getting closer too. I could see it in my peripheral vision. The creature was at least six feet long and looking straight at me, its tongue flicking in and out, tasting the air, as its black claws reached out and touched the ground next to my left arm. For a second time, our faces were separated by mere centimetres. I was exposed and vulnerable but, like the plan to confront my PTSD, there was no way I was going to back down and give up.

Fortunately, the instructors startled the animal and it again retreated. I could hear Perro calling out, "Holy shit man, get a look at that."

"Fuck me, now that's a big bastard! You don't even get 'em that big back home," the other instructor said, still unable to find me. It was none other than my mate Pauly.

*****

Exposure therapy really was like having a goanna in your face—profoundly confronting although it did give me some new insights. One day, Angela told me that she believed that I was 'torturing' myself over Katrina Dawson's death because, 'I believed that I deserved to suffer for what happened to her'. "So, let me get this straight Ben," Angela said leaning forward in her chair. "Another operator at Lindt fired five rounds inside the café. Katrina Dawson's wounds all came from bullet fragments that were non-traceable. The rounds you were issued with and fired on the day were specifically designed to fragment and could've come from anywhere ... and you still blame yourself for her death? Ben, have you read the coroner's report?"

"I couldn't bring myself to," I replied.

"I want to read you some of the findings and then I want you to tell me how these words make you feel. Is that okay?

"Sure," I replied.

"Ben, this is what he said. "I can't stress too heavily that the deaths and injuries that occurred because of the siege weren't the fault of police. All the blame rests on Man Monis."

I just nodded. Angela then asked, "Will I continue?" I nodded again.

"'He ... Monis ... created an intensely dangerous situation. He maliciously executed Tori Johnson. He barricaded himself in a corner of the café and his actions forced police to enter the café in circumstances where the risk of hostages being wounded or killed was very high.'"

"You okay"?

"Yep."

"'Monis deserves to be the sole focus of our denunciation and condemnation,'" she said putting the document back down on the table.

I just looked at the floor. "Ben, the Prime Minister came out publicly stating the legal system had let the public down, 'This monster shouldn't have been allowed in our community, he shouldn't have been allowed into the country, he shouldn't have been out on bail'," she continued reading from another document.

"Yeah," I replied.

"And the new commissioner said in an interview, "In hindsight, with everything we know, we should have gone in earlier," Angela continued, now reading from what appeared to be a newspaper clipping.

I just said, "Okay," and nodded as I thought to myself, the commissioner had conducted comprehensive reviews following the coroners' findings also consulting with TOU operators and snipers. Because of that process, police powers during terrorism incidents were strengthened and bail legislation reformed. But I wasn't going to tell Angela. She was already on a roll.

"So, how do you feel about all that?"

"To be honest," I replied, "I know, truly I do, but facts and feelings are very different." This was difficult for me to admit.

"Yes Ben, they are," she replied, relieved to hear me say it but, now clearly unsure of where the conversation was going.

I sat silently for what seemed like a long time before I continued. "So, Angela, tell me, throughout my stint in the psych hospital and all our chats, I've sussed out nearly all of my symptoms, but I just can't figure out why I have this constant pain in my chest."

"Tell me Ben. Have you ever had your heart broken?" Angela asked, surprising me.

"Well yes, I suppose I have," I said, now intrigued.

"And does it feel like that?"

"Yes ... it feels exactly like that," I said as the idea ticked over in my mind. "Angela, it's true!" I suddenly exclaimed.

"Yes, and what's that?" she persisted.

"My heart literally broke the night Katrina Dawson died in my arms," I said as the realisation hit me.

I noticed that tears were welling up in Angela's eyes as she reached for a tissue. "Then I think it's time we did something about that don't you?" Angela gently insisted, wiping her eyes.

"I just wish that I could see her one last time and say sorry," I replied now fighting back my own emotions.

"Ben, I want you to write Katrina a letter and tell her everything. What do you think?"

Katrina,

I'm sorry that I never knew you. Everything I've heard about you tells me that you were a remarkable person. I'm sorry that your children will be raised without their mother and that you will never hold them again or tuck them in at night as I do with my three girls. I'm sorry that you will never share the big or even the small things in their lives. I'm sorry that your children will never again be able to share these moments with their mother. I'm sorry that you will never be with your husband, your brothers and your parents again. I'm sorry that you can never go for morning coffee with your friends before arriving at your important job, a job that you were obviously very good at.

We never knew each other but, we shared the most intimate moment in time. You died in my arms as we looked into each other's eyes. I sincerely hope that I was able to comfort you in that final moment. Katrina, I am reminded of you every single day through the pain I have in my heart. When you were dying, I desperately wanted to hold you, just like I now hold my girls when they are in pain.

I blame myself for your death. I relive it over and over. I torture myself every waking moment with the memory of it. I have had many people tell me that I couldn't have done anything differently, but I can't help thinking this way. I wish that I could see you one last time, just to tell you how sorry I am. I am so truly sorry Katrina. I hope that there is a better place after death because you deserve to be there. But Katrina, I can't go on like this any longer. I can't be a constant burden on my family. They don't deserve that. I hope that you can forgive me for wanting to begin the long process of repairing my broken heart.

You will always be with me until the end of my life.

With love and immense sorrow.

Ben ■■■.

*****

The police medical panel sat on April fool's day 2021 and the decision was final. 'Ben ■■■, badge number ■■■/TOU Operator number ■, medical discharge'. I was no longer a cop and no longer a TOU operator-sniper. The grief hit me harder than I could ever imagine. I felt I'd lost my identity, my sense of belonging and a higher purpose in life. Being in the TOU and my career in policing, was more than a job to me. I lived by the TOU motto, 'Courage, Teamwork, Duty and Honour'. I was entrusted by the community to protect and serve, and I did so proudly—and professionally.

"You know what daddy, I've been thinking," my eldest daughter said with a thoughtful frown on her face. "I want you to go back to being a policeman. I was so proud of you doing that cool job and I liked telling all my friends about it too."

I swallowed hard before replying, "To be honest sweetheart, I'd love to go back. I miss it every single day. But I just can't."

What I couldn't bear to tell her was what I missed the most: the unfailing mateship—that precious loyalty forged through adversity and, in the case of the TOU, constant exposure to danger.

Within days, I slipped into a deep depression. The realisation hit me that after putting my life and soul into the job, as far as the police hierarchy were concerned, I was just another number. After what felt like so many positive steps in my battle with PTSD, this knocked me for six. I quickly withdrew into myself and avoided everyone, ignoring texts and phone calls. I stopped exercising, drank constantly, and grew a huge, ungroomed beard and a thatch of wild uncombed hair, which I covered with my black TOU cap. "When was the last time you had a shower and changed your clothes?" Lisa questioned me.

I had zero motivation and chewed my way through boxes of Nicorette gum. It seemed like the only time I was able to feel any level of happiness was when I drank excessively. If I had my way, I'd have stayed in bed all day. I just couldn't shake it. It was like a fog that I couldn't see a way through or out of. There were many times that I thought that ending it all would just be so much easier. My PTSD symptoms and cognitive issues skyrocketed, and I struggled with the stigma of my diagnosis. The goanna was back! Was I now seen as a victim? I could never tolerate that. (And there's a very real belief within police ranks that PTSD is just a way to get out with a financial advantage.)

Lindt impacted everyone involved. After the siege, eight TOU operators left the police force with PTSD with many others leaving the Unit. And it changed Gus too. He wasn't so easy going, social or carefree anymore. (Gus was later diagnosed with PTSD and he too was medically discharged.) Our long friendship was now more important than ever especially in the 'everyday things'. One day, he came around after I repeatedly ignored his calls. "████, to be honest, I've always loved how you never seemed to give a shit about what people thought but, seriously man, this is next level. You look like a fat Tom Hanks out of *Cast Away*." I just laughed it off.

But my situation was becoming worse than it appeared. Lisa's family and many of her friends were in Ireland and so, for most of our relationship, I was her main support. And I was happy to be that, especially as she had a stressful job too. (Funnily enough, she's also known as a 'shit magnet' in her work as well.) My worsening PTSD changed me. I became numb to the point where I was no longer capable of providing her with any level of emotional comfort or support. One day she told me that, although I wasn't killed at Lindt, the siege had changed me, and changed her life and the life of our three girls too.

Lisa and I became distant from each other. She now had to look after three kids and cope with me as well—especially my increasingly dark moods and outbursts and self-imposed social isolation. It seemed that all we did was argue. Most of the time I wouldn't even fight; I didn't care enough. I'd just turn up the television or ignore her and walk away. This made everything worse. Sometime after Botany we stopped being kind to each other. It was like walking on eggshells when we were both at home. I never spoke to her about what I was going through. I didn't want to show weakness. I'd already burdened her enough. But, in reality, I didn't know how to. (On top of that Lisa had to face uncomfortable questions from friends and school mums as to why I wasn't at work anymore.) I decided to apologise for all the hurt I'd caused her. When I did, I felt a sense of burden had lifted, for both of us.

However, it was my girls who saved me with their unconditional love. Lisa had returned to work. I was driving them to school one morning and our baby was along for the ride. We were already late. My second daughter couldn't find her favourite unicorn toy, the most important thing in the world to her and, in that very moment, in her overwhelmingly emotional state, she realised that she'd forgotten her school bag. My eldest called her an 'idiot' before a fight broke out between the two of them in the back seat. Then my baby started crying.

I snapped. I yelled until I was red in the face and the veins bulged out of my neck. All three were now crying. I felt nothing. At school, I walked them across the road and dropped them at the front gate. My eldest wouldn't even look at me. My second daughter, now in kindergarten, began to walk off, still in tears, holding her sister's hand. Then she paused before returning to give me a cuddle. "I still love you daddy," she said in her softly spoken voice.

I glanced into the rear vision mirror, looking directly at my reflection and didn't look away for a long time. I knew what it was to be irritable and emotionally numb but never with my princesses. In that precise moment I decided that PTSD and depression weren't going to define me. They wouldn't defeat me. I had Lisa and my three girls, and they were now my only priority.

There was just no time to wallow in my own misery. Just like the gruelling selection pack march, it was going to be one step in front of the other. I'd gone headlong into my exposure therapy and come out the other side. But having to leave the job I loved was compounding my PTSD. Drawing inspiration from my professional training, I refocused. I was determined to confront threat, just as I'd done when I was firing on the terrorist at Lindt.

*****

"So, Ben, have you heard of TMS?" Angela questioned me.

"Ah no, not another shrink acronym?" I said smiling back at her.

"Ha ha, well yes," she continued. It's called transcranial

magnetic stimulation."

"The psychiatrist said that she'd like me to have a go at that; sounds like some sort of weird Frankenstein shit to me," I replied.

"Not quite Ben, they still do shock therapy but this isn't like that. It's basically neural stimulation through a magnetic field that targets certain parts of your brain," she explained patiently.

"Yeah righto. So, what can it do for me?" I queried.

"It's been shown to have good results in motivated patients like you with severe depression and PTSD."

"Yeah, sweet. Let's give it a run then. I can't do this whole sad sack bullshit anymore anyway," I grinned. (Angela had got a new office. I complimented her on the relaxed beachy feel, the neutral colours, and the comfortable furniture, as well as a couple of live healthy plants, not to mention the filtered natural light that forced its way through the glass wall tiles.)

I doubled my efforts with Angela and kept myself constantly busy. I began writing again and used brain training apps to minimise cognitive impairment. I got back into training and started a healthy diet—and despite a natural reluctance, I agreed to undertake other 'psychotherapies and therapeutic measures' with proven benefits to patients like me: Cognitive Behavioural Therapy (CBT), Eye Movement Desensitisation and Reprocessing (EMDR), and Emotional Freedom Techniques (EFT). I even completed the course of Transcranial Magnetic stimulation (TMS). I knew that every day was going to be a battle; but to win the war I had to overwhelm the 'enemy' in a multi-pronged attack, striking from all angles, never retreating, with as many resources as I could muster.

And so, after five years, I made the decision to return to the

Lindt Café and, although Angela agreed with the idea, I was still apprehensive. I caught the train into the city with a good mate. Coincidentally and completely by chance, it was Remembrance Day—the 11th of November. As we walked through the station concourse and up into Martin Place, a solemn commemoration was being held in front of the cenotaph. Just before 11.00 a.m., I stood quietly at a distance and watched. The memorial service was beautifully concluded with the playing of the Last Post by a soldier in a sharp dress uniform, with the distinctive notes of the bugle echoing off the surrounding buildings. As people began to leave, I saw someone from police rescue. I could see recognition in his eyes despite my full beard and baseball cap and quickly turned away. I didn't want to have to explain why I was there.

My friend and I decided to take a walk as we waited for another mate to arrive from the mountains. We passed by the Lindt Café's honey-coloured exterior and the four large display windows; and there it was—the truck loading bay—where I'd spent 16 hours of my life before hearing those fateful words—'Tiger! Tiger! Tiger!' It was just the way I remembered it. Then, suddenly, I realised how nervous I was. In a moment of deliberate distraction, I decided to look for the place where Pauly had poached something for us to eat and drink. In a side alley, I found a small shopfront with a big counter. Sure enough, in a glass display jar, the very same café style choc chip biscuits and a refrigerator full of ice-cold water bottles.

Our mate's train was running late, so we grabbed a table at a sidewalk café, ordered drinks and looked out and along Phillip Street towards Lindt. At the table next to us were two smartly dressed 30-something female barristers and a tall man in court robes. They were sipping lattes and enjoying the sunshine. A gentle sea breeze blew from the northeast, and I again noticed the sound of the streetscape palm fronds rustling above me.

My other friend's train finally arrived from Katoomba and so, it was time. I hung back, letting the other two go ahead with the door closing behind them. My heart was racing, and my breathing was becoming more rapid. I stopped short of the weathered concrete landing and looked at the large double glass doors, embossed as they were on the day of the siege, with the Lindt chocolate logo. I took a deep breath, reached out and, grabbed hold of one of the solid brass handles. I momentarily hesitated, before I pulled it open and stepped inside.

The place was bustling with customers, all completely relaxed, chatting, laughing and enjoying their coffee and chocolates—just as it must have been in the minutes before the terrorist entered the café. At my request, the three of us were given a table near the front door so I could sit with my back against the wall. We sat on the same long bench where I'd found the badly injured Louisa Hope and under the very same windows where terrified hostages were forced at gunpoint to hold up Islamist black flags. I took a deep breath and looked around the room.

Management had renovated after the siege. The interior was somewhat different from what I remembered; the colour scheme had changed but, in most ways, it was just the same: the large green marble pylons, the high ornate ceilings, the chandeliers and chocolate displays, as well as the staff walking around in the same aproned uniforms. I panned the room before my eyes were drawn to the back corner. My heart skipped a beat. The tables and chairs were stacked exactly as they were when I found Katrina Dawson. I turned my head away before forcing myself to look under them. I closed my eyes and was instantly back at the siege, looking down in horror at the critically injured young woman; but when I reopened them—she wasn't there.

With the support of my friends, I continued to take in everything—feelings and memories and now fresh recollections. Then, while we waited for another round of drinks, I walked around the café on my own. There was so much that I hadn't seen on that day. I found the kitchen area and then the toilets where hostages had been making their secret calls to distraught family and friends. I ventured into the Art Nouveau foyer where Gus and the Bravo team had made entry. Then I investigated the stairs where six hostages had escaped into Martin Place as the enraged terrorist fired on them.

Returning to the table, I sat back down and enjoyed the last of my hot chocolate. As the bill was paid, I took one final look at that corner. One of my companions put a hand on my shoulder and kindly asked, "Are you okay Ben?"

I replied with a smile, "I'm okay guys, thanks. You're good mates." And with those simple words an unusual calmness came over me. As the three of us got up together and walked towards the entrance, I momentarily glanced at the plaster wall, just above the entrance doors. I noticed the very average job someone had done in patching the terrorist's shotgun blasts. I stepped out onto the street as the glass doors slowly closed behind me.

*****

A year later, I met Louisa Hope in her home for lunch. I was anxious about how I'd feel when I saw her again. She was even lovelier than I could've imagined. "Thank you so much for saving me ... ," she said with a serious look. We gave each other a long, hard hug. It was something that I'd wanted to do all those many years before. Meeting Louisa, and discovering the person she is, and then becoming friends, provided closure for both of us.

*****

It was summer and, some time after the unprecedented bush fires that devastated Australia from Perth to Sydney. A new weather pattern, a La Nina, had brought rain and the grass in our local park was green again. We were sitting in the shade of two gnarled coastal Tea trees looking at the ocean. I was drinking my take-a-way coffee and the girls were sipping their banana smoothies. My baby was trying to chase seagulls while spilling babycino all over herself. Out of the corner of my eye, I saw a blonde, fair, 30s-something woman walk past on the bike track. I immediately recalled Lindt—but to my surprise, my heart didn't begin to race as I expected it to. I smiled and went back to enjoying time with my daughters.

Hope

My new role was a stay-at-home dad. And I embraced it (including the day-to-day insanity of Covid home schooling). I spent a lot of one-on-one time with my baby girl and her zest for life began to rub off on me. She taught me to again appreciate the small and best things in life. My afternoons were soon filled with kid's basketball, hip hop dancing, gymnastics, soccer, swimming, and boxing. I bravely took on coaching my six-year old's soccer team—a real lesson in patience and self-control. I even got a motorbike for the older girls, much to Lisa's protests—just like with Mum all those years ago.

I engaged in a lot of self-reflection. Thinking back to my PTSD group I'd been too judgemental. I could see that now. As I spent more time with people from all walks of life suffering from the same condition, I discovered that I was listening more and learning from their experiences.

One evening, I found myself watching yet another of my girl's dance productions in our lounge room to the teeny bopper muzak of Taylor Swift and 'YouTube sensation' JoJo Siwa. My baby daughter was squirming on my lap, trying her best to join in. I thought how much my life had changed—and how quickly—from adrenaline-soaked TOU mayhem to daddy day care—and from being in the constant company of Alpha males—to being surrounded by some very girly girls.

And then I turned 40. I just couldn't contemplate the idea of a party, let alone manage a mid-life crisis. But I wasn't given a choice when Gus turned up at my front door. "Grab a bag of clothes and you my friend are coming with me," he said with a look that told me there was no point in arguing. Lisa and Gus had hired a house down the coast overlooking the water: 'A boys' weekend'. My good mates surprised me there—Browny, Stevey, Jimmy, Perro and 'Big Stu', a mate from the SPSU. My new mate Steve-o was also there, (my daughter's friend's dad, an ex-bank manager who now works at the airport.) It was just like old times, with endless banter and plenty of stories. Steve-o fitted right in. But where was Pauly?

The following day the boys took me to a swanky restaurant. Then I saw him. 'Mad dog' Pauly was dressed in a long red cape resembling Captain America, with a top hat wrapped in tin foil which had multi-coloured chenille stem pipe cleaners holding up a crown of white polystyrene balls.

"You didn't think I'd miss this did you Benny boy?" he called out, strolling up to the table.

"Of course not," I replied, looking around at everyone in the restaurant, now staring at Pauly.

"You see this hat bro? It's my 'PTSD protection hat'. I don't want to end up catching the bastard from you now do I?"

"Pretty sure you're already there mate," I replied, raising one eyebrow, as the boys erupted into fits of raucous laughter. Everyone else in the restaurant just looked stunned.

"If you're in the moment, fuck it—own it," Pauly beamed.

*****

On the way to the park, my two eldest were racing each other on their bikes along the beach side cycle path near our home. I glanced back at my little girl strapped in the carrier behind me. As always, she had a huge happy grin, her blonde locks gently blowing in the breeze. A loud noise caught her attention, and she looked up. An army Black Hawk helicopter was directly overhead. I remembered once being up there too, with the special forces snipers. I'd had a good innings; there was no question of that. I'd worn both the 'blues' and the 'blacks' with pride and, as I said to Angela that very morning, I loved being in the cops. It had been a privilege. I looked back down at my little girl. She was pointing upwards, giggling, without a care in the world. But it was going to be a long, hard road for me—I knew that. It was time to move on.

And so, these days when someone asks me, "Who are you?" I answer, "My name is Ben ▇▇▇▇ and I do a bit of everything. I'm a stay-at-home dad with three beautiful daughters; I do a bit of carpentry; I dabble in property investment, the stock market and crypto … and I'm a writer."

"Have you always been a writer?" they ask because this seems to attract the most interest.

"No, I'm new to it. To be honest I was in the cops for nearly 20 years."

"You must have some crazy stories?" they continue, always pressing me for one.

"Sure have. You should read my book."

ABOUT THE AUTHOR

Ben ███, 'Officer A' VA (Medal of Valour), was brought up in the Hawkesbury north-west of Sydney. He is married with three daughters. He was in the New South Wales Police Force for nearly 20 years. *Tiger! Tiger! Tiger!* is his first book.

www.tigertigertigerbook.com